ALAND

BUSINESS INTELLIGENCE REPORT

STRATEGIC, PRACTICAL INFORMATION AND OPPORTUNITIES

International Business Publications, USA
Washington DC, USA - Finland

ALAND

BUSINESS INTELLIGENCE REPORT

STRATEGIC, PRACTICAL INFORMATION AND OPPORTUNITIES

UPDATED ANNUALLY

We express our sincere gratitude to all government agencies and international organizations which provided information and other materials for this report

Cover Design: **International Business Publications, USA**

2018 Updated Reprint International Business Publications, USA
ISBN 1-4330-0039-3

For additional analytical, business and investment opportunities information,
please contact Global Investment & Business Center, USA
at (703) 370-8082. Fax: (703) 370-8083. E-mail: ibpusa3@gmail.com
Global Business and Investment Info Databank - www.ibpus.com

Printed in the USA

For additional analytical, business and investment opportunities information,
please contact Global Investment & Business Center, USA
at (703) 370-8082. Fax: (703) 370-8083. E-mail: ibpusa3@gmail.com
Global Business and Investment Info Databank - www.ibpus.com

ALAND

BUSINESS INTELLIGENCE REPORT

STRATEGIC, PRACTICAL INFORMATION AND OPPORTUNITIES

TABLE OF CONTENTS

STRATEGIC AND DEVELOPMENT PROFILES

Capital and largest city	Mariehamn 60°07′N 019°54′E60.117°N 19.900°E
Official languages	Swedish
Demonym	○ Ålandic ○ Ålandish ○ Åländning ○ Åländare • Ahvenanmaalainen
Government	Autonomous region of Finland
• Governor[a]	Peter Lindbäck
• Premier	Katrin Sjögren
Legislature	Lagting
	Autonomy
• Act on the Autonomy of Åland	7 May 1920
• Recognized	1921[b]
	Area
• Total	1,580 km² (unranked) 610 sq mi
	Population
• 2016 estimate	29,013
• Density	18.36/km² 46.98/sq mi
GDP (PPP)	2007 estimate
• Total	$1.563 billion
• Per capita	$55,829
HDI	0.967[5] very high
Currency	Euro (€)[d] (EUR)
Time zone	EET (UTC+2)
• Summer (DST)	EEST (UTC+3)
Calling code	+358
ISO 3166 code	AX
Internet TLD	.ax

The **Åland Islands** form an archipelago in the Baltic Sea. They are situated at the entrance to the Gulf of Bothnia and form an autonomous, demilitarised, monolingually Swedish-speaking region of Finland. The islands collectively constitute the smallest region of Finland, with only 0.49% of its land area, and 0.50% of its population.

Åland comprises *Fasta Åland* (the "Main Island," with 90% of the population), together with an archipelago to the east that comprises over 6,500 skerries and islands. *Fasta Åland* is separated from the coast of Sweden by 38 kilometres (24 mi) of open water to the west. In the east, the Åland archipelago is contiguous with the Finnish Archipelago Sea. Åland's only land border is located on the uninhabited skerry of Märket,[5] which it shares with Sweden.

Because of the autonomous status of the Åland Islands, the powers exercised at the provincial level by representatives of the central state administration in the rest of Finland are largely exercised by the Government of Åland in Åland.

BASIC FACTS & INFORMATION

The Åland Islands form an autonomous, demilitarized and unilingually Swedish province of Finland. They consist of more than 6,500 islands and skerries, 6,400 of which are larger than 3,000 square metres.

The **Åland Islands**, or *Landskapet Åland* in Swedish (*Åland* pronounced /'ɔː.læn/or /'ɔː.lænd/ in English), or *Ahvenanmaan maakunta/Ahvenanmaa* (literally Perch's Island) in Finnish are an archipelago at the entrance of the Gulf of Bothnia in the Baltic Sea. They form an autonomous, demilitarised, monolingually Swedish-speaking administrative province of Finland. The Åland Islands consist of a Main Island, *Fasta Åland,* with 90% of the population, and east thereof an archipelago of more than 6,500 skerries and islands at the entrance to the Gulf of Bothnia. *Fasta Åland* is separated by open water from the coast of Sweden, 40 kilometres (25 mi) to the west. In the east, the Åland archipelago is virtually contiguous with the Finnish Archipelago Sea.

By reason of Åland's autonomous status, the powers exercised at provincial level by representatives of the central state administration in the rest of Finland are here largely in the remit of the Government of Åland *(Ålands landskapsregering).*

The autonomous status of the islands was affirmed by a decision made by the League of Nations in 1921, and in a somewhat different context, reaffirmed in the treaty on Finland's admission to the European Union. By law, Åland is politically neutral and entirely demilitarised. The islands were granted extensive autonomy by the Parliament of Finland in an Act on the Autonomy of Åland of 1920, last revised in 1991.

In connection with Finland's admission to the European Union a protocol on the Åland Islands provides, among other things, that provisions of the European Community Treaty shall not force a change of the existing restrictions for foreigners (i.e. persons who do not enjoy "home region right" *(hembygdsrätt)* in Åland) to acquire and hold real property or to provide certain services, implying a recognition of a separate nationality.

The largest island is "Fasta Åland" (the Main Island), where 90 per cent of the population live. It extends over more than 70 per cent of the total land area of Åland, and its greatest distance is 50 km from north to south and 45 km from east to west. In spite of its small land area, Åland can boast 905 km of public roads.

Population. Today Åland has the largest population it has ever had. According to a travel book written by F.W. Radloff in the 18th century, the population of Åland at that time was about 11,000, inhabiting 80 of the islands. In 1905 there were some 22,000 inhabitants, living in 150 islands altogether. In time many of the islands have been joined together or with the Main Island by means of bridges and causeways, while others are depopulated, and the 25,000 inhabitants live in only 65 of the islands. Slightly over 40 per cent of the population now live in the only town, Mariehamn.

The province of the Aland Islands enjoys considerable autonomy by virtue of the Autonomy Act of 1951 that guarantees the way of life and the preservation of Swedish traditions on the islands. The 1951 law was supplemented by a 1975 law that restricts the acquisition of real estate on the islands. Both laws have constitutional status, and they may be altered only in accordance with the strict parliamentary provisions that protect the Constitution.

In addition to this protection against legislation prejudicial to its interests, the archipelago's provincial assembly, the Landsting, has the right to ratify laws affecting it. The Landsting consists of thirty members elected on the basis of proportional representation for four-year terms. Voters must be eighteen years of age by the year of the election and must have the right of domicile on the islands, a right acquired by living for at least five years in the province. Those with this right may also exercise certain professions and may acquire real estate, and they may not be conscripted if they have been residents of the islands since before their twelfth year. This last provision resulted from the demilitarized and neutral status of the islands established by a decision of the League of Nations in 1921.

The Landsting has the right to pass laws that touch on administration, provincial taxation, police matters, transportation, health care, and cultural matters. Issues relating to the Constitution, national defense, foreign affairs, the judiciary, family law, and civil law are outside its competence. All laws passed by the Landsting must be approved by the president of the republic, who may veto those laws judged to exceed the Landsting's competence or to damage the country's internal or external security.

The highest executive authority in the province is the Provincial Executive Council, consisting of seven members elected by, and from within, the Landsting. The council must enjoy the confidence of the Landsting to carry out its duties, and the president of the council can be forced to resign if this is not the case.

The governor of the province represents the national government. He is appointed by the president of the republic, but only after the approval of the Landsting, and is responsible for those administrative functions beyond the competence of provincial authorities. Another link between the islands and the national government is the Aland Delegation, usually headed by the provincial governor; its other four members are chosen by the Council of State and the Landsting. The delegation's chief duties are supervising transfers of funds from the national government to the provincial government, to pay for the costs of selfgovernment , and examining laws passed by the Landsting, before sending them to the president. In addition to these ties between the archipelago and the mainland, the province has one representative in the Eduskunta who usually has a seat on the Constitutional Committee in order to protect the islands' rights. Since 1970 the province has had one delegate at the annual meeting of the Nordic Council.

During the late 1980s, changes of a constitutional nature in the relations between the Aland Islands and the national government were under review in the Eduskunta. The projected legislation touched on increased provincial control of the taxes the archipelago pays or generates and on greater control over radio and television reception, with the aim of increasing access to programming from Sweden and to the Swedish-language programs of the Finnish broadcasting system. Having secured the right to issue their own stamps in 1984, the archipelago's inhabitants also wanted to have their own postal system, a right still reserved to the national government. Under discussion, too, were international guarantees for the islands' security.

The province of the Aland Islands enjoys considerable autonomy by virtue of the Autonomy Act of 1951 that guarantees the way of life and the preservation of Swedish traditions on the islands. The 1951 law was supplemented by a 1975 law that restricts the acquisition of real estate on the islands. Both laws have constitutional status, and they may be altered only in accordance with the strict parliamentary provisions that protect the Constitution.

In addition to this protection against legislation prejudicial to its interests, the archipelago's provincial assembly, the Landsting, has the right to ratify laws affecting it. The Landsting consists of thirty members elected on the basis of proportional representation for four-year terms. Voters must be eighteen years of age by the year of the election and must have the right of domicile on the islands, a right acquired by living for at least five years in the province. Those with this right may also exercise certain professions and may acquire real estate, and they may not be conscripted if they have been residents of the islands since before their twelfth year. This last provision resulted from the demilitarized and neutral status of the islands established by a decision of the League of Nations in 1921 (see Finnish Security Policy Between the Wars , ch. 1).

The Landsting has the right to pass laws that touch on administration, provincial taxation, police matters, transportation, health care, and cultural matters. Issues relating to the Constitution, national defense, foreign affairs, the judiciary, family law, and civil law are outside its competence. All laws passed by the Landsting must be approved by the president of the republic, who may veto those laws judged to exceed the Landsting's competence or to damage the country's internal or external security.

The highest executive authority in the province is the Provincial Executive Council, consisting of seven members elected by, and from within, the Landsting. The council must enjoy the confidence of the Landsting to carry out its duties, and the president of the council can be forced to resign if this is not the case.

The governor of the province represents the national government. He is appointed by the president of the republic, but only after the approval of the Landsting, and is responsible for those administrative functions beyond the competence of provincial authorities. Another link between the islands and the national government is the Aland Delegation, usually headed by the provincial governor; its other four members are chosen by the Council of State and the Landsting. The delegation's chief duties are supervising transfers of funds from the national government to the provincial government, to pay for the costs of selfgovernment , and examining laws passed by the Landsting, before sending them to the president. In addition to these ties between the archipelago and the mainland, the province has one representative in the Eduskunta who usually has a seat on the Constitutional Committee in order to protect the islands' rights. Since 1970 the province has had one delegate at the annual meeting of the Nordic Council.

During the late 1980s, changes of a constitutional nature in the relations between the Aland Islands and the national government were under review in the Eduskunta. The projected legislation touched on increased provincial control of the taxes the archipelago pays or generates and on greater control over radio and television reception, with the aim of increasing access to programming from Sweden and to the Swedish-language programs of the Finnish broadcasting system. Having secured the right to issue their own stamps in 1984, the archipelago's inhabitants also wanted to have their own postal system, a right still reserved to the national government. Under discussion, too, were international guarantees for the islands' security.

NATURE

The landscape of the Åland Islands is the result of lengthy, still continuing processes of natural forces, which have shaped it into a typical archipelago landscape consisting of thousands of islands, islets, skerries, rocks and shoals. Its fundamental character is displayed in rapid alternations between land and water scenes and between light cultivated areas and dark hills and forests, as well as in the remarkable profusion of flora and fauna species and the many types of vegetation and animal colonies which have evolved. The mosaic-like patterns of islands, with their fantastic waterways and land formations and their teeming flocks of sea fowl, make an unforgettable impression upon visitors to Åland.

From the phytogeographical aspect Åland lies in the socalled oak zone of Scandinavia, possessing relatively large elements of deciduous trees such as the oak, ash, elm, maple and linden, as well as southern European varieties of flowers. The mild climate and calcareous soil also contribute to an abundant flora. Large numbers of orchids are to be found, and the wooded meadows contain more varieties of vegetation than any others in the whole of Finland.

Nature conservancy is fairly well developed. Åland has its own conservancy law, and there are special regulations for protecting wild flora and fauna. Common right of access in Åland is more limited in certain aspects than in surrounding regions.

Some fifty kinds of plants, including most orchid species, are protected in Åland, as well as the majority of birds and mammals, with the exception of various kinds of game which are hunted at specified periods.

A ruling of the Åland Government protects certain endangered species of butterflies, as well as all species of batrachia and reptiles except the adder.

ÅLAND'S OWN FLAG FOR NEARLY 50 YEARS

Already 1937 there were suggestions that Åland should get its own flag but the suggestion was postponed for a variety of reasons for many years. In 1951, the new law of independence allowed the "lagting" to make it's own decision of the new flag's features, independently of Finland.

The layout suggestions were all similar to the Swedish flag with a narrow blue cross in the centre of the Swedish flag's yellow cross or a blue cross on a yellow base. These suggestions were all rejected due to their similarity to the Swedish flag. In 1953 another flag suggestion was presented, this time a red cross on the yellow cross and the new Åland flag was approved in 1954.

Its interesting to note that the old Swedish king Karl Knutsson Bonde's royal banner has proved to have the same pattern as the Åland flag. This in turn means that when the king visited the castle of Castelholm in the 1400's, his banner was flying high on the tower as an early Åland flag. The Åland flag day is celebrated the last Sunday in April.

AUTONOMY

THE LAGTING – ÅLAND'S OWN PARLIAMENT

Thanks to their autonomy, the Ålanders possess the right to pass laws themselves concerning their own internal matters and to exercise budgetary powers. The legislative assembly or "parliament" of Åland is called the Lagting. The Lagting appoints the Landskapsstyrelse, Åland's "government." Rules on the autonomy are contained in the Act on the Autonomy of Åland, which can only be altered by the Parliament of Finland in constitutional order and with the consent of the the Åland Lagting. The current Autonomy Act came into force on 1 January 1993.

In which spheres can the Lagting pass laws?
The Autonomy Act specifies the spheres in which the Åland Lagting has the right to pass laws. The most important sectors are
– education, culture and preservation of ancient monuments
– health and medical services
– promotion of industry
– internal communications
– municipal administration
– the police service
– the postal service
– radio and television.

We may say that in these spheres Åland functions in just about the same way as an independent state with its own legislation and administrative machinery.

Which spheres belong to the authorities of Finland?
In spheres where the Lagting does not possess legislative competence, the laws of Finland apply just like in the rest of the country.
Examples of such sectors are
– administration of foreign affairs
– most aspects of civil and penal law
– courts of justice
– customs and monetary services.

To enable the interests of Åland to be safeguarded in these matters as well, Åland has its own representative in the Parliament of Finland, who is elected in the same way as other Members of Parliament in Finland.

How is the Lagting elected?
The Lagting, consisting of 30 members, is elected every four years by means of secret,

proportional ballot, the voting age being 18. Only persons possessing regional citizenship in Åland may vote and stand in such elections.

The Lagting assembly hall

Politics

After the election in October 1999 there are six groups represented in the Lagting:
Liberals in Åland
Åland Centre
Moderates (''Frisinnad Samverkan'')
The Independents
Åland Social Democrats
Progressive Group
9 seats
9 seats
4 seats
4 seats
3 seats
1 seat

The political groups in Åland are all quite independent from parties outside Åland, but naturally they have borrowed their ideological features from equivalent groups in neighbouring countries.

ECONOMIC AUTONOMY

Besides passing laws, the main duty of the Lagting is to adopt the budget of Åland. The new Autonomy Act has entailed great changes for the autonomy in economic aspects. As previously, the State of Finland collects taxes, customs duty and charges in Åland like in the rest of Finland. In return the outlays of Åland are compensated through an allocation in the State budget being placed at the disposal of the Lagting. This allocation amounts to 0.45 % of the income of the State budget with the exception of State loans. This lump sum is to enable Åland to manage such affairs which otherwise would be administered by the State authorities. The Lagting is free to decide how to apportion the lump sum.

LEGISLATIVE SUPERVISION

Laws passed by the Lagting are submitted to the President of Finland, who may impose his veto. The President has a veto only in two cases: if the Lagting has exceeded its legislative competence, or if the law affects the external or internal security of the country.

The President bases his decision upon statements from the Åland Delegation, and sometimes also upon statements from the Supreme Court. Half of the members of the Åland Delegation are appointed by the Government of Finland and half by the Åland Lagting.

How is it that such a small people possesses such extensive autonomy?

As far back as is known the Ålanders have been Swedish-speaking, their culture closely resembling that of Sweden, with local variations. The Åland Islands belonged to the Kingdom of Sweden, occasionally with a fairly independent administration, right up to the

1808-1809 war, when Sweden was forced to relinquish Finland and Åland to Russia. Åland then became part of the Grand Duchy of Finland.
When the Russian Empire started disintegrating, a meeting was held at the Åland Folk High School in August 1917, with secret discussions between representatives of all the Åland districts, who resolved to work for reunion with the old mother country of Sweden. This wish was conveyed to the King and Government of Sweden by Åland representatives, being supported by a mass petition signed by an overwhelming majority of the resident adult population.

In December 1917 Finland proclaimed itself an independent republic – by virtue of the same principle of national self-determination which was being invoked by the Ålanders in support of reunion with Sweden. However, the Finns were not prepared to comply with the Ålanders' demand for reunion with Sweden; instead they wanted to give them a certain form of internal self-government. In 1920 the Parliament of Finland passed an autonomy act, but the Ålanders were unwilling to accept it at that stage.

Because of its international character, the Åland Islands question was referred to the newly-formed League of Nations, and in June 1921 the Council of the League decided that Finland should receive sovereignty over the Åland Islands. Finland undertook, however, to guarantee the inhabitants of the Åland Islands their Swedish language, culture and customs. The decision was supplemented by a treaty between Finland and Sweden on how the guarantees were to be effected.

At the same time the League of Nations decided that a treaty should be drawn up on Åland's demilitarization and neutralization. This meant that none of the three parties in the conflict, Finland, Sweden and Åland, was left without any benefits. Finland received sovereignty over the Åland Islands, Åland received its autonomy combined with guarantees for its language and culture, and Sweden received guarantees that Åland would not constitute a military threat to Sweden.

Stipulations concerning voting rights and the acquisition of land were added to the Autonomy Act, and in 1922 the first election to the Åland Parliament was held. The Landsting, as the Lagting was previously named, assembled for its first plenary session on 9 June, which date is now celebrated as Åland's Autonomy Day. Since then the Autonomy Act has been completely revised twice, in 1951 and 1993.

GOVERNMENT AND ADMINISTRATIVE BOARD

Administration

To assist it the Landskapsstyrelse has an administrative machinery, consisting of the central board with its six departments. This body is also commonly called the Landskapsstyrelse.

The Landskapsstyrelse exercises administration in all the spheres which, under the Autonomy Act, devolve upon the Åland authorities instead of upon the State of Finland. It has charge of matters which in Finland itself come under the Cabinet and various ministries, county administrative boards and various central administrative boards.

Government

The Åland Landskapsstyrelse, which is the government of Åland, drafts and gives effect to matters belonging to the autonomy. It may consist of five to seven members, and its chairman bears the title of "lantråd".

The Landskapsstyrelse is appointed by the Lagting upon parliamentary principles after discussions between the political groups. The purpose of these negotiations is to ensure that the Landskapsstyrelse is supported by as broad a majority as possible – a minority government cannot be appointed.

DEMILITARIZATION

The Åland Islands are demilitarized, which means that no armed forces may be stationed there and no fortifications may be built in Åland. The Islands are also neutralized, so they must not become a battlefront.

After the incorporation of Åland with the Russian Empire in 1809, Russia began building a fortress at Bomarsund in the eastern part of the Main Island. During the Crimean War the fortress was attacked and captured by forces from France and Britain. At the Peace of Paris in 1856 the Åland Islands were demilitarized for the future, thanks to a unilateral undertaking on the part of Russia.

In 1921, when the League of Nations decided the question of Åland's national status, a decision was also made to draw up an international convention confirming the 1856 demilitarization of Åland and neutralizing the Islands as well.

The 1921 convention was signed by ten States, but the Soviet Union was not a party to it. The 1940 Moscow Treaty on Åland and the 1947 Peace Treaty of Paris contain provisions on Åland's demilitarization but do not mention its neutralization.
Persons possessing regional citizenship and who have moved to Åland before the age of 12 are exempted from military service.

REGIONAL CITIZENSHIP

It is necessary to possess Åland regional citizenship in order to
– vote in and stand for elections to the Lagting
– own and hold real estate in Åland
– carry on business in Åland.

Restrictions upon the right of owning and holding real estate have been imposed with a view to preserving land in the possession of the Ålanders.

Regional citizenship is acquired by a child at birth if one of its parents possesses Åland citizenship. Immigrants who have lived in Åland for five years and have satisfactory knowledge of Swedish can obtain Åland citizenship upon application. Only Finnish citizens may acquire regional citizenship.

In individual cases the Landskapsstyrelse may grant exemptions from the rule that only possessors of Åland citizenship may own real estate and carry on business.

Persons who have been resident outside Åland for longer than five years lose their regional citizenship.

LANGUAGE

Under the Autonomy Act the Province of Åland is unilingually Swedish. This means that Swedish is the official language of the Islands, being used in provincial, municipal and State administration in Åland. Official letters and other documents sent to Åland by the State authorities of Finland must be in Swedish.

The teaching language in schools receiving public support is Swedish.

NORDIC COOPERATION

Since 1970 Åland has had its own representation in the Nordic Council. The Lagting elects two of its members to be members of the Council. Together with the representatives appointed by the Landskapsstyrelse they form the Åland delegation to the Nordic Council. The Landskapsstyrelse also participates in the work of the Nordic Council of Ministers.

ALAND AND EUROPE

Although the administration of foreign affairs is a matter devolving upon the State of Finland, there are provisions concerning international treaties in the Act on the Autonomy of Åland.

If Finland contracts an international treaty which contains a provision coming under the sphere of competence of Åland, the consent of the Lagting is required to enable the treaty to apply in Åland too.

When Finland joined the European Union, the consent of the Åland Lagting was required for Åland to join the EU too. Membership of the Union means that some of Åland's legislative competence is transferred to the legislative body of the EU. Åland's special relationship to the rules of the EU is regulated in all important respects in a separate protocol included in the Accession Treaty. Under the protocol Åland as a member of the EU stands outside the EU tax union. The Union has also consented to Åland retaining its special provisions for the purchase of real estate and the right of carrying on business in Åland. In addition, a note in the protocol confirms Åland's special status under international law.

ADMINISTRATION

Under the Autonomy Act the Åland administration has charge of many duties which devolve upon the State in the rest of Finland. However, Finnish Government authorities deal with such matters as the judicial system, collection of taxes, customs and land surveying. The County Administrative Board, which has charge of matters belonging to the general administration of the country, has more limited duties in Åland than in the rest of Finland.

The Government of Finland is represented in Åland by the County Governor, who is appointed by the President upon agreement with the Speaker of the Åland Lagting.

Special duties of the County Governor include being chairman of the Åland Delegation and opening and closing the Lagting.

MUNICIPALITIES

Åland is divided into 16 municipalities. Since municipal administration comes under the competence of the Åland authorities, there are provisions on local self-government in a special Åland law.

Right of decision is exercised by the municipal councils, which are appointed for 4 years in general elections. In order to vote and stand in municipal elections a person must possess regional citizenship or else have been resident in Åland for 3 years.

Åland's largest municipality is its only town, Mariehamn, where almost half of the population lives. Founded in 1861, Mariehamn is the centre of politics and business life in Åland. Jomala, which surrounds Mariehamn, is the largest country municipality, with nearly 3,000 inhabitants. The smallest municipality – and also the smallest in all Finland – is the outer island municipality of Sottunga, with some 130 inhabitants.

CULTURE

The goals of Åland cultural policy are:
– to stimulate and create conditions for an all-round cultural life irrespective of economic, social and geographical factors
– to secure the continued existence of genuine Åland culture and
– to strengthen feeling for the Åland identity.
Cultural life in Åland is mainly fostered by various societies, while responsibility for public cultural work is divided between the Åland authorities and the municipalities. Many societies are supported by funds from the income of the Ålands Penningautomatförening (slotmachine society). Visiting professionals provide a complement to local activities, which are based upon the work of amateurs. An arts festival is held every autumn, some of the performers coming from outside Åland.

Musical activity flourishes, with a large number of choirs and small orchestras. Annual events include a high-class organ festival. Tuition for musically talented adolescents is provided by a music institute, which also has dance tuition on its curriculum. Theatrical activity has its roots in the youth society movement and amateur clubs. Professional drama is provided by visiting companies from neighbouring regions. The archipelago landscape has inspired many writers throughout the ages. Among Åland writers who have reached a wide circle of readers outside Åland too are Sally Salminen and Anni Blomqvist.

The Åland landscape has been a source of inspiration in the visual arts as well. Many subjects from Åland may be seen in collections in places far outside these islands. The Åland Art Museum has a permanent collection of Åland art. There are also several art galleries in various places.

The strong maritime traditions are documented in the Åland Maritime Museum, which contains large collections from the sailing-ship epoch. The Åland Museum covers local history from prehistoric times up to the present day. The Museum Office administers the many ancient monuments of Åland. There are several small museums in the countryside.

Local shipbuilding traditions have been preserved in recent years by the building of several small ships, following old-time models.

The Nordic Institute in Åland functions within the framework of the Nordic Council of Ministers. Its task is to consolidate the cultural life of Åland and to maintain and develop cultural connections between Åland and the rest of the Nordic countries.

ECONOMY

Being a small community with an open economy, Åland is greatly dependent upon exchanges of goods and services with surrounding regions. In many branches there is a low degree of self-sufficiency, and the local market is limited. Åland's geographical situation between two economic centres, southern Finland and the Stockholm region, affords certain advantages but also makes the Islands vulnerable. On the one hand, there are two large market regions at close quarters, to the benefit not least of the shipping industry. On the other hand, Åland is extremely dependent upon economic conditions in adjacent markets, and the population movement varies considerably with fluctuations in the economy. It is primarily to Sweden that people move when times become worse.

The long-standing basic industries in the Åland economy have been shipping, agriculture and fishing. Tourism has been an expanding branch ever since the 1960s, but it is strongly seasonal. In pace with the increase in tourism, primary industries have declined, though they are still of importance, particularly for employment in the outer islands. Because of the small areas available, as well as the favourable climate, agriculture has concentrated upon special crops such as onions, Chinese cabbage, cucumbers, sugarbeet, potatoes and apples.

Shipping is of great significance to the Åland economy, being strongly linked to land-based industries, affecting tourism, trade and industry. The financial sector too is closely connected to shipowning operations. Thanks to the capital-intensive shipping industry, the gross national product per person in Åland is high, while the level of income does not exceed the average for the whole of Finland. However, developments in ferry operations have stagnated in recent years, a factor which has had great effects upon the economy as a whole.

It is thanks to the ferry services that tourism has undergone such vigorous expansion. Today the number of arri-vals considerably exceeds a million per year, and tourism creates many jobs. Hotels and guest-houses offer some 2,600 beds, and there are more than 2,000 vacation cottages for hire. Trippers often choose accommodation on board a cruise ship. In the summertime many visitors arrive in their own yachts or motorboats, when they can moor at any of the almost 30 marinas in Åland.

Industries in Åland are on a relatively small scale. The main industries, which involve processing of fish and agricultural produce, have an important indirect effect upon employment. In addition there are plastic, metal and manufacturing industries, joinery and carpentry factories, printing works and electronics industries.

THE LABOR MARKET

The labour market in Åland is seasonal. Due to the large number of tourists visiting Åland in the summer, service industries are commonly dependent upon labour from other places during the peak season. Unemployment is usually low in the summertime. However, the restructuring of the shipping industry in the 1990s has left distinct traces in unemployment figures. Otherwise businesses in Åland are generally on a small scale, so any restructuring does not cause such an upheaval on the labour market.
Emigration has always been an alternative to unemployment in Åland, with the result that the employment situation has generally been better there than in surrounding regions. The people who move away from Åland during recessions are mainly young and relatively well-educated. Opportunities for tertiary education are limited, so most young people who aim at academic degrees leave Åland for a time, and then they are less inclined to return when unemployment increases.

Traditionally trade union activity has not attracted much interest in Åland, but the situation has changed considerably during the last 15 years. Nowadays more than half of the employees belong to some labour market organization. One factor contributing to this increased interest is that in a large part of the public sector Åland employees can negotiate and enter into agreements independently. In addition the deterioration in the employment situation during the 1990s has led to more people joining unemployment bene-fit societies.

In sectors with compulsory trade union membership, mainly in shipping, employers have also organized themselves. Primary producers are also well organized, while employers in other industries have a low degree of organization.

EDUCATION

Åland has extensive autonomy in the sphere of education. The only matters concerning the authorities in Finland are the requirements which a school should fulfil to enable its pupils to qualify for tertiary education.

The teaching language in all schools in Åland is Swedish. The nine-year comprehensive school, for which the local districts are responsible, provides a general basic education. The English language is a compulsory subject at comprehensive school, while the Finnish language is optional.

Schools in Åland are relatively small, the smallest having as few as three pupils. The establishment of small senior level schools in the outer island districts has proved a successful idea, since it enables the majority of pupils to receive tuition in their places of domicile during the whole period of compulsory school attendance.

Training is provided in sectors like shipping, commerce, tourism, technology and agriculture, all of which are important to the economy of Åland. In addition there is a three-year theoretical secondary school which qualifies pupils for university and other tertiary studies. Nursing training is provided at the Åland Nursing Institute.

Certain academic courses are arranged under the auspices of the Åland Institute of Higher Education, but most young people wishing to pursue higher studies leave Åland for a while in order to study in Sweden or Finland.

TRAVEL TO ALAND

DISCOVER ARCHIPELAGO CULTURE WITH THE ARCHIPELAGO FERRIES

The Northern line

A trip with the northern line will take you through the municipalities Vårdö, Kumlinge and Brändö with their islands at the same time as it takes you on a journey following the old mail route.

Staring point is lush Vårdö and the author Anni Blomqvist's childhood home at Simskäla. You then travel further to Kumlinge's four main islands, where you easily can travel by bicycle. At Kumlinge you can discover the history of the archipelago at the museum farm Hermas. Enjoy good food at Restaurant Glada Laxen at Bärö where you also can participate in fishing guiding, excursions and orienteering or arrange conferences and stay overnight.

From Kumlinge, the ferry will take you further to Brändö where you may go for a seal safari, visit the archipelago museum or island hop along bridges and banks in the beautiful nature of Brändö.

The Southern line

The southern parts of the Åland archipelago are also worth a visit. The southern ferry line will take you on a journey through the archipelago municipalities of Föglö, Sottunga and Kökar. You begin in Långnäs, Lumparland and Föglö, with its varied nature, is the first stop. From the southern line you can get off in Överö, Föglö and travel by means of bicycle or car across Föglö to Degerby, where the ferry will take you back to the main island.

At Föglö you can go hiking, horseback riding or do craft activities at Sundblom's nursery. You can also visit the Inn Enigheten, the Föglö museum or the fish restaurant Seagram with its swimming pool.

If you choose to continue with the Southern line, the smallest municipality of Finland, namely Sottunga is next in turn. Sottunga has a beautiful wooden church at walking distance from the ferry harbour. There are also beautiful hiking trails at Sottunga. By boat you can also visit the small island Södö that has ancient monuments and an old ore mine, and the old pilot's house and lighthouse at Sälsö. Contact Nordbergs Taxibåt to charter a boat. Phone: +358-18-55211 or +358-400 823647.

From Sottunga, the Southern line will take you to Kökar, Åland's and Finland's southernmost municipality, that has mighty shores and a untamed nature. At Kökar you can visit the homestead museum, the Franciscus chapel and the church and make an excursion to the harsh island of Källskär, where Baron Åkerhjelm built a house and a garden. You can then treat yourself to good food and rest at Hotel & Restaurant Brudhäll.

The Transverse line makes it possible to change route between the Northern and the Southern lines. A tip for a successful trip - plan it ahead and adjust the programme to suit the ferries arrival and departure times. Book your accommodations in advance.

Welcome to the Åland archipelago!

Further information: See Ålandstrafiken for information about the ferries departures and booking.

GUIDES

Nåtö TuristService
Järsövägen 447, Nåtö, 22100 Mariehamn, +358 18 54127, [0]457 548 3107
email: gun.styrstrom@nato-turistservice.inet.fi
http://personal.inet.fi/koti/gun.styrstrom

Kaptensgatan 18, 22100 Mariehamn, +358 18 526262
email: info@guideformedling.aland.fi
http://www.guide.aland.fi Ålands Guideklubb r.f.
Mek-Mattesgränd 9, 22100 Mariehamn, +358 457 3425333

HISTORY

About 8000 B.C.
The highest parts of Åland emerge from the sea.

4200 B.C.
The first human beings, hunters and fishermen, come from the east. They belong to the comb ceramic culture. Seasonal settlement.

2500 B.C.
New immigrants come from the west, belonging to the pitted ware culture. Hunting and fishing are still the main sources of livelihood. First signs of primitive agriculture and cattle raising. Permanent habitations.

1500-400 B.C.
The Bronze Age. Cairn graves on hills, typical of this period. Ship settings on the main island.

400 B.C. - 500 A.D.
A deterioration in climate affects living conditions. Åland is sparsely populated. At the end of the period population increases again through immigration, mainly from the west.

500-800 A.D.
Population increases rapidly. Settlement spreads over the main island.

10th century
Dense settlement on the main island. Large numbers of farmstead cemeteries and house foundations exist from this period. Extensive trade connections with neighbouring countries. First traces of Christianity emerge.

13th century
Several churches originate from this period. Åland is subject to the Swedish Crown.

14th century
1309
Åland comes under Åbo bailiwick and belongs to the diocese of Åbo.

1388
Kastelholm Castle is mentioned for the first time.

15th century
Åland constitutes a special administrative region with Kastelholm as its centre.

1442
King Christopher's national law code is ratified. The people of Åland are permitted to trade only with Åbo and Stockholm.

1472
Kökar monastery is mentioned for the first time.

16th century
1507
A Danish naval force under Sören Norrby ravages Kastelholm.

1521 - 1523
Fights and battles on Åland between Swedes and Danes during Gustav Wasa's war of liberation.

1556
Duke John of Sweden receives Åland and Åboland in fief.

1571
Eric XIV of Sweden and Karin Månsdotter are held prisoners in Kastelholm's Castle.

17th century
1634
Åland becomes part of the newly-formed County of Åbo and Björneborg with the Province of Åland.
1638
Regular mail services across Åland are organized between Sweden and Finland. Farmers have the duty of maintaining the post rota system.

1639
A school, "Ålands pedagogi", is established in Saltvik.

18th century
1714
Åland is devastated by the Russians (the Great Wrath). The majority of the population flees to Sweden.

1718
Peace negotiations between Russians and Swedes at Lövö village, Vårdö.

1742 - 1743
Russian troops occupy Åland again (the Lesser Wrath).

1765
Farmers are granted the right to sell their goods where they wish.

1795
F.W. Radloff publishes an account of Åland.

1796
An optical telegraph system is established between Grisslehamn and Signildskär.

19th century
1808
The Russians invade Åland. Their main force is stationed in Kumlinge. A peasant uprising, however, puts the Russian forces out of action.

1809
Åland is conquered by the Russians. Sweden loses Finland and Åland at the Peace of Fredrikshamn.

1828
The Eckerö Post and Customs House, designed by C.L. Engel, is completed.

1829
Work begins on Bomarsund Fortress with the township of Skarpans.

1835
A navigation college is founded in Godby.

1854
Bomarsund Fortress is captured by British and French naval forces (the Crimean War).

1856

At the peace negotiations after the Crimean War the Åland Islands are declared a demilitarized zone.
Freedom of trade is introduced, resulting in a vigorous development of peasant seafaring.

1861
The town of Mariehamn is founded on land belonging to Övernäs village in Jomala.

1886
The Önningeby colony, an artists' colony round Victor Westerholm, is formed.

1895
The Åland Folk High School begins its activities in Finström.

2000th century
1915
Russian troops are moved to Åland. Coastal batteries and field fortifications are built.

1917
The Russian Revolution. The desire of the people of Åland for reunion with Sweden is announced publicly for the first time at a meeting at the Folk High School on August 20th. Finland proclaims its independence on December 6th.

1918
The Civil War affects Åland. Fighting in the region of Godby between the Red Guard and the Nystad (Uusikaupunki) Corps. Swedish troops of about 600 men land and commence negotiations to prevent further clashes. A German naval squadron intervenes, after which all military units leave Åland.
A non-legalized "parliament" is constituted.

1919
A deputation of three representatives submits the cause of Åland at the peace conference in Paris.

1920
The Parliament of Finland adopts an autonomy act for Åland. The Åland Landsting attends upon the Swedish Government and declares that Åland still adheres to the concept of reunion. The situation is aggravated when the Åland leaders Julius Sundblom and Carl Björkman are prosecuted for high treason and are taken away from Åland. The Åland Islands question is referred to the Council of the League of Nations.

1921
The Åland Islands question is settled in the Council of the League of Nations. Finland is awarded sovereignty over the Åland Islands. Åland receives guarantees for the preservation of its language, culture and its local customs. In the autumn ten states sign a convention on the demilitarization and neutralization of Åland.

1922
The application of the Autonomy Act from 1920 begins. A "landsting" is elected, with Julius Sundblom as its speaker. The landsting assembles for the first time on June 9th(now Åland's Autonomy Day).

1938
The people of Åland protest vigorously against plans of Sweden and Finland to fortify Åland (the Stockholm Plan). Those plans are, however, shelved because of opposition from the Soviet Union.

1939-44
Åland is mainly spared from military operations. Fortifications are built in several places on Åland but are demolished directly after the end of the war.

1951
A revised Autonomy Act is adopted.

1954
Åland receives its own flag.

1970
Åland becomes a member of the Nordic Council.

1978
The Self-Government building is opened.

1984
The first Åland postage stamps are issued.

1988
Appointment of the Landskapsstyrelse is effected on a parliamentary basis for the first time.

1993
A new Autonomy Act, the third, comes into effect.

1993
Åland's own postal administration commences operations.

1995
Together with Finland, Åland joins the EU.

1996
Åland's Radio & TV Ab is formed.

SPECIAL MEMBER STATE TERRITORIES AND THE EUROPEAN UNION

Several **European Union member states** have **special territories** which, for historical, geographical, or political reasons, enjoy special status within or outside of the European Union. These statuses range from no or limited derogation from EU policies, limited inclusion in EU policies or none at all. Most of the territories which are outside the EU nonetheless enjoy a special relationship with the EU.

OUTERMOST REGIONS

The **outermost regions** (OMR) are nine regions of EU member states which are part of the EU. According to the EC Treaty, European Union law applies to these territories with possible derogations to take account of their "structural social and economic situation ... which is compounded by their remoteness, insularity, small size, difficult topography and climate, economic dependence on a few products, the permanence and combination of which severely restrain their development ...". There were initially seven outermost regions, as established by the EC Treaty, but the Treaty of Lisbon included two additional territories, both of which seceded from one of the original outermost regions.

AZORES AND MADEIRA

Azores and Madeira are two groups of Portuguese islands in the Atlantic. While derogations from the application of EU law could apply, none do. Their VAT is lower than the rest of Portugal, but they are not outside the European Union Value Added Tax Area.

CANARY ISLANDS

The Canary Islands are a Spanish archipelago off the African coast which forms one of the Spanish Autonomous Communities, thus having the status of being part of Spanish territory. They are outside the European Union Value Added Tax Area. The Canary Islands are the most populated and economically strongest territory of all the outermost regions in the European Union. The outermost regions office for support and information is located in these islands, in the city of Las Palmas de Gran Canaria (Gran Canaria).

FRENCH OVERSEAS DEPARTMENTS OF FRENCH GUIANA, GUADELOUPE, MARTINIQUE, AND RÉUNION

French Guiana, Guadeloupe, Martinique, and Réunion are four French overseas departments which under French law are, for the most part, treated as integral parts of the Republic. Each also forms a French overseas region. The euro is legal tender and they are part of the European Union Customs Union. However they are outside the Schengen area and the VAT area.

A fifth French Overseas Department, Mayotte, was created on 31 March 2011 when its status was changed from being a overseas collectivity. While Mayotte is currently an overseas country or territory, it is due to become an overseas region and thus part of the EU on 1 January 2014.

SAINT BARTHÉLEMY AND SAINT MARTIN

On 22 February 2007, Saint Barthélemy and Saint Martin were broken away from the French overseas department of Guadeloupe to be formed into two new overseas collectivities. As a consequence their status was unclear for a time. While a report issued by the French parliament suggested that both islands remained within the EU as outermost regions,[5] European Commission documents listed them as being outside the European Community. The legal status of the islands was clarified on the coming into force of the Lisbon Treaty which lists them as outermost regions.

In October 2010 the French government announced that Saint Barthélémy would cease to be an outermost region and instead become an OCT on 1 January 2012, a change which, they say, should facilitate trade with countries outside the EU, notably the United States. The change in Saint Barthélémy's status was made possible by a provision of the Lisbon Treaty which allow the European Council to change the EU status of a Danish, Dutch or French territory on the initiative of the member state concerned.

OVERSEAS COUNTRIES AND TERRITORIES

The overseas countries and territories (OCT) are twenty one territories that have a special relationship with one of the member states of the EU: twelve with the United Kingdom, six with France, two with the Netherlands and one with Denmark. They are listed in Annex II acc. to Article 198 of the Treaty on the Functioning of the European Union and were invited to form association agreements with the EU and may opt in to EU provisions on freedom of movement for workers (Article 202 (ex Article 186)) and freedom of establishment (Article 199(5) (ex Article 183(5))). They are not subject to the EU's common external tariff (Article 200(1) (ex Article 184(1))) but may claim customs on goods imported from the EU on a non-discriminatory basis (Article 200(3) and 200(5) (ex Article 184(3) and (5))). They are not part of the EU, and EU law applies to them only insofar is necessary to implement the association agreements.

BRITISH OVERSEAS TERRITORIES

Twelve overseas territories of the United Kingdom (all but Gibraltar, which, unlike the other territories, is part of the European Union (see below), and the Sovereign Base Areas of Akrotiri and Dhekelia on Cyprus), namely:

- Anguilla
- Bermuda
- British Antarctic Territory
- British Indian Ocean Territory
- British Virgin Islands
- Cayman Islands
- Falkland Islands
- Montserrat

- Pitcairn Islands
- Saint Helena, Ascension and Tristan da Cunha
- South Georgia and the South Sandwich Islands
- Turks and Caicos Islands

These are counted as Overseas Countries and Territories under the Treaty of Rome; however, Bermuda has chosen not to apply for this status. All citizens of the British overseas territories – including those connected to Bermuda, but excluding those connected to Britain's sovereign bases in Cyprus – were granted full British citizenship by the British Overseas Territories Act 2002 and are consequently citizens of the European Union.

FRENCH OVERSEAS COLLECTIVITIES, MAYOTTE, NEW CALEDONIA AND THE FRENCH SOUTHERN LANDS

Saint-Pierre and Miquelon, French Polynesia and Wallis and Futuna are overseas collectivities (formerly referred to as overseas territories) of France, while New Caledonia is a "*sui generis* collectivity". Mayotte has recently become an overseas department on 31 March 2011, having previously been an overseas collectivity. While Mayotte is due to become an overseas region and part of the European Union on 1 January 2014, it remains an OCT and outside the EU until then.

Mayotte and Saint-Pierre and Miquelon are both part of the Eurozone, while New Caledonia, French Polynesia and Wallis and Futuna use the CFP Franc, a currency which is tied to the euro and guaranteed by France. Natives of the collectivities are European citizens owing to their French citizenship and elections to the European Parliament are held in the collectivities. A declaration (43) annexed to the final act of the Treaty of Lisbon stated that upon request from the French government, the European Council would have to make a decision in order to make Mayotte an outermost region when "the evolution currently under way in the internal status of the island so allows". (In March 2011, Mayotte became an overseas department and overseas region of France, a *collectivité unique*, and the French government anticipates its becoming an Outermost Region. French president Nicolas Sarkozy is expected to make a formal request to the Council of the European Union for Mayotte to become an OMR.

The French Southern and Antarctic Territories (which include the French Scattered Islands in the Indian Ocean) is a French Overseas Territory but have no permanent population. Both have *sui generis* statuses within France. It has overseas countries and territories status within the European Union.

DUTCH OVERSEAS TERRITORIES

After the dissolution of the Netherlands Antilles on 10 October 2010, Aruba, Curaçao, and Sint Maarten are now autonomous countries within the Kingdom of the Netherlands. As the Netherlands Antilles, they were initially specifically excluded from all association with the EEC by reason of a protocol attached to the Treaty of Rome, allowing the Netherlands to ratify on behalf of the Netherlands and Netherlands New Guinea only, which it subsequently did. Following the entry into force of the Convention on the association of the Netherlands Antilles with the European Economic Community on 1

October 1964, however, the Netherlands Antilles were counted as overseas territories. The inhabitants of the islands are EU citizens owing to their Dutch nationality, but most of them were not, until recently, entitled to vote in European Parliamentary Elections. This has been recently ruled to be contrary to EU law by the European Court of Justice as Dutch citizens resident outside the EU, other than those resident in either the former Netherlands Antilles and Aruba, were entitled to vote in the Dutch elections to the European Parliament.

Bonaire, Sint Eustatius, and Saba — collectively known as the BES islands or the Caribbean Netherlands — are now special municipalities of the Netherlands. They will remain OCTs at least until 2015.

Aruba and the former Netherlands Antilles are listed in the OCT list in Annex II to the Treaty on the Functioning of the European Union, the latter with enumerating her former five component territories Curaçao, Sint Maarten, Bonaire, Sint Eustatius, and Saba.

GREENLAND

Greenland is a special case among the overseas countries and territories as it is the only one which was once part of the Union (then called the European Community). Greenland had a referendum on membership and subsequently left in 1985. Greenlanders are, nonetheless, full European Union citizens owing to their Danish citizenship.

SPECIAL CASES

While the outermost regions and the overseas counties and territories fall into structured categories to which common mechanisms apply, this is not true of all the special territories. Some territories enjoy ad-hoc arrangements in their relationship with the EU. Some of these could be called "protocol territories" as their status is governed by protocols attached to their respective countries' accession treaties. The rest owe their status to European Union legislative provisions which exclude the territories from the application of the legislation concerned. Many opt out from either the VAT area or the customs union or both.

ÅLAND ISLANDS

Åland, a group of islands belonging to Finland, but with partial autonomy, located between Sweden and Finland, with a Swedish-speaking population, joined the EU along with Finland in 1995. The islands had a separate referendum on accession and like the Finnish mainland voted in favour.

While most EU law applies to Åland it is outside the VAT area and is exempt from common rules in relation to turnover taxes, excise duties and indirect taxation. There are also restrictions on the freedom of movement of people and services, the right of establishment, and the purchase or holding of real estate in Åland.

BÜSINGEN AM HOCHRHEIN

The German exclave town of Büsingen am Hochrhein, fully surrounded by Switzerland, is in customs union with the latter non-EU country. The euro is legal tender, although the Swiss franc is preferred. Büsingen is excluded from the EU customs union and VAT area. Swiss VAT and sales taxes are paid.

CAMPIONE D'ITALIA AND LIVIGNO

The Italian enclave village of Campione d'Italia is totally surrounded by Switzerland's Ticino (Tessin) canton as well as Lake Lugano (Lake Ceresio) and is in the Province of Como, whilst Livigno, a small and remote mountain resort town, is in the Italian province of Sondrio. Although part of the EU, they are excluded from the customs union and VAT area, with Livigno's tax status dating back to Napoleonic times. Moreover, legal tender in Campione d'Italia is the Swiss Franc, even with the euro widely accepted.

CEUTA AND MELILLA

Ceuta and Melilla are two Spanish cities on the North African coast. They are excluded from the common agricultural and fisheries policies. They are also outside the customs union and VAT area, but no customs are levied on goods exported from the Union into either Ceuta and Melilla, and certain goods originating in Ceuta and Melilla are exempt from customs charges.

THE CHANNEL ISLANDS AND THE ISLE OF MAN

Jersey, Guernsey and the Isle of Man are British Crown dependencies, the former two being just off the French coast and the latter being in the middle of the Irish Sea. The islands take part in the EU freedom of movement of goods but not people, services or capital. The Channel Islands (as they were defined in 1972, when the UK joined the European Communities, now Jersey and Guernsey) are outside the VAT area (since they have no VAT), while the Isle of Man is inside it. Both areas are inside the customs union.

Channel Islanders and Manx people are British citizens and hence European citizens. However, they are not entitled to take advantage of the freedom of movement of people or services unless they are directly connected (through birth, descent from a parent or grandparent, or five years' residence) with the United Kingdom.

CYPRUS

When the Republic of Cyprus became part of the European Union on 1 May 2004, the northern third of the island was outside of the effective control of its government, a United Nations buffer zone of varying width separated the two parts, and a further 3% of the island was taken up by UK sovereign bases (under British sovereignty since the Treaty of Establishment in 1960). Two protocols to the Treaty of Accession 2003 – numbers 3 and 10, known as the "Sovereign Base Areas Protocol" and the "Cyprus Protocol" respectively – reflect this complex situation.

EU law only applies fully to the part of the island that is effectively controlled by the government of the Republic of Cyprus. EU law is suspended in the northern third of the island (the Turkish Republic of Northern Cyprus, whose independence is recognised only by Turkey) by article 1(1) of the Cyprus Protocol. Turkish Cypriots living there are nonetheless European citizens and are entitled, at least in principle, to vote in elections to the European Parliament; however, elections to that Parliament are not organised in northern Cyprus.

UNITED KINGDOM SOVEREIGN BASES

The United Kingdom has two sovereign bases on Cyprus, namely Akrotiri and Dhekelia. Unlike other British overseas territories, they are not listed as Overseas Countries and Territories under the Treaty of Rome and their inhabitants (who are entitled to British Overseas Territories Citizenship) have never been entitled to British citizenship.

Prior to Cypriot accession to the EU in 2004, EU law did not apply to the sovereign bases. This position was changed by the Cypriot accession treaty and EU law, while still not applying in principle, applies to the extent necessary to implement a protocol attached to that treaty.

In practice this protocol applies a substantial portion of EU law to the sovereign bases including provisions relative to agricultural policy, customs and indirect taxation. The UK also agreed in the Protocol to keep enough control of the external (i.e. off-island and northern Cyprus) borders of the sovereign bases to ensure that the border between the sovereign bases and the Republic of Cyprus can remain fully open and will not have to be policed as an external EU border. Consequently the sovereign bases will become a *de facto* part of the Schengen Area if and when Cyprus implements it. The bases are already *de facto* members of the eurozone due to their previous use of the Cypriot pound before it was replaced by the euro in 2008.

As pointed out above, inhabitants of the sovereign bases have never been entitled to British citizenship or the European Union citizenship that would go with it. However, apart from those temporarily living there in connection with the British forces, the majority of the inhabitants are nationals of the Republic of Cyprus and therefore European citizens.

UNITED NATIONS BUFFER ZONE

The United Nations buffer zone between north and south Cyprus ranges in width from a few metres in central Nicosia to several kilometres in the countryside. While it is nominally under the sovereignty of the Republic of Cyprus, it is effectively administered by the United Nations Peacekeeping Force in Cyprus (UNFICYP).

The population of the zone is 8,686 (as of October 2007), and one of the mandates of UNFICYP is "to encourage the fullest possible resumption of normal civilian activity in the buffer zone". Article 2.1 of the Cyprus Protocol allows the European Council to determine to what extent the provisions of EU law apply in the buffer zone.

FAROE ISLANDS

The Faroe Islands are not part of the EU. Danish citizens residing on the islands, who hold Faroese-Danish passports (modelled on the pre-EU green Danish passports), are not considered as citizens of a member state within the meaning of the treaties or, consequently, citizens of the European Union. However Faroese may become EU citizens by changing their residence to the Danish mainland.

The Faroe Islands are not part of the Schengen Area, and Schengen visas are not valid. However, the islands are part of the Nordic Passport Union. This means that there is an identity check upon arrival on the islands where Nordic citizens on intra-Nordic travel need no passport, only showing the ticket plus identity card.

GIBRALTAR

Gibraltar is a British overseas territory located near the southernmost tip of the Iberian Peninsula and overlooking the Strait of Gibraltar, sharing a border with Spain to the north. It is part of the EU, having joined the European Economic Community under the United Kingdom in 1973. Article 355(3) (ex Article 299(4)) applies the treaty to "the European territories for whose external relations a Member State is responsible", a provision which in practice only applies to Gibraltar. Notwithstanding its being part of the EU, Gibraltar is outside the customs union and VAT area and is exempted from the Common Agricultural Policy. As a separate jurisdiction to the UK, Gibraltar's government and parliament are responsible for the transposition of EU law into local law.

Owing to a declaration lodged by the United Kingdom with the EEC in 1982 Gibraltarians were to be counted as British nationals for the purposes of Community law. This was notwithstanding that they were not all, at the time, British citizens but many were British Overseas Territories citizens. As such Gibraltarians have enjoyed European Union citizenship from its creation by the Maastricht Treaty. All Gibraltarians have since been granted full British citizenship.

Despite their status as EU citizens resident in the EU, elections to the European Parliament were not held in Gibraltar until 2004. The inclusion resulted from the European Court of Human Rights' ruling in *Matthews v. United Kingdom* which deemed that Gibraltar's exclusion violated Article 3 of Protocol 1 to the European Convention on Human Rights. In the 2004 European Parliament election the territory formed part of the South West England constituency of the United Kingdom. The inclusion was unsuccessfully challenged by Spain before the European Court of Justice.

Like the UK, Gibraltar does not form part of the Schengen Area and as a result the border between Spain and Gibraltar is an external Schengen border through which Spain is legally obliged to perform full entrance and exit controls. However Gibraltar does participate in certain police and judicial cooperation aspects of the Schengen *acquis* in line with the UK's request to participate in the same measures.

With respect to the application of EU law to Gibraltar, the Governments of Spain and the United Kingdom made the following Declaration which is appended (as Declaration 55) to the Treaty on European Union: "The Treaties apply to Gibraltar as a European territory for whose external relations a Member State is responsible. This shall not imply changes in the respective positions of the Member States concerned."

HELIGOLAND

Heligoland is a German island situated 70 km (43 mi) off the German north-western coast. It is part of the EU, but is excluded from the customs union and the VAT area.

MOUNT ATHOS

Mount Athos is an autonomous monastic region of Greece. Greece's EU accession treaty provides that Mount Athos maintains its centuries-old special legal status, guaranteed by article 105 of the Greek Constitution. It is part of the customs union but outside the VAT area. Notwithstanding that a special permit is required to enter the peninsula and a prohibition on the admittance of women, it is part of the Schengen Area. A declaration attached to Greece's accession treaty to the Schengen Agreement states that Mount Athos's "special status" should be taken into account in the application of the Schengen rules.

SAIMAA CANAL AND MALY VYSOTSKY ISLAND

Finland leases the Russian part of the Saimaa Canal and the island of Maly Vysotsky from Russia. The area is not part of the EU; it is a special part of Russia, and under the treaty signed by Finnish and Russian governments, as of 2010 Maly Vysotsky is managed by Russian authorities. Russian law is in force, with a few exceptions concerning maritime rules and the employment of canal staff, which fall under Finnish jurisdiction. There are also special rules concerning vessels travelling to Finland via the canal. Russian visas are not required for just passing through the canal, but a passport is needed and it is checked at the border. Euros are accepted for the canal fees.

ÅLAND AND THE EU

THE AUTONOMOUS REGIME OF ÅLAND

The town hall in Mariehamn, capital of Åland province

The guarantees for the special status of the Åland Islands, a province consisting of more than 6,500 islands in the Gulf of Bothnia between Finland and Sweden, are to be found in international agreements and international regional customary law as well as national legislation. The islands were demilitarised and neutralised under the 1856 Paris Treaty that brought the Crimean War to an end. Finland is also under an obligation to ensure the residents of the Åland Islands the right to maintain the Swedish language as well as their own culture and local traditions. Guarantees for the extensive self-government of the islands form part of regional European customary law and have been confirmed in the Finnish Constitution and regulated in detail by the Autonomy Act of 1920, as amended in 1922, 1951 and 1991. (See also the previous section on the Swedish-speaking Finns in this article). The latest amendments to the 1991 Act will enter into force in June 2004. The Autonomy Act can be amended only by consistent decisions supported by qualified majority votes taken in the Finnish Parliament and the Legislative Assembly of Åland.

Wide legislative and executive powers are vested in the Provincial Legislative Assembly (*Lagting/ Maakuntapäivät*) and the Provincial Government (*Landskapsregering/ Maakunnan hallitus*). The Autonomy Act lists the matters falling within the competence of Åland on the one hand and the Finnish State on the other. Matters that belong to the competence of the Ålandic Legislative Assembly are, for example, municipal taxation, building and planning, and the protection of nature and the environment. The Finnish State maintains legislative competence for foreign relations and foreign trade, family and inheritance law, and general criminal law. Under a general clause, the Finnish State has legislative competence in other matters that are deemed to be within its legislative power.

At the end of 2002, the total population of Åland was 26,347. Regional citizenship or the right of domicile (*hembygdsrätt/ kotiseutuoikeus*) is a prerequisite for the right to vote or stand as a candidate in elections to the Legislative Assembly, to own and hold real estate in Åland or to exercise without restriction a trade or profession in Åland. Exceptions to this rule may be made by an Ålandic law.

The official language of the authorities in the Islands, the Province and its municipalities, is Swedish. However, a citizen of Finland may use Finnish before a court of law or Ålandic officials in Åland in matters concerning the citizen personally. The language of instruction in publicly financed schools is Swedish, but an Ålandic municipality is free to provide teaching of Finnish. The Ålandic authorities have the right to communicate in Swedish with any administrative authority in mainland Finland. Consequently, measures taken to improve the status of the Swedish language in mainland Finland, in particular measures taken to improve the language skills of judicial and administrative authorities, have relevance in view of the obligations assumed by Finland in relation to the authorities and population of Åland.

As a result of the demilitarisation and neutralisation of the Åland Islands, military service is not obligatory for persons who have the right of domicile in the Islands. Such persons may, instead of being conscripted for military service, serve in a corresponding manner in the pilotage or lighthouse services or in other civilian administration in Åland.

Åland's autonomy made it possible for the Ålanders to make their own decision about joining the European Union or not after Finland had decided to join. The Parliament of Åland resolved that Åland should also join the EU, since it was given special legal exemptions which safeguard its autonomy and the population's livelihood.

ÅLAND AND INTERNATIONAL AGREEMENTS

According to the Autonomy Act, foreign policy falls within the authority of the Republic of Finland. Åland has therefore no authority to enter into international agreements on its own.

But Åland is not totally without influence in international affairs. If an international treaty entered into by Finland contains a provision which is in conflict with the Autonomy Act or which falls within the authority of Åland, the Parliament must approve such a provision for it to be valid in Åland.

The President has to seek the consent of the Parliament to international agreements. There are about ten such cases every year. So far agreements have contained regulations for the avoidance of double taxation or regulations relating to social security. The Parliament has given its consent more or less as a matter of routine.

The Autonomy Act also contains provisions which enable the Government of Åland to approach authorities of the Republic of Finland and propose negotiations about new treaties.

ÅLAND IN THE EU

When Finland was preparing its application for membership of the EU, Åland put forward certain desiderata that it saw as important for the safeguarding of Åland's autonomy and the future development of its economy. The negotiations between Finland and the European union resulted in a treaty of accession which, from the point of view of Åland, must be regarded as successful. In other words, Åland was given a sympathetic ear by the EU.

Åland's relation to the European Union's legal system is regulated by a special protocol, known as **the Åland Protocol.** The protocol is included in Finland's treaty of accession and is thus part of the EU's primary laws. This means that the provisions of the protocol cannot be altered by EU regulations, directives or resolutions, but that an amendment must be approved by all the membership states jointly. The Åland Protocol has thus a very strong formal position within the EU's legal system.

According to the Åland Protocol, membership of the EU does not prevent Åland from retaining its domicile status requirement for the purchase of land, for the right of establishment and for the right to provide services in Åland.

Furthermore, Åland is to be classified as a so-called third territory, which remains outside the application of the EU's harmonization directive for indirect taxation.

This exemption makes tax-free sales possible between Sweden and Åland even after the abolition of such sales in the EU in 1999. It further makes tax-free sales between Åland and Finland possible. The aim of this exemption is to maintain the future viability of the Åland economy.

The taxation provision contains two so-called safety clauses which enable the EU to take measures to annul the exemption if it no longer appears justifiable. The safety clauses in combination with the regulations requiring the right of domicile for the purchase of land and the establishment of a business make it difficult for Åland to develop into a tax haven. There is, of course, no political will in Åland to create such a situation.

The introduction to the Åland Protocol refers to Åland's position in international law as an autonomous, demilitarized, and neutral territory.

In addition to the Åland Protocol, the member states of the EU have committed themselves in a special **declaration** to respecting the regulations governing franchise and elegibility in local council elections in Åland. Furthermore, in a **unilateral declaration** the Government of Finland has confirmed Åland's special status in international law. Thus Åland's autonomy, its demilitarized status, and its neutrality have been confirmed both in the Åland Protocol and in a declaration by the Government of Finland.

ÅLAND'S INFLUENCE IN THE EU

The question of ensuring that Åland has sufficient influence in EU matters is regarded by the EU as an internal Finnish issue.

On joining the EU, Åland, like Finland, surrendered some of its legislative power. The view in Åland is that Åland, like Finland, should have been compensated for this loss of authority by being given represenation in the European Parliament. However, the Finnish Parliament resolved not to allocate any of its sixteen seats in the European Parliament to Åland, a decision which Åland opinion has labelled as unacceptable.

On the other hand, Åland's participation in the national decision-making process relating to the EU is satisfactorily provided for. New rules have been introduced into the Autonomy Act which give the Government of Åland the right of access to information about business which is in preparation in the EU's institutions, if such business is of special importance to Åland. The Government also has the right to participate when such business is being prepared in the Finnish Council of State. Furthermore, the Autonomy Act empowers the Government of Åland to formulate Finland's response in so far as it concerns the application of common EU policy in Åland. The Autonomy Act also gives the Government of Åland the right to choose a representative for the EU's regional committee.

To enable Åland to participate in the Finnish Parliament's discussions of issues of European integration, the legislation on parliamentary procedure has been amended to allow Åland's member always to be present at the meetings of the Grand Committee. Each ministry also ha a civil servant with special responsibility for EU parliamentary business which concerns Åland. Finally, the Government of Åland has its own special adviser at Finland's permanent representation in Brussels.

THE IMPLEMENTATION OF THE ÅLAND PROTOCOL

The question of how the exemption from the harmonization of taxation contained in the Åland Protocol is to be implemented is still open. According to the present autonomy legislation, it falls to the Republic of Finland to legislate on both direct and indirect state taxation. The Finnish parliament has not as yet resolved to use the opportunity to introduce the special legislation on taxation that the Åland Protocol allows for.

The technical solution chosen to enable tax-free sales to continue has brought with it certain disadvantages for Åland. Because Åland as a third territory is outside the taxation union, a tax border with the EU came into being which threatened to put Åland producers at a competitative disadvantage. However, a special law passed by the

Finnish Parliament removed for the time being the border formalities for the trade between Åland and Finland, but in the trade with the rest of the EU the tax border involves formalities which are at variance with the trade formalities within the rest of the EU and which put producers in Åland to some extent at a competitative disadvantage.

THE EU DECISION

The decision by the Parliament of Åland to seek EU membership was preceded by an advisory referendum. In the referendum 74 % voted for membership on the conditions laid down in the Åland Protocol. After that the Parliament of Åland resolved with 26 votes to 4 to follow Finland's example and seek membership of the European Union.

ÅLAND AND THE NEW EUROPEAN CONSTITUTION

The positions of the Region of Åland in relation to the work of the European Convention

(Approved by the Committee for Autonomy Issues at the Åland Parliament on 4 August 2002)

1. Åland's primary objective

Recognition of Åland's regional legislative and administrative competence

The key problem for the Region of Åland in respect to its membership of the European Union is that the EU consists of and only recognises the Member states as parties to the EU's legislative and administrative business, and that so far the EU has regarded intra-State divisions of legislative powers as a purely internal, national concern. This is particularly inappropriate in view of the lack of legitimacy that this creates in regions with legislative power, adding to the existing lack of legitimacy in the Union.
Åland's primary objective is therefore that the EU treaties be amended to the effect that the EU recognises a regionally-based legislative and administrative authority within the EU.

Åland is thus seeking to obtain recognition of all the EU's legislative regions. In case such recognition does not prove possible, the Committee for Autonomy Issues considers that a number of provisions which relate to the special position of the Åland Islands and contain a recognition by the EU of Åland's legislative and administrative authority should be introduced. Such special treatment of the Region of Åland is warranted by the Region's special position in the Finnish Constitution, which not only delegates power to the Region of Åland but provides for a division of power between Åland and Finland. Åland also occupies a special position in international law and, as a consequence of the "Åland Protocol," also to some extent in the EU's founding treaties.

2. Key issues

The principle of subsidiarity. In future treaties the principle of subsidiarity should be binding also with respect to the legislative regions.

Regional parliaments in regions with legislative authority. The role of regional parliaments should be clarified and above all strengthened. In particular, this means that parliaments in regions with legislative powers would be given an opportunity to participate in the co-operation process between the European Parliament and the national parliaments.

Participation in the Council of Ministers and other parts of the decision-making process. The EU's legislative regions should be given representation in the Council of Ministers as well as in other parts of the decision-making process, where their representation should correspond to the extent to which their competence is affected. The legislative regions should also be given an insight into and opportunities to participate in the Commission's drafting work through consultation and by other means.

The right to take legal action before the European Court. The legislative regions should be given the right to take legal action before the European Court insofar as the case touches upon their areas of competence.

Constituencies in elections to the European Parliament. In deciding the boundaries of constituencies consideration should be given to the territorial division into legislative regions. This principle should be introduced in the treaty.

Simplification of treaties and clarification of the division of authority. The Region of Åland is willing to support the process of simplifying treaties, provided that such amendments do not alter the status of the Åland Protocol.

The Committee of the Regions. As a consequence of the recognition of the legislative and administrative authority of regions within the EU that constitutes the primary objective of the Region of Åland, the Committee of the Regions should be accorded the status of an EU institution. The Committee of the Regions should be developed into an agency that deals with issues relating to local and regional self-government and seeks to promote the interests of the EU's regions.

The Charter of Fundamental Rights of the European Union. Any amendment that makes the Charter a binding legal instrument must not lead to a weakening of Åland's autonomy.

Defence-related issues. Åland's demilitarised and neutralised status must be retained, irrespective of the future development of European structures of defence co-operation.

3. Other

The Region of Åland advocates the establishment of a special working group for the regional dimension.

4. Åland's position in the EU

The positions of the Region of Åland in relation to the constitutional treaty that is currently being drawn up are as follows:

1) The Åland Protocol's status as part of the founding treaties of the EU must be retained.

2) The contents of the Åland Protocol must be retained, both in respect of derogations and mechanisms for change. The preamble to the Protocol, which refers to "Åland's position under international law", must be retained unaltered.

3) The new constitutional treaty must include an express provision stating that the treaty does not conflict with the international decisions and agreements regulating the Ålandic population's special rights, Åland's autonomy or the international agreements regulating Åland's demilitarised and neutralised status.

ACT ON THE AUTONOMY OF ÅLAND

This is an unofficial translation.
The original text in Swedish and Finnish:
16 August 1991/1144 amended 31 December 1994/1556 and 12 July 1996/520
(in Swedish also in Ålands författningssamling 1991/71,1995/6 and 1996/59)
This translation was published in March 1997

ACT ON THE AUTONOMY OF ÅLAND

In accordance with the Decision of Parliament, reached in the manner prescribed in section 67 of the Parliament Act, the following is enacted with the approval of the Åland Legislative Assembly:

CHAPTER 1 GENERAL PROVISIONS

Section 1
Autonomy of Åland

The Åland Islands are autonomous, as hereby enacted.

Section 2
Territory of Åland

Åland comprises the territory it has at the time of the entry into force of this Act and the territorial waters directly adjacent to its land territory according to the enactments in force on the limits of the territorial waters of Finland.
If the jurisdiction and sovereignty of the State are extended beyond the limits of the territorial waters the jurisdiction and sovereignty of Åland may be likewise extended, as agreed by the State and Åland.

Section 3
Organs of Åland

The Åland Legislative Assembly shall represent the people of the Åland Islands in matters relating to its autonomy.
The administration of Åland is vested in the Government of Åland and the officials subordinate to it.

Section 4
Governor

The Governor shall represent the Government of Finland in Åland. He shall be appointed in the manner prescribed in section 52.

Section 5
Åland Delegation

The Åland Delegation shall be a joint organ of Åland and the State. Its composition, duties and expenses are as provided by sections 5557.

CHAPTER 2
RIGHT OF DOMICILE IN ÅLAND

Section 6
Right of domicile by virtue of law

The right of domicile in Åland shall belong to
1) a person who at the time of the entry into force of this Act had the right of domicile under the Autonomy Act for Åland (28 December 1951/670); and
2) a child under 18 years of age who is a citizen of Finland and a resident of Åland, provided that his father or mother has the right of domicile.

Section 7
Right of domicile on application

The power to grant the right of domicile is vested in the Government of Åland.
Unless there are persuasive reasons for not granting the right of domicile, it shall be granted on application to a citizen of Finland
1) who has taken up residence in Åland;
2) who has without interruption been habitually resident in Åland for at least five years; and

3) who is satisfactorily proficient in the Swedish language.
For a special reason the right of domicile may also be granted to a person who does not fulfil the requirements of paragraph 2, subparagraphs 2 and 3, subject to the provisions of an Act of Åland.

Section 8
Forfeiture of the right of domicile

A person who forfeits the citizenship of Finland shall likewise forfeit the right of domicile. The forfeiture of the right of domicile of a person who moves his permanent residence from Åland shall be as provided by an Act of Åland.

Section 9
Participation in elections and eligibility for office

Only a person with the right of domicile may participate in the elections of the Legislative Assembly, the municipal councils and the other positions of trust in the Åland and municipal administration. Only a person with the right of domicile shall be eligible for such positions of trust.
The right to vote and the eligibility for office in certain cases shall be governed by the provisions of section 67.

Section 10
Right to acquire real property

The limitations on the right to acquire real property or property of a similar nature in Åland with full legal title or with the right to enjoy are as provided by the Act on the Acquisition of Real Property in Åland (3 January 1975/3). The limitations shall not apply to a person with the right of domicile.

Section 11
Right of trade

The right of a person without the right of domicile to exercise a trade or profession in Åland for personal gain may be limited by an Act of Åland. However, such an Act of Åland may not be used to limit the right of trade of a person residing in Åland, if no person other than a spouse and minor children is employed in the trade and if the trade is not practiced in business premises, an office or any other special place of business.

Section 12
Service of conscription

A person with the right of domicile may in place of conscription for military service serve in a corresponding manner in the pilotage or lighthouse services or in other civilian administration.
Service in the pilotage and lighthouse services shall be as provided by a State Act after the Legislative Assembly has been reserved an opportunity to submit an opinion on the matter. Service in other civilian administration shall be provided by a State Act with the

consent of the Legislative Assembly. Until such service has been organised, the residents of Åland referred to in paragraph 1 shall be exempt from conscription for military service.
Paragraph 1 shall not apply to a person who has taken up residence in Åland after having reached the age of twelve years.

CHAPTER 3 LEGISLATIVE ASSEMBLY AND THE GOVERNMENT OF ÅLAND

Section 13
Election of the members of the Legislative Assembly

The members of the Legislative Assembly shall be elected by direct and secret ballot. The suffrage shall be universal and equal.

Section 14
Opening and closing the sessions of the Legislative Assembly

The sessions of the Legislative Assembly shall be opened and closed by the President of the Republic or, on his behalf, by the Governor. The Governor shall present the proposals and statements of the President to the Legislative Assembly.

Section 15
Dissolution of the Legislative Assembly

After consultation with the Speaker of the Legislative Assembly, the President of the Republic may dissolve the Legislative Assembly and order an election. The right of the Legislative Assembly to decide on a dissolution and the ordering of an election shall be provided by an Act of Åland.

Section 16
Government of Åland

The Government of Åland shall be appointed as provided by an Act of Åland.

CHAPTER 4 AUTHORITY OF ÅLAND

Section 17
Legislation of Åland

The Legislative Assembly shall enact legislation for Åland (*Acts of Åland*).

Section 18
Legislative authority of Åland

Åland shall have legislative powers in respect of
1) the organisation and duties of the Legislative Assembly and the election of its members, the Government of Åland and the officials and services subordinate to it;
2) the officials of Åland, the collective agreements on the salaries of the employees of

Åland and the sentencing of the officials of Åland to disciplinary punishment;
2 a) the employment pensions of the employees of Åland and the elected representatives in the administration of Åland, as well as of the head teachers, teachers and temporary teachers in the primary and lower secondary schools in Åland; (12 July 1996/520)
3) the flag and coat of arms of Åland and the use thereof in Åland, the use of the Åland flag on vessels of Åland and on merchant vessels, fishing-vessels, pleasure boats and other comparable vessels whose home port is in Åland, without limiting the right of State offices and services or of private persons to use the flag of the State;
4) the municipal boundaries, municipal elections, municipal administration and the officials of the municipalities, the collective agreements on the salaries of the officials of the municipalities and the sentencing of the officials of the municipalities to disciplinary punishment;
5) the additional tax on income for Åland and the provisional extra income tax, as well as the trade and amusement taxes, the bases of the dues levied for Åland and the municipal tax;
6) public order and security, with the exceptions as provided by section 27, subparagraphs 27, 34 and 35; the firefighting and rescue service;
7) building and planning, adjoining properties, housing;
8) the appropriation of real property and of special rights required for public use in exchange for full compensation, with the exceptions as provided by section 61;
9) tenancy and rent regulation, lease of land;
10) the protection of nature and the environment, the recreational use of nature, water law;
11) prehistoric relics and the protection of buildings and artifacts with cultural and historical value;
12) health care and medical treatment, with the exceptions as provided by section 27, subparagraphs 24, 29 and 30; burial by cremation;
13) social welfare; licences to serve alcoholic beverages;
14) education, apprenticeship, culture, sport and youth work; the archive, library and museum service, with the exceptions as provided by section 27, subparagraph 39; (12 July 1996/520)
15) farming and forestry, the regulation of agricultural production; provided that the State officials concerned are consulted prior to the enactment of legislation on the regulation of agricultural production;
16) hunting and fishing, the registration of fishing vessels and the regulation of the fishing industry;
17) the prevention of cruelty to animals and veterinary care, with the exceptions as provided by section 27, subparagraphs 3133;
18) the maintenance of the productive capacity of the farmlands, forests and fishing waters; the duty to transfer, in exchange for full compensation, unutilised or partially utilised farmland or fishing water into the possession of another person to be used for these purposes, for a fixed period;
19) the right to prospect for, lay claim to and utilise mineral finds;
20) the postal service and the right to broadcast by radio or cable in Åland, with the limitations consequential on section 27, subparagraph 4;
21) roads and canals, road traffic, railway traffic, boat traffic, the local shipping lanes;
22) trade, subject to the provisions of section 11, section 27, subparagraphs 2, 4, 9, 12-15, 1719, 26, 27, 2934, 37 and 40, and section 29, paragraph 1, subparagraphs 35, with

the exception that also the Legislative Assembly has the power to impose measures to foster the trade referred to in the said paragraphs;
23) promotion of employment;
24) statistics on conditions in Åland;
25) the creation of an offence and the extent of the penalty for such an offence in respect of a matter falling within the legislative competence of Åland;
26) the imposition of a threat of a fine and the implementation thereof, as well as the use of other means of coercion in respect of a matter falling within the legislative competence of Åland;
27) other matters deemed to be within the legislative power of Åland in accordance with the principles underlying this Act.

Section 19
Supervision of legislation

The decision on the adoption of an Act of Åland shall be delivered to the Ministry of Justice and to the Åland Delegation; the latter shall give its opinion to the former before the decision is presented to the President of the Republic. (31 December 1994/1556)
After having obtained an opinion from the Supreme Court the President of the Republic may order the Act of Åland annulled in full or in part, if he considers that the Legislative Assembly has exceeded its legislative powers or that the Act of Åland relates to the internal or external security of the State. The President shall order the annulment within four months of the date when the decision of the Legislative Assembly was delivered to the Ministry of Justice. (31 December 1994/1556)
For purposes of uniformity and clarity an Act of Åland may contain provisions on matters relating to the legislative powers of the State, provided that in their substance they agree with the corresponding provisions of a State Act. The inclusion of such provisions in an Act of Åland shall not alter the separation of the legislative powers of the State and Åland.

Section 20
Entry into force of an Act of Åland

If the President of the Republic has annulled an Act of Åland, or if he has decided not to use his veto, the Government of Åland shall be so informed.
Where the Presidential veto concerns only a part of an Act of Åland, the Government of Åland shall decide, as provided by an Act of Åland, whether the remaining part of the Act shall enter into force or whether the entire Act is annulled.
Acts of Åland shall be published by the Government of Åland. If the Legislative Assembly has not specified the day on which the Act shall enter into force the Government of Åland shall do so.

Section 21
Decrees of Åland

By virtue of an authorisation in an Act of Åland the Government of Åland may issue Decrees of Åland on the organisation and activities of the Åland administration, on the implementation and application of the Act and on other matters within the powers of Åland.

The provisions of section 19, paragraph 3 on Acts of Åland shall apply correspondingly to Decrees of Åland.

Section 22
Initiatives of the Legislative Assembly and the Government of Åland

The Legislative Assembly may submit initiatives on matters within the legislative power of the State. The Government of Finland shall present the initiative for the consideration of the Parliament of Finland.
The Government of Åland may submit initiatives on matters referred to in paragraph 1 for the issuance of administrative provisions and regulations for Åland.

Section 23
Administrative authority of Åland

Åland officials shall conduct the administration of matters within the legislative power of Åland, subject to the following:
1) statistical information that is necessary for the State and in the possession of Åland officials shall on request be made available for State officials;
2) statistical information for the use of Åland shall be collected in cooperation with the State officials concerned;
3) the Government of Åland shall obtain opinions from the State officials concerned before undertaking measures regarding a non-movable prehistoric relic;
4) the Government of Åland shall obtain an opinion from the National Archives before the Åland officials or the municipal or ecclesiastical officials render a decision on the destruction of documents in an archive located in Åland.

Section 24
Citizenship of officials

A citizen of Finland, Iceland, Norway, Sweden or Denmark may be employed as an official of Åland or of a municipality in Åland. The employment of other aliens for such service shall be as provided by an Act of Åland.
Only a citizen of Finland may be employed in the police force.

Section 25
Administrative procedure

An appeal may be brought to the Government of Åland against an administrative decision made by a body subordinate to the Government of Åland, provided that the decision does not concern a tax or dues. An appeal against a decision of the municipal authorities may be brought before a County Administrative Court, or another instance as provided by a State Act. Notwithstanding this, an Act of Åland may provide that an appeal against a decision by a municipal authority on a matter within the competence of Åland may be brought to the Government of Åland.
An appeal as to the legality of a decision of the Government of Åland may be brought before the Supreme Administrative Court. A decision of the Government of Åland relating to appointments shall not be subject to appeal.

Section 26
Establishment of an administrative court

An administrative court may be established in Åland by a State Act. Notwithstanding section 25 such a court may by an Act of Åland be granted jurisdiction over administrative matters within the competence of Åland.

CHAPTER 5 AUTHORITY OF THE STATE

Section 27
Legislative authority of the State

The State shall have legislative power in matters relating to
1) the enactment, amendment, explanation and repeal of a Constitutional Act and an exception to a Constitutional Act;
2) the right to reside in the country, to choose a place of residence and to move from one place to another, the use of freedom of speech, freedom of association and freedom of assembly, the confidentiality of post and telecommunications;
3) the organisation and activities of State officials;
4) foreign relations, subject to the provisions of chapter 9;
5) the flag and coat of arms of the State and the use thereof, with the exceptions provided by section 18, subparagraph 3;
6) surname and forename, guardianship, the declaration of the legal death of a person;
7) marriage and family relations, the juridical status of children, adoption and inheritance, with the exceptions provided by section 10;
8) associations and foundations, companies and other private corporations, the keeping of accounts;
9) the nationwide general preconditions on the right of foreigners and foreign corporations to own and possess real property and shares of stock and to practice a trade;
10) copyright, patent, copyright of design and trademark, unfair business practices, promotion of competition, consumer protection;
11) insurance contracts;
12) foreign trade;
13) merchant shipping and shipping lanes;
14) aviation;
15) the prices of agricultural and fishing industry products and the promotion of the export of agricultural products;
16) the formation and registration of pieces of real property and connected duties;
17) mineral finds and mining, with the exceptions as provided by section 18, subparagraph 19;
18) nuclear energy; however, the consent of the Government of Åland is required for the construction, possession and operation of a nuclear power plant and the handling and stockpiling of materials therefor in Åland;
19) units, gauges and methods of measurement, standardisation;
20) the production and stamping of precious metals and trade in items containing precious metals;
21) labour law, with the exception of the collective agreements on the salaries of the Åland and municipal officials, and subject to the provisions of section 29, paragraph 1,

subparagraph 6, and section 29, paragraph 2;
22) criminal law, with the exceptions provided by section 18, subparagraph 25;
23) judicial proceedings, subject to the provisions of sections 25 and 26; preliminary investigations, the enforcement of convictions and sentences and the extradition of offenders;
24) the administrative deprivation of personal liberty;
25) the Church Code and other legislation relating to religious communities, the right to hold a public office regardless of creed;
26) citizenship, legislation on aliens, passports;
27) firearms and ammunition;
28) civil defence; however, the decision to evacuate residents of Åland to a place outside Åland may only be made with the consent of the Government of Åland;
29) human contagious diseases, castration and sterilisation, abortion, artificial insemination, forensic medical investigations;
30) the qualifications of persons involved in health care and nursing, the pharmacy service, medicines and pharmaceutical products, drugs and the production of poisons and the determination of the uses thereof;
31) contagious diseases in pets and livestock;
32) the prohibition of the import of animals and animal products;
33) the prevention of substances destructive to plants from entering the country;
34) the armed forces and the border guards, subject to the provisions of section 12, the actions of the authorities to ensure the security of the State, state of defence, readiness for a state of emergency;
35) explosive substances, as to the part relating to State security;
36) taxes and dues, with the exceptions provided by section 18, subparagraph 5;
37) the issuance of paper money, foreign currencies;
38) statistics necessary for the State;
39) archive material derived from State officials, subject to the provisions of section 30, subparagraph 17;
40) telecommunications; however, a State official may only grant permission to engage in general telecommunications in Åland with the consent of the Government of Åland;
41) the other matters under private law not specifically mentioned in this section, unless the matters relate directly to an area of legislation within the competence of Åland according to this Act;
42) other matters that are deemed to be within the legislative power of the State according to the principles underlying this Act.

Section 28
State Acts of special importance to Åland

The amendment of a Constitutional Act or another State Act shall not enter into force in Åland without the consent of the Legislative Assembly, insofar as it relates to the principles governing the right of a private person to own real property or business property in Åland.
An opinion shall be obtained from Åland before the enactment of an Act of special importance to Åland.

Section 29
Delegation of legislative authority to Åland

In addition to the provisions of section 27, the following matters come under the legislative power of the State:
1) the population registers;
2) the trade register, the association register and the shipping register;
3) the employment pensions of the employees of the municipalities and the elected officials of the municipalities, and the employment pensions of other persons, with the exceptions as provided by section 18, subparagraph 2 a, as well as other social insurance; (12 July 1996/520)
4) other alcohol legislation than that referred to in section 18, subparagraph 13;
5) the banking and credit services;
6) employment contracts, with the exception provided for apprenticeship by section 18, subparagraph 14, and cooperation in enterprises. (12 July 1996/520)
With the consent of the Legislative Assembly an Act may be enacted to the effect that the legislative authority referred to in paragraph 1 be delegated to Åland in full or in part. Such an Act shall contain provisions on the measures consequent on the delegation of authority.
A person whose contract of service with the State is affected by the delegation of authority referred to in paragraph 2 shall with his consent be transferred to the service of Åland to comparable duties and with his former benefits, as further provided by Decree.

Section 30
Administrative authority and procedure

State officials shall conduct the administration of matters within the legislative power of the State, with regard to the following:
1) when making an appointment to a State office in Åland, special weight shall be given to the fact that the appointee has knowledge of the local conditions in Åland or resides in Åland;
2) the word "Åland" shall be incorporated in a passport issued in Åland, if the holder of the passport has the right of domicile;
3) the Åland officials shall partake in civil defence, as provided by Consentaneous Decree;
4) a person with the right of domicile may be assigned only to civilian duties within Åland by virtue of the general obligation of the citizenry to work;
5) statistics relating to the local conditions in Åland that are in the possession of State officials shall on request be handed over to the appropriate Åland officials;
6) State officials shall ensure that Åland gain access to the necessary frequencies for radio and television broadcasts;
7) the Government of Åland shall decide on granting foreigners or foreign corporations permission to acquire ownership or possession of real property in Åland or to practice a trade in Åland; before making a decision it shall request an opinion from the State official concerned;
8) the duties that according to legislation on contagious diseases in humans or pets and livestock, legislation on the prevention of substances destructive to plants from entering the country and legislation on the production and use of poisons belong to State officials, shall in Åland be performed by the Government of Åland or by another official as provided by an Act of Åland;
9) (repealed by the Act of 31 December 1994/156);
10) the duties that in the State belong to the Consumer Complaint Board shall in Åland

be performed by a special board appointed by the Government of Åland;
11) the duties that according to legislation on consumer counselling belong to a municipality shall in Åland be performed by Åland officials, as agreed by Åland and the municipalities;
12) a new merchant shipping lane may only be opened in Åland with the consent of the Government of Åland, subject to the provisions of section 62;
13) a matter relating to the permission to conduct merchant shipping in Åland or between Åland and the rest of Finland in a foreign vessel shall be negotiated on with the Government of Åland;
14) the speed limits for merchant vessels on the lanes in Åland and the other matters relating to shipping that are of special importance to Åland shall be negotiated on with the Government of Åland;
15) matters relating to the right to practice air traffic in Åland shall belong to the Government of Åland; however, an opinion on such matters shall be obtained from a State official;
16) when considering matters relating to air traffic that are of special importance to Åland, State authorities shall consult the Government of Åland;
17) archive material deriving from State authorities in Åland may be removed from Åland only after negotiations with the Government of Åland;
18) a decision of the Bank of Finland that may be presumed to be especially important for the economic life or for employment in Åland shall, if possible, only be made after negotiations with the Government of Åland;
19) the Government of Åland shall have the right to be represented together with the Council of State in the negotiations with the central organisations of the producers on income from agriculture and the fishing industry and on the regulation of agricultural production and the fishing industry;
20) the Government of Åland shall be heard before a decision is reached on changes in import regulations that may be especially important to the agricultural production or fishing industry in Åland;
21) an opinion shall be obtained from the Government of Åland before granting a licence to practice a licenced trade, if a State official has the competence to grant the licence;
22) the Government of Åland shall be heard before a decision is reached on closing down an institution or permanent post of local administration of the State in Åland;
23) statistics on Åland that are necessary for the State shall be collected in cooperation with the appropriate Åland officials.

Section 31
Obligation of State officials to aid the Åland officials

On request of the Government of Åland, State officials are obliged as within their general competence to aid the Åland officials in the performance of duties relating to autonomy .

Section 32
Consentaneous Decrees

In agreement with the Government of Åland, duties belonging to State administration may be transferred by Decree (*Consentaneous Decree*) to an Åland official for a fixed period or until further notice. Correspondingly, duties belonging to Åland administration may be transferred to a State official.

If notice is given on the agreement, the Decree shall be amended or repealed as soon as possible and in any case within one year from the date of the notice. Unless the Decree is amended or repealed within the said time, the agreement shall be deemed to have been terminated one year after the notice. An Act of Åland contrary to a Consentaneous Decree shall not apply for the part contrary to the Consentaneous Decree while the Decree is in force.

An opinion on a proposition for a Consentaneous Decree shall be requested from the Åland Delegation. The Consentaneous Decree shall be issued by the President of the Republic. (31 December 1994/1556)

Section 33
Obtaining an opinion from the Government of Åland

Before the President of the Republic or the Council of State issue provisions that only concern Åland or that otherwise are especially significant to Åland, an opinion on the matter shall be obtained from the Government of Åland. The above provision shall apply also to regulations issued by other officials.

Section 34
Decision and presentation

The President of the Republic shall make his decision on matters relating to the autonomy of Åland as provided by section 34 of the Constitution.

Matters relating to autonomy shall be presented to the Council of State from the Ministry of Justice. However, matters relating to the economy of Åland shall be presented from the Ministry of Finance.

The Council of State shall appoint persons with good knowledge of the autonomy of Åland as presenting officials for matters referred to in paragraph 2.

Section 35
Administration of the law

The administration of the law in Åland shall be conducted by the courts and officials as provided by State legislation, unless otherwise provided by section 25 or 26.

CHAPTER 6 LANGUAGE PROVISIONS

Section 36
Official language

The official language of Åland shall be Swedish. The language used by the State and Åland officials and in the municipal administration shall be Swedish.

The official language of the Åland Delegation shall be Swedish. The opinions and decisions of the Supreme Court referred to in this Act shall be written in Swedish.

The provisions of this Act on the language used in State administration shall also apply, where appropriate, to the officials of the Evangelical Lutheran Church, unless otherwise provided by the Church Code.

Section 37
Right to use Finnish

In a matter concerning himself a citizen of Finland shall have the right to use Finnish before a court and with other State officials in Åland.

Section 38
Language of correspondence

Letters and other documents between Åland officials and the State officials in Åland shall be written in Swedish. The same provision shall apply also to correspondence between the said authorities and the Åland Delegation, on one hand, as well as the Council of State, the officials in the central government of Finland and the superior courts and other State officials to whose jurisdiction Åland or a part thereof belongs, on the other hand.

However, a treaty referred to in section 59 that is submitted for approval of the Legislative Assembly may be sent to Åland in the original language, if the treaty by law is not to be published in Swedish. A document referred to in section 59 a that is notified to Åland may be sent to Åland in the original language, if it has not yet been translated into Swedish. (31 December 1994/1556)

The provisions of paragraph 1 on Åland officials shall also apply to municipal officials in Åland.

Section 39
Translations

On the request of a party, the courts and the County Government of Åland shall enclose a Finnish translation in their documents.

If a document submitted to a court or another State official is written in Finnish, the official shall see to its translation into Swedish, if necessary.

A private party in Åland shall have the right to receive an enclosed Swedish translation with his copy of the document in matters that are considered by a State official in the State, referred to in section 38, paragraph 1, and on which the document shall according to general language legislation be written in Finnish.

Section 40
Language of education

The language of education in schools maintained by public funds or subsidised from the said funds shall be Swedish, unless otherwise provided by an Act of Åland.

Section 41
Proficiency in Finnish

A graduate of an educational institution in Åland may, as further provided by Decree, be admitted to a State-maintained or State-subsidised Swedish or bilingual educational institution and be graduated therefrom, even if he does not have the proficiency in Finnish required for admittance and graduation.

Section 42
Linguistic proficiency of State officials

Provisions on the linguistic proficiency of a State official in Åland shall be issued by Decree with the consent of the Government of Åland.
The State shall organise training in Swedish for the persons in its service in Åland.

Section 43
Information and regulations issued in Swedish

The Council of State shall take measures to have the necessary product and service information distributed to the consumers in Åland in Swedish, where possible.
The Council of State shall also see to the availability in Swedish of the regulations to be followed in Åland.

CHAPTER 7 FINANCIAL MANAGEMENT OF ÅLAND

Section 44 (12 July 1996/520)
Budget

The Legislative Assembly shall confirm a budget for Åland. More detailed provisions on the budget for Åland shall be given by an Act of Åland
When confirming a budget, the Legislative Assembly shall strive to ensure at least the same level of social benefits for the people of Åland as enjoyed by the people in the State.
The right of the Legislative Assembly to legislate on taxes and the bases of the dues levied in Åland administration is as provided by section 18, subparagraph 5.

Section 45
Equalisation

Åland shall every year receive a sum of money from State funds to cover the costs of autonomy. The sum (*amount of equalisation*) shall be determined in a special equalisation procedure.
The equalisation shall take place retroactively for every calendar year. Advance payments of the amount of equalisation shall be made every year.

Section 46
Calculation of the amount of equalisation

The amount of equalisation shall be calculated by multiplying the State income for the appropriate year, not including new State loans, as established in the State final accounts, by a certain index (*basis for equalisation*).

Section 47
The basis for equalisation and the alteration thereof

The basis for equalisation shall be 0.45 per cent.
The basis for equalisation shall be altered if the bases for the State final accounts change in a manner that has a considerable effect on the amount of equalisation.
The basis for equalisation shall be raised if
1) the expenditures of Åland have increased because administrative duties of the State have been transferred to Åland, or because Åland by agreement with the State pursues in full or for a considerable part an activity that is in the interest of the State
2) the realisation of the purposes of autonomy causes substantial additional expenditures;
3) other significant expenditures which have not been taken into notice when enacting this Act are caused to the Åland administration.
The basis for equalisation shall be lowered if administrative duties of Åland have been transferred to the State and the expenditures of Åland have hence decreased.
The alteration of the basis for equalisation shall be provided by a State Act with the consent of the Legislative Assembly.

Section 48
Extraordinary grant

An extraordinary grant may be given on the proposition of the Government of Åland for particularly great non-recurring expenditures that may not justifiably be expected to be incorporated in the budget of Åland. An extraordinary grant may only be given for purposes within the competence of Åland.

Section 49
Tax retribution

If the income and property tax levied in Åland during a fiscal year exceeds 0.5 per cent of the corresponding tax in the entire country, the excess shall be retributed to Åland (*tax retribution*).

Section 50
Loans

Bond loans may be issued and other loans taken out for the needs of Åland.

Section 51
Special subsidy

Åland shall be subsidised from State funds in order to
1) prevent or remove substantial economic disorders that affect especially Åland;
2) cover the costs of a natural disaster, nuclear accident, oil spill or another comparable incident, unless the costs are justifiably to be borne by Åland.
The Government of Åland shall initiate the proceedings for a subsidy at the latest on the year following the emergence of the costs. A decision on the matter shall, if possible, be made within six months of the initiation of the proceedings.

CHAPTER 8 GOVERNOR AND THE ÅLAND DELEGATION

Section 52
Appointment of the Governor

A person who has the necessary qualifications for conducting the administration of Åland well and for attending to State security shall be appointed Governor.
The President of the Republic shall appoint the Governor after having agreed on the matter with the Speaker of the Legislative Assembly. If a consensus is not reached, the President shall appoint the Governor from among five candidates nominated by the Legislative Assembly.

Section 53
Acting Governor

When the office of Governor is vacant or when the Governor is prevented from attending to his duties the President may, after having agreed on the matter with the Speaker of the Legislative Assembly, appoint a suitable person as Acting Governor.

Section 54
Dismissal of the Governor

The Speaker of the Legislative Assembly shall be heard before making a decision on a matter relating to the dismissal of the Governor.

Section 55
Composition and competence of the Åland Delegation

The duties of the Chairman of the Åland Delegation shall be performed by the Governor or another person, whom the President of the Republic has appointed after having agreed on the matter with the Speaker of the Legislative Assembly. When the Chairman is prevented from attending to his duties, they shall be performed by the Vice Chairman, also appointed by the President after having agreed on the matter with the Speaker. The Council of State and the Legislative Assembly shall both elect two persons as Members of the Delegation and two Deputy Members for each Member.
The Delegation shall only have a quorum when all the Members are present.
The Delegation may hear expert opinions.

Section 56
Duties of the Åland Delegation

Upon request the Delegation shall give opinions to the Council of State, the ministries thereof, the Government of Åland and the courts.
The Delegation shall decide upon the matters referred to in section 62.
In addition, the Delegation shalL
1) carry out the equalisation referred to in section 45;
2) determine the tax retribution in accordance with section 49;
3) give the extraordinary grant referred to in section 48 and award the subsidy referred to in section 51, and decide upon the possible conditions therefor.
The Delegation shall determine the amount of the advance payments referred to in

section 45, paragraph 2.
The President of the Republic shall confirm the decision of the Delegation on a matter referred to in paragraph 3. The decision shall within three months be confirmed unaltered or left unconfirmed. If the decision is not confirmed, the matter shall be returned to the Delegation for reconsideration.

Section 57
Expenses of the Åland Delegation

Åland shall bear the expenses of the Åland Delegation derived from the Delegates elected by the Legislative Assembly. The other expenses shall be covered from State funds.

CHAPTER 9 INTERNATIONAL TREATIES

Section 58
Negotiations on international treaties

The Government of Åland may propose negotiations on a treaty with a foreign State to the appropriate State officials.
The Government of Åland shall be informed of negotiations on a treaty with a foreign State if the matter is subject to the competence of Åland. If the negotiations on a treaty with a foreign State otherwise relate to matters of special importance to Åland, the Government of Åland shall be informed of the negotiations, if appropriate. For a special reason the Government of Åland shall be reserved the opportunity to participate in the negotiations.

Section 59
Entry into force of international treaties

If a treaty that Finland has concluded with a foreign State contains a provision contrary to this Act, the provision shall enter into force in Åland only if so provided by an Act enacted in accordance with sections 67 and 69 of the Parliament of Finland Act and section 69 of this Act.
If the treaty contains a provision that according to this Act is subject to the authority of Åland, the Legislative Assembly must consent to the statute implementing the treaty in order to have the provision enter into force in Åland.
The Legislative Assembly may authorise the Government of Åland to give the consent referred to in paragraph 2.

CHAPTER 9 A (31 DECEMBER 1994/1556) MATTERS RELATING TO THE EUROPEAN UNION

Section 59 a
(31 December 1994/1556)
Preparation of EU matters

The Government of Åland shall be notified of matters under preparation in the institutions of the European Union, if the matters are within the legislative power of Åland or may for other reasons be especially important to Åland.
The Government of Åland shall have the right to participate in the preparation of the matters referred to in paragraph 1 within the Council of State.

Section 59 b
(31 December 1994/1556)
Application of a Common Policy of the European Community

In so far as the matter belongs to the legislative power of Åland, the Government of Åland shall formulate the national position of Finland relating to the application of a Common Policy of the European Community in Åland.

Section 59 c
(31 December 1994/1556)
The Committee of the Regions of the European Community

A candidate designated by the Government of Åland shall be nominated as one of the representatives of Finland in the Committee of the Regions of the European Community.

CHAPTER 10 MISCELLANEOUS PROVISIONS

Section 60
Legality of Decrees, conflicts of authority

If a provision of a Decree of Åland conflicts with an Act of Åland or a State Act applied in Åland, it shall not apply.
If a conflict of authority arises between Åland officials and State officials on a given administrative function, a decision on the matter shall be rendered by the Supreme Court on the proposal of the Government of Åland or the State official. Before rendering the decision the Supreme Court shall obtain opinions from the appropriate official and the Åland Delegation.

Section 60 a
(31 December 1994/1556)
Confidentiality

State legislation shall apply on confidentiality and access to documents in matters referred to in chapters 9 and 9 a.

Section 61
State land and State buildings

If the State requires land in the Åland Islands for regular State administration, Åland shall allocate suitable lots for the purpose. If Åland does not allocate the lots, the State may acquire the required land without the cooperation of Åland.
If the land referred to in paragraph 1 is no longer required for regular State

administration, the right of the State to the land shall pass to Åland. Åland shall also acquire the buildings and facilities rendered unnecessary, unless they are removed.
The allocation of land according to paragraph 1 and the transfer of land and other property to Åland according to paragraph 2 shall be agreed upon by the appropriate ministry and the Government of Åland.
State legislation shall apply to the redemption, for full compensation, of real property for State needs.

Section 62
Controversy in certain situations

If controversy arises in situations referred to in section 30, subparagraph 12, or section 61, paragraph 1 or 2, the matter shall be resolved by the Åland Delegation.

Section 63
Right of Åland to inheritance

If a person habitually resident in the Åland Islands dies without an heir, the inheritance shall pass to Åland. However, real property and comparable property inherited by Åland not located in the Åland Islands and not required to cover the debts of the estate shall be handed over to the State.

Section 64
Degree earned in another Nordic country

A Decree may be issued to the effect that a degree required for a State office in Åland may be substituted with a comparable degree earned in Iceland, Norway, Sweden or Denmark.

Section 65
Trade activity of the State and certain offices in Åland

If the right to practice a trade, regulated in State legislation according to section 27 or section 29, is reserved to the State, an independent State institution or a corporation where the State holds the power of decision, a Decree may be issued to the effect that Åland or a corporation where Åland holds the power of decision be entitled to practice the same trade in the Åland Islands, unless there are substantial reasons for the contrary.
The provisions of section 30, subparagraph 1, section 42, paragraph 1 and section 64 on State offices shall apply also to service in independent State institutions in Åland and, as further provided by a Decree, in corporations where the State holds the power of decision.

Section 66
Exemption from taxes

Åland shall have the same right of exemption from taxes and for comparable benefits as the State.

Section 67
Implementation of municipal suffrage in certain cases

A citizen of Finland without the right of domicile and citizens of Iceland, Norway, Sweden and Denmark shall be awarded the suffrage and eligibility for office in municipal elections on the prerequisites provided by an Act of Åland. Citizens of other states may be awarded the suffrage and eligibility for office in the same manner. (31 December 1994/1556)

A decision to enact an Act of Åland referred to in paragraph 1 shall require at least a two thirds' majority of the votes cast.

Section 68
Electoral district

In Parliamentary and Presidential elections Åland shall constitute an electoral district. Provisions on the said elections shall be enacted separately.

Section 69
Amendment of the Autonomy Act and the Enactment of an Act of Åland by qualified majority

This Act may be amended, explained, repealed or exceptions to it may be made only by consistent decisions of Parliament of Finland and the Legislative Assembly. In Parliament of Finland the decision shall be made as provided for the amendment, explanation and repeal of Constitutional Acts and in the Legislative Assembly by at least a two thirds' majority of votes cast.

An Act of Åland may be enacted to the effect that the Legislative Assembly is to enact an Act of Åland by at least a two thirds' majority of votes cast. An Act of Åland containing such a provision shall be enacted in the same manner.

CHAPTER 11 ENTRY INTO FORCE AND TRANSITORY PROVISIONS

Section 70
Entry into force

This Act shall enter into force on 1 January 1993.

This Act shall repeal the Autonomy Act for Åland (28 December 1951/760), as later amended (*the previous Act*), the Act on the Application of the Administrative Appeals Act in The Åland Islands (16 February 1979/182) and the other provisions contrary to this Act.

Measures required for the implementation of this Act may be undertaken before its entry into force. When enacting an Act of Åland, the Legislative Assembly may apply the provisions of this Act even before its entry into force. However, such an Act of Åland shall not enter into force before this Act has entered into force.

The Åland Delegation elected in accordance with this Act shall perform also the duties of the Åland Delegation provided by the previous Act.

Section 71
Application of previous provisions

If an area of legislation that has previously been regulated by Acts of Åland has been transferred to the legislative power of the State or if an area previously subject to the legislative power of the State has been transferred to the legislative power of Åland by this Act or on the basis of this Act, an Act of Åland or State Act enacted before the entry into force of this Act, relating to the said area of legislation, shall apply in Åland until the Act of Åland has been repealed by Decree and the State Act by an Act of Åland.

Section 72
Right of domicile

A person habitually resident in Åland at the time of the entry into force of this Act shall upon request to the Government of Åland have the right to gain the right of domicile according to the provisions of the previous Act.
The right of domicile of an adopted child shall be determined according to the adoptive parents also in cases where the adoption has taken place before the entry into force of this Act.

Section 73
Trade

A person habitually resident in Åland at the time of the entry into force of this Act shall, after having resided in Åland for five years without interruption, have the right to practice a trade in Åland in accordance with the provisions of the previous Act.
The private persons, companies, co-operations, associations and other corporations and foundations that at the time of the entry into force of this Act practice a trade in Åland in accordance with the provisions of the previous Act shall have the right to continually practice the said trade in accordance with the provisions of the previous Act.

Section 74
Dealing with matters at transfer of authority

A matter, where the authority is transferred between officials in accordance with this Act, shall be dealt with by the officials with whom the matter was pending at the time of the transfer of authority. The matter shall be dealt with in accordance with the provisions of force before the transfer of authority.
The previous Act and the other applicable former Acts shall apply to an appeal against an official decision made before the transfer of authority.

Section 75
State officials

A person whose duties in a State office are in accordance with this Act transferred to the authority of Åland shall, if he so consents, be transferred with equal benefits to corresponding duties in an Åland office, as provided by Decree.
Until the issuance of the Decree referred to in section 42, paragraph 1, the previous Act

and the legislation on the linguistic proficiency of State officials, in the form they were at the time of the entry into force of this Act, shall apply to the required linguistic proficiency of a State official in Åland.
A person in a State office in Åland at the time of the entry into force of this Act shall be continually qualified for the said office, regardless of the provisions of the Decree issued in accordance with section 42, paragraph 1.

Section 76
Impeachment

The provisions of the previous Act on the impeachment of the Chairman or a member of the Government of Åland, a presenting official thereof or another Åland official shall be continually applied, until otherwise provided by Decree.

Section 77
Regular equalisation, extraordinary grants and the alteration of the basis for equalisation

The regular equalisation referred to in the previous Act shall be carried out for the last time for the year preceding the entry into force of this Act.
An extraordinary grant given before the entry into force of this Act may be supplemented on the two years following the entry into force of this Act.
The basis for equalisation shall be altered if the bases for the State final accounts change before the entry into force of this Act in a manner referred to in section 47, paragraph 2.

Section 78
Land, buildings and facilities

The provisions of section 61, paragraph 2 shall apply also to land, buildings and facilities used in regular State administration at the time of the entry into force of this Act.
A Decree may be issued to the effect that the State land, building or facility not referred to in paragraph 1 be handed over to Åland.

Section 79
Movable property

When the duties of a State official are transferred to an Åland official in accordance with this Act, the State movable property in Åland necessary for the carrying out of the said duties shall pass to Åland without compensation.

PROTOCOL

11994N/PRO/02
ACT concerning the conditions of accession of the Kingdom of Norway, the Republic of Austria, the Republic of Finland and the Kingdom of Sweden and the adjustments to the Treaties on which the European Union is founded, Protocol No 2 - on the Åland islands
Official Journal C 241 , 29/08/1994 p. 0352

MORE INFO TEXT:

Protocol No 2
on the AAland islands

Taking into account the special status that the AAland islands enjoy under international law, the Treaties on which the European Union is founded shall apply to the AAland islands with the following derogations:

Article 1
The provisions of the EC Treaty shall not preclude the application of the existing provisions in force on 1 January 1994 on the AAland islands on:
- restrictions, on a non-discriminatory basis, on the right of natural persons who do not enjoy hembygdsraett/kotiseutuoikeus (regional citizenship) in AAland, and for legal persons, to acquire and hold real property on the AAland islands without permission by the competent authorities of the AAland islands;
- restrictions, on a non-discriminatory basis, on the right of establishment and the right to provide services by natural persons who do not enjoy hembygdsraett/kotiseutuoikeus (regional citizenship) in AAland, or by legal persons without permission by the competent authorities of the AAland islands.

Article 2
(a) The territory of the AAland islands - being considered as a third territory, as defined in Article 3 (1) third indent of Council Directive 77/388/EEC as amended, and as a national territory falling outside the field of application of the excise harmonization directives as defined in Article 2 of Council Directive 92/12/EEC - shall be excluded from the territorial application of the EC provisions in the fields of harmonization of the laws of the Member States on turnover taxes and on excise duties and other forms of indirect taxation. This exemption shall not have any effect on the Community's own resources. This paragraph shall not apply to the provisions of Council Directive 69/335/EEC, as amended, relating to capital duty.
(b) This derogation is aimed at maintaining a viable local economy in the islands and shall not have any negative effects on the interests of the Union nor on its common policies. If the Commission considers that the provisions in paragraph (a) are no longer justified, particularly in terms of fair competition or own resources, it shall submit appropriate proposals to the Council, which shall act in accordance with the pertinent articles of the EC Treaty.

Article 3
The Republic of Finland shall ensure that the same treatment applies to all natural and legal persons of the Member States in the AAland islands.

EU ISLANDS

Åland Islands

The Åland Islands form an autonomous and demilitarized province of Finland, which acceded to the European Union on January 1, 1995. Åland's special relationship with the EU is regulated by Protocol 2 to the Finnish Act of Accession.

Regulation 82/97/EC stipulates that the Åland Islands are part of the **customs territory** of the European Union. The Euro is the currency in the Åland Islands.

Åland's official website is: http://www.ls.aland.fi

For an English language overview of the Åland Islands, see http://www.aland.fi/virtual/eng/frame.html

Azores

The Azores, located 740 miles west of Portugal, are part of Portugal and entered the EU when Portugal and Spain became members in 1986. As such, the Azores are part of the **customs territory** of the EU, and the Euro is their currency. The Azores have no separate agreements with the EU, but as one of the "remote regions," they benefit from special Community support. The *POSEIMA* program was established to this end to benefit the Azores and Madeira.

The Amsterdam Treaty introduced Article 299 (2), which defines and characterizes the EU's "outermost regions." This article provides for the application of the Treaty while "taking into account the special characteristics and constraints of these outermost regions without undermining the integrity and coherence of the Community legal order…."

The Azores regional government's Portuguese language website follows:

http://www.azores.gov.pt/

Canary Islands

The Canary Island archipelago consists of seven main islands of volcanic origin, situated over six hundred miles from the Iberian Peninsula. The Canary Islands are part of the territory of Spain and, as such, part of the territory of the European Union. The Euro is the official currency.

Initially, the Canary Islands were specifically excluded from the customs territory of the EU (Article 1(2) of Protocol 2 to the Spanish and Portuguese accession agreement). However, Regulation 1911/91/EEC changed that status and included the Canary Islands in the EU's **customs territory** from July 1, 1991, introducing a gradual application of the common customs tariff (CCT) from that date until its full application in 2000.

The Canary Islands are excluded from the EU VAT in Article 3 (3) of the EU's Sixth Council Directive on the common system of VAT (77/388/EEC, as amended).

As with the Azores, the Canary Islands benefit from the EU's efforts to support the outermost regions, as stated in Article 299 (2) of the Amsterdam Treaty. To this end, the EU's *POSEICAN* program was established.

The official website of the Canary Islands is: http://www.gobcan.es

Channel Islands

The Channel Islands are situated off the northwest coast of France in the Bay of St. Malo. The Channel Islands (Alderney, Guernsey, Herm, Jersey and Sark) are self-governing Crown dependencies with their own legislative assemblies, systems of local administration and law and their own courts. The British government is responsible for their defense and international relations, including relations with the European Union.

Protocol 3 to the UK act of accession applies EU customs rules to the Channel Islands, and Article 3 of the Customs Code (EU Regulation 2913/92/EEC, as amended) includes the Channel Islands as part of the EU's **customs territory**. The islands are excluded from the provisions of the EC Treaty, apart from those ensuring the proper functioning of free trade with the European Union (Article 25 (c) of the UK Act of Accession).

EU **VAT** requirements do not apply in the Channel Islands.

Both the UK and the Channel Islands issue notes and coinage. Although Channel Islands currency is of equal value to UK money, travelers should exchange it before returning home, as this currency does not circulate widely. Alderney issues its own commemorative coins. Guernsey has been issuing its own currency since 1816 (although this currency is tied to the UK Sterling) and has coins shaped similarly to those of the UK. The currency in Jersey is Sterling, although the Island has its own coins and notes. English money is readily accepted, as are UK and Euro-cheques supported by a bank card, and most credit cards. Sark is in the UK currency area. UK, Guernsey and Jersey currencies are in circulation in Sark.

Faroe Islands

The Faroe Islands are an island group located in northern Europe, between the Norwegian Sea and the North Atlantic Ocean, about one-half of the distance from Iceland to Norway. The Faroes, part of the Kingdom of Denmark, have been a self-governing overseas administrative division of Denmark since 1948.

The currency is the Danish krone. Unlike Denmark, the Faroe Islands are not part of the European Union. Article 299 (6a) of the *Treaty establishing the European Community* states that "this Treaty shall not apply to the Faroe Islands." In 1974, the Faroese Parliament decided by a unanimous vote not to apply for EU membership. Instead, a trade agreement was concluded between the Faroe Islands and the EU.

Article 3 (1) of the EU's Customs Code, as amended, specifically excludes the Faroe Islands from the **customs territory** of the European Union.

The English portion of the official website for the Parliament of the Faroe Islands is: http://www.logting.fo/Pdf/logen.pdf

French Overseas Departments

The French Overseas Departments consist of the Caribbean islands of Guadeloupe and Martinique, the island of Reunion in the Indian Ocean and French Guiana on the northeast coast of South America. The French Overseas Departments are part of France and part of the customs territory. The Euro is their currency. The provisions of EU treaties apply to these departments and, because of their remoteness, they also benefit from special EU assistance under Article 299 (2) of the *Treaty Establishing the European Community.* The *Poseidom* program was established by Council Decision 89/687EEC to achieve these objectives.

French Overseas Territorial Collectivities

St. Pierre-et-Miquelon is located near the southwest coast of Newfoundland, Canada, and Mayotte is a volcanic island located in the Indian Ocean northwest of Madagascar.

These two French territorial communities (collectivités territoriales), Saint Pierre-et-Miquelon and Mayotte, are not part of the EU and are excluded from the **customs territory** in Article 3 (1) of the EU's Customs Code, as amended.

Council Decision 1999/95/EC (see also this location) stipulates that the Euro shall be the currency in both of these overseas territorial collectivities.

Greenland

Greenland is the world's largest island with more than 80 percent of its area covered by ice. Cape Morris Jesup at the northernmost extremity of Greenland is the northernmost land area in the world, situated fewer than 500 miles from the North Pole. Greenland's southernmost point, Cape Farewell, is 1,600 miles to the south of Cape Morris Jesup.

Greenland, like the Faroe Islands, is part of the Kingdom of Denmark. All three areas have in common: the Danish Royal Family, the Constitution, foreign policy, defense, the judicial system and the currency. Greenland does exercise a certain amount of autonomy through "home rule," approved by the Danish legislature and effective in 1979.

Greenland entered the EU in 1973 as part of Denmark, however a 1982 referendum on EU membership was narrowly defeated, and Greenland left the Community. The Treaty of withdrawal (of March 13, 1984), or "*Greenland Treaty*" (*Official Journal* L 29 of February 1, 1985), came into force on February 1, 1985, and granted Greenland the status of an **Overseas Country and Territory (OCT).** This arrangement is spelled out in Articles 182-188 and Annex II of the *Treaty Establishing the European Community.* One of the most important applications of the OCT status for Greenland is the non-reciprocal trade regime, the most generous granted to any Community partner. Greenland is ensured of unlimited duty-free access to the EU market for its fisheries products.

The Danish krone is used in Greenland. Greenland is not part of the **customs territory** of the EU, as spelled out in Article 3 (1) of the EU's Customs Code, as amended.

A recent Commission Communication [COM(2002) 697 of December 3, 2002] assesses EU relations with Greenland, particularly in the fisheries sector, while considering future possibilities for the bilateral relationship.

Greenland's official website (English version) is:
http://dk.nanoq.gl/enhed.asp?page=enhed&objno=522

Isle of Man

The Isle of Man, a British Crown dependency, is located in the Irish Sea between Northern Ireland, Scotland and England. The island is an internally self-governing dependent territory of the British Crown that is not part of the United Kingdom.

The Isle of Man has a special relationship with the European Union set out in Protocol 3 to the United Kingdom's Treaty of Accession. The Isle of Man is not a Member State of the European Union.

Under Protocol 3 of the EU's Customs Code (Article 3, as amended), the Isle of Man is part of the **customs territory** of the Union. It follows that there is free movement of industrial and agricultural goods in trade between the island and the Union. The Isle of Man neither contributes nor receives funds from the European Union, thus guaranteeing the island's fiscal independence. Any proposal to change Protocol 3 would require the unanimous approval of all Member States of the EU, including the UK.

The Isle of Man does impose a Value Added Tax (VAT) (EU Directive 92/111/EEC—Article 1) as though it were part of the EU, but it is administered through its own Office of Customs and Excise.

Apart from the requirements of Protocol 3, in particular that the Isle of Man authorities shall apply the same treatment to all natural and legal persons of the Union, the other EU rules do not apply.

The island's relationship with the EU allows it to trade with countries in the European Economic Area in a fashion generally similar to its trade with the EU itself.

The Isle of Man issues its own currency.

The official website of the Isle of Man is: http://www.gov.im/

Madeira

The Madeira Islands are located 350 miles off the northwest coast of Africa. While part of Portugal, Madeira does enjoy partial autonomy. To the outside world Madeirans are, to all intents and purposes, Portuguese. They carry Portuguese passports, vote in Portuguese elections and pay Portuguese taxes. Where they differ from the rest (with the exception of their island brethren on the Azores) is that they are also represented at a local level by the Regional Government.

The Madeira Islands entered the EU as part of Portugal in 1986. There is no separate agreement. As such, Madeira is part of the **customs territory** of the EU and uses the Euro as its currency.

Article 299 (2) of the *Amsterdam Treaty (Treaty Establishing the European Community)* states that the Treaty applies to the Madeira Islands, and it provides for the same supportive measures applicable to other remote Community regions. Madeira, like the Azores, benefits from the provisions of the *POSEIMA* program.

POLITICAL AND GOVERNMENT SYSTEM

Landscape government's public administration consists of six departments, moreover, there is a law drafting. Each section consists of one or more agencies and is, within its management area and for the preparation of matters, and for administration verksamhet.Varje agency may also consist of different units. Audit Office, which is independent of the overall management, manages the internal audit and reports directly the Government of Åland in addition to those that were examined.

Landscape government has adopted an environmental policy for the internal operations of public administration. The introduction of an environmental management system aimed at reducing the negative environmental impact of provincial government.

Politics of the Åland Islands takes place in a framework of a parliamentary representative democratic autonomous, demilitarised and unilingually Swedish territory of Finland, whereby the Lantråd is the head of government, and of a multi-party system.

The Åland Islands are governed according to the Act on Åland Autonomy and international treaties, which guarantees autonomy and demilitarized status. The Government of Åland, or *Landskapsregering*, is dependent on the Parliament of Åland, or *Lagting*, according to the principles of parliamentarism.

In 1634, Åland was made part of the Åbo and Björneborg County as a part of the grand administrative reforms initiated by count Axel Oxenstierna. The county became part of the Russian Empire within the Grand Duchy of Finland in 1809, when Sweden was forced to cede vast areas in the Napoleonic Wars. When Finland declared its independence in 1917, the newly established state inherited the Åland islands.

During the Civil War in 1918, some Russian troops were still stationed on the islands, causing serious instability and nervousness. This anxiety in the local population, and in the other Scandinavian states, resulted in a Swedish occupation and 7,135 people (of a total population of approximately 22,500 at the time) signing the address for Åland joining the kingdom of Sweden. The fear of Russia finally resulted in a German occupation of the islands. In the mean time, the Finnish press was playing with the idea of an exchange of land areas between Sweden and Finland. The areas in question of this exchange would have been the Swedish speaking Åland to Sweden and some Finnish speaking areas of Norrbotten and Västerbotten to Finland. The response from the Swedish government was bluntly negative to any exchanges of this nature.

In 1921 the question of Åland was brought to the council of League of Nations. The council decided unanimously, that the islands would remain under Finland's sovereignty, but stated that the native population's rights to their own language had to be preserved, that the area had to stay demilitarized and that Åland was granted autonomy during peace time.

Åland has its own national flag, has issued its own postage stamps since 1984, has its own police force, and is a member of the Nordic Council. The islands are demilitarised, and the male population is exempted from conscription. Parliamentarism has been the custom since 1988. The Åland autonomy preceded the creation of the Regions of Finland, but the autonomous government of Åland also handles what the regional councils do.

The sovereignty over Åland belongs to Finland, and Åland is thus not independent. The Åland Islands are guaranteed representation in the Finnish parliament, and elect one representative.

EXECUTIVE BRANCH

Main office holders

Office	Name	Party	Since
Lantråd	Viveka Eriksson	LÅ	2003
Other Government parties		ÅC	

Åland does not only have its own Government of Åland (*Ålands Landskapsregering*), there is also a Åland State Provincial Office (*Länsstyrelsen på Åland*), led by a governor, Peter Lindbäck.

LEGISLATIVE BRANCH

The Parliament of Åland (*Lagtinget*, which means Law Thing) has 30 members, elected for a four year term by proportional representation.

POLITICAL PARTIES AND ELECTIONS

Summary of the 21 October 2007 Parliament of Åland election results

Parties	Votes		%		Seats	
	2007	+/–	2007	+/–	2007	+/–
Liberals for Åland (Liberalerna på Åland)	4,173	+1,203	32.6	+8.5	10	+3
Åland Centre (Ålands Center)	3,106	+126	24.2	+0.1	8	+1
Non-aligned Coalition (Obunden Samling)	1,571	+408	12.3	+2.9	4	+1
Åland Social Democrats (Ålands Socialdemokrater)	1,512	-826	11.8	-7.2	3	-3
Freeminded Co-operation (Frisinnad Samverkan)	1,235	–424	9.6	–4.0	3	-1
Future of Åland (Ålands Framtid)	1,069	+269	8.3	+1.8	2	±0
Hut Group (Hutgruppen)	153	-	1.2	-	0	-
Total (turnout 67.8%)	13,166		100		30	

Sources: JCI Mariehamn, Parties and Elections in Europe

THE PARLIAMENT OF ÅLAND

Åland Parliament, P.O. Box 69, AX-22101 Mariehamn, Finland, phone +358-18-25000, fax +358-18-13302, http://www.lagtinget.aland.fi.

SECRETARIAT

Visiting address: Strandgatan, The Parliament Building, floor 3, Mariehamn, Åland
Post address: The Parliament of Åland, P.O. Box 69, AX-22101 Mariehamn, Finland

Phone: +358-18-25000
Fax: +358-18-13302

STAFF:
Secretary General: Mr Lars Ingmar Johansson, phone +358-18-25331, GSM +358 457 5267475, e-mail: Larsingmar.Johansson@lagtinget.aland.fi

Deputy Secretary General: Susanne Eriksson, phone +358 18 25472, GSM +358-457-5230416, e-mail: susanne.eriksson@lagtinget.aland.fi

Committee Secretary and Secretary of the Åland Delegation to the Nordic Council, Ms Marine Holm-Johansson, phone +358-18-25474, GSM +358-457-5267474 e-mail: Marine.Holm-Johansson@lagtinget.aland.fi

Librarian: Ms Lilian Norring-Öhman, phone +358 18 25354, e-mail: lilian.norring-ohman@lagtinget.aland.fi

Assistant, archivist: Ms Annette Gammals, phone +358-18-25332, e-mail: Annette.Gammals@lagtinget.aland.fi

Assistant: Ms Maj Falck, phone +358-18-25353, e-mail: Maj.Falck@lagtinget.aland.fi

Stenographer: Ms Anita Karrento, phone +358-18-25333, e-mail: Anita.Karrento@lagtinget.aland.fi

Messenger: Mr Hans Grönvall, phone +358-18-25334, +358-18-25337, GSM 0457-5267463, e-mail: Hans.Gronvall@lagtinget.aland.fi

IN WHICH SPHERES CAN THE LAGTING PASS LAWS?
Thanks to their autonomy, the Ålanders possess the right to pass laws themselves concerning their own internal matters and to exercise budgetary powers. The Parliament of Åland is called the Lagting. The Lagting appoints the Landskapsstyrelse, Åland's "government." Rules on the autonomy are contained in the Act on the Autonomy of Åland, which can only be altered by the Parliament of Finland in constitutional order and with the consent of the the Åland Lagting. The current Autonomy Act came into force on 1 January 1993.
The Autonomy Act specifies the spheres in which the Åland Lagting has the right to pass laws. The most important sectors are
education, culture and preservation of ancient monuments
health and medical services
promotion of industry
internal communications
municipal administration
the police service
the postal service
radio and television.

We may say that in these spheres Åland functions in just about the same way as an independent state with its own legislation and administrative machinery.

THE SESSION HALL OF THE LAGTING

WHICH SPHERES BELONG TO THE AUTHORITIES OF FINLAND?
In spheres where the Lagting does not possess legislative competence, the laws of Finland apply just like in the rest of the country.
Examples of such sectors are
 administration of foreign affairs
 most aspects of civil and penal law
 courts of justice
 customs and monetary services.
To enable the interests of Åland to be safeguarded in these matters as well, Åland has its own representative in the Parliament of Finland, who is elected in the same way as other Members of Parliament in Finland.

HOW IS THE LAGTING ELECTED?
The Lagting, consisting of 30 members, is elected every four years by means of secret, proportional ballot, the voting age being 18. Only persons possessing regional citizenship in Åland may vote and stand in such elections.

POLITICS
After the election in October 1999 there are six groups represented in the Lagting:
Åland Centre, 9 seats
Liberals in Åland, 9 seats
Moderates ("Frisinnad Samverkan"), 4 seats
Åland Social Democrats, 3 seats
Independents, 4 seats
The Åland Progressive Group, 1 seat

The political groups in Åland are all quite independent from parties outside Åland, but naturally they have borrowed their ideological features from equivalent groups in neighbouring countries.

ECONOMIC AUTONOMY

Besides passing laws, the main duty of the Lagting is to adopt the budget of Åland. The new Autonomy Act has entailed great changes for the autonomy in economic aspects. As previously, the State of Finland collects taxes, customs duty and charges in Åland like in the rest of Finland. In return the outlays of Åland are compensated through an allocation in the State budget being placed at the disposal of the Lagting. This allocation amounts to 0.45 % of the income of the State budget with the exception of State loans. This lump sum is to enable Åland to manage such affairs which otherwise would be administered by the State authorities. The Lagting is free to decide how to apportion the lump sum.

LEGISLATIVE SUPERVISION

Laws passed by the Lagting are submitted to the President of Finland, who may impose his veto. The President has a veto only in two cases: if the Lagting has exceeded its legislative competence, or if the law affects the external or internal security of the country.

The President bases his decision upon statements from the Åland Delegation, and sometimes also upon statements from the Supreme Court. Half of the members of the Åland Delegation are appointed by the Government of Finland and half by the Åland Lagting.

PARLIAMENT OF ÅLAND 1 NOVEMBER 1999 - 31 OCTOBER 2003

STANDING COMMITTEES 1999-2003

THE LEGAL COMMITTEE	**THE FINANCE COMMITTEE**	**THE COMMITTEE FOR INDUSTRY, TRADE AND AGRICULTURE**	**THE CULTURAL COMMITTEE**
Lotta Wickström-Johansson (chair) Fredrik Lindqvist (v.ordf) Mats Perämaa Olof Salmén Christer Jansson Secretary: Lars-Ingmar Johansson	Folke Sjölund (chair.) Lars Holmberg (v.chair.) Dennis Jansson Anne-Helena Sjöblom Jan-Erik Mattsson Secretary: Marine Holm-Johansson	Anne-May Pehrsson (chair) Leo Sjöstrand (v.chair) Gun-Mari Lindholm Harriet Lindeman Anders Englund Secretary: Susanne Eriksson	Jörgen Strand (chair) Britt Lundberg (v.chair) Per-Erik Eriksson Hasse Svensson Barbro Sundback Secretary: Susanne Eriksson
THE SOCIAL AND ENVIRONMENTAL COMMITTEE	THE GRAND COMMITTEE	THE REVIEW COMMITTEE	THE PARLIAMENT OFFICE COMMISSION

Ulf Andersson (chair) Lasse Wiklöf (v.chair) Raija-Liisa Eklöw Sune Mattsson Danne Sundman Secretary: Marine Holm-Johansson	Barbro Sundback (chair) Harriet Lindeman (v.chair) Bert Häggblom Ronald Boman Lisbeth Eriksson Raija-Liisa Eklöw Lotta Wickström-Johansson Per-Erik Eriksson Ulf Andersson Britt Lundberg Secretary: Pehr Karlström	Ronald Boman (chair) Harriet Lindeman (v.chair) Anne-May Pehrsson Secretary: Lars-Ingmar Johansson	Speaker Viveka Eriksson I v. Speaker Christer Jansson II v. Speaker Bert Häggblom Ragnar Erlandsson Anne-Helena Sjöblom Secretary: Lars-Ingmar Johansson
THE AUTONOMY COMMITTEE	THE SPEAKERS' CONFERENCE	THE DELEGATION OF ÅLAND AT THE NORDIC COUNCIL	
Speaker Viveka Eriksson (chair) Christer Jansson (v.chair) Bert Häggblom Lasse Wiklöf Roger Jansson Folke Sjölund Britt Lundberg Secretary: Lars-Ingmar Johansson and Susanne Eriksson	Speaker Viveka Eriksson v.speaker Christer Jansson II v.speaker Bert Häggblom Ulf Andersson Ronald Boman Anne-May Pehrsson Folke Sjölund Jörgen Strand Lotta Wickström-Johansson	Ragnar Erlandsson (chair) Harriet Lindeman Hasse Svensson Lasse Wiklöf	

THE STRUCTURE OF THE PARLIAMENT

The Parliament has thirty members, who participate in the Chamber as well as in the work of the Parliaments seven committees and other special bodies.

THE PRESIDIUM

The Presidium of the Parliament consists of the Speaker and the two Deputy Speakers, all of whom are elected for one year at a time. The Speaker conducts the business in the Chamber but may not participate in the debate. In the Speaker's absence the business in the Chamber is conducted by one of the Deputy Speakers. The Deputy Speakers may participate in the debate except when they chair the session.

THE STANDING COMMITTEES

The Parliament has seven standing committees. Most items of Parliament business are examined by one of the six special standing committees, each of which is responsible for a specific area.The Special Standing Committees have five members each plus five deputy members. The Review Committee has three members and three deputy members.

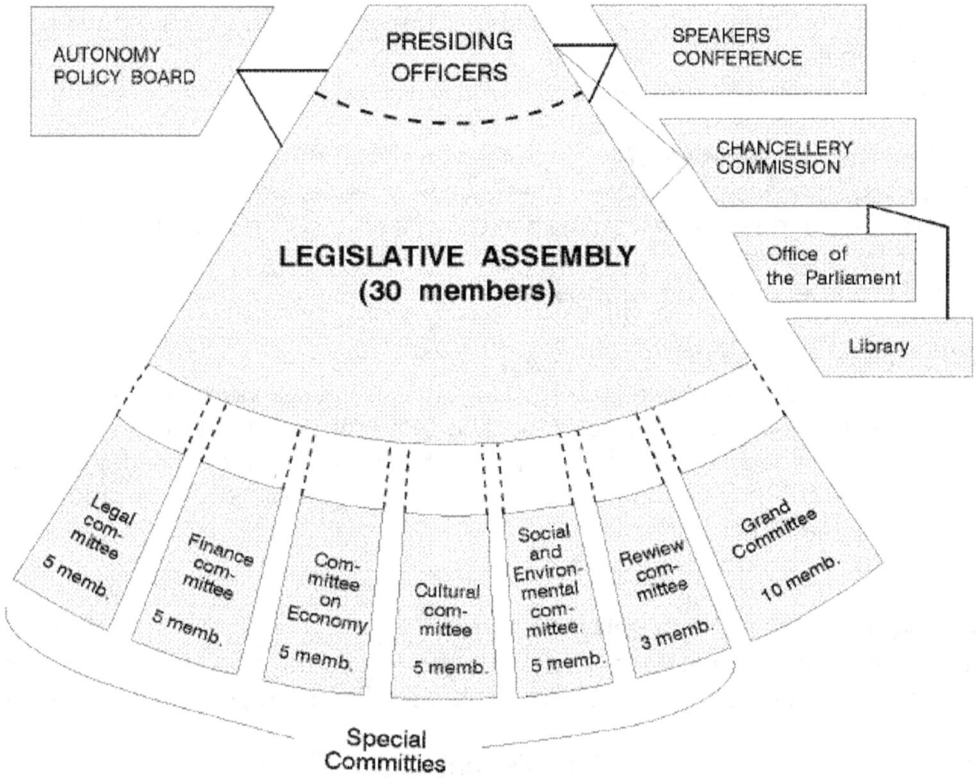

The Legal Committee prepares all legal business which relates to the autonomy of Åland and to international treaties which are applicable to Åland. The Legal Committee also prepares business which involves legislation relating to the administration of Åland, to local authorities, traffic, the police force, elections, and the civil service.
The Finance Committee examines the Åland Government's budget proposals, finance motions, the auditors' reports, requests for extra budgetary grants, local authority finance, and collective wage agreements. The Committee may also prepare bills which apply to the budget or the audit.

The Committee for Industry, Trade and Agriculture prepares business which relates to industry, trade agriculture, taxation, fishing, wild game hunting and regional policy.
The Cultural Committee deals with education, cultural activities, sport, museums, archives, libraries, radio and television.

The Social and Environmental Committee prepares business relating to social welfare, health care, building and housing legislation, as well as nature conservation and environmental issues.

The Review Committee ensures that the formal wording of the Parlaiments resolutions is correct.

In addition to the Special Committees, **the Grand Committee** examines legal matters or international treaties which have already been before one of the Special Committees. Business of this kind may be sent to the Grand Committee at the request of at least eiight members of the Parliament. In practice, matters are sent to the Grand Committee only if they are complicated or controversial or if they require further legal preparation. The Grand Committee has ten members.
[Members of the Standig Committees]

THE SPEAKERS' CONFERENCE

The Speakers' Conference consists of the Presidium of the Parliament and the chairmen of the Special Committees. The Conference deals with the Parliaments working practices and procedures.
[Members of the Speakers' Conference]

THE AUTONOMY COMMITTEE

The Autonomy Committee advises the Parliament and the Government of Åland on important matters relating to the autonomy. The Government of Åland presents a yearly report which is examined by the Autonomy Committee, after which it is put before the Parliament. The Autonomy Committee consists of the Speaker and four members elected by the Parliament.
[Members of the Autonomy Committee]

THE PARLIAMENT OFFICE COMMISSION

The Parliament Office Commission consists of the Presidium and two members chosen by the Parliament. It deals with the running of the Parliaments economy and the Parliament Office.
[Members of the Parliament Office Commission]

THE PARLIAMENT LIBRARY

The Parliament has a library for the use of its own members and the officials of the Åland administration. It mainly holds books on political science, law and territorial autonomy.

THE DELEGATION OF ÅLAND AT THE NORDIC COUNCIL

The Delegation works in conjunction with the Parliament. It consists of two representatives from Åland chosen by the Parliament, their deputies, and the members of the Åland Government. The Delegation deals with matters which concern the work of the Nordic Council and the Nordic Ministerial Council.
[Members of the Delegation of Åland at the Nordic Council]

BUSINESS IN THE PARLIAMENT

WHO MAY INTRODUCE AN ITEM OF BUSINESS?

The work of the Parliament is highly formalized. Only certain individuals or bodies are entitled to introduce items of business in the Parliament. The rules specify that only the President of Finland, the Government of Åland and the members of the Parliament may introduce business.

Representations
Proposals made by the Government of Åland to the Parliament are called representations. Representations from the Government of Åland may concern proposals for items in the Åland budget as well as issues concerning guarantees for Åland, initiatives in the Parliament of Finland and requests for extra budgetary expenditure.

The Government of Åland is assisted by its civil service in the preparation of parliamentary business and is consequently the Parliament main "client". The Government of Åland submits approximately fifty representations every year to the Parliament. **The President of Finland** also submits representations to the Parliament. In accordance with the Autonomy Act, the Parliament shall give its consent to laws which bring into effect international treaties which affect Åland's legal position. If the Parliament withholds its consent, such treaties remain invalid for Åland. The most common international treaties to which the Parliament has given its consent concern social benefits and health care as well as the avoidance of double taxation. The Parliaments consent was also necessary for the ESS Treaty. When Finland joined the EU, the Parliament had to give its consent for Åland, otherwise the Åland Islands would have remained outside the Union like the autonomous areas of Denmark, the Faroes and Greenland.

Finally, the Parliaments own organ, the **Speakers' Conference,** may submit representations to it. The representations of the Speakers' Conference concern internal legislation.

Motions
Proposals from the Parliaments own members are called motions. They are of three kinds: legal motions, finance motions, and petitions.

Legal motions contain ready-drafted legislative proposals. **Finance motions** contain proposals for grants to be included in the budget of Åland. **Petitions** are requests that the Government of Åland should take specific measures. Besides to the Government of Åland, such requests may be submitted to the Parliament of Finland, to the Speakers' Conference, or to the Autonomy Committee.

Notification
The Government of Åland may notify the Parliament of matters which it considers to fall within the Parliaments purview for comment but about which it does not wish make specific proposals for action. Such notification often concerns major reforms which are still at the planning stage.

Reports
The Parliament receives and considers a number of reports. The following bodies are required by law to submit yearly reports on their activities: Åland's Delegation at the Nordic Council, the Åland Government'a Auditors, and the Parliaments Library Commission.

When May Business Be Introduced?
Submissions to the Parliament may be made at any time. This also applies, in principle, to legal motions. However, there are strict rules governing the timing of petitions and finance motions as well as the different categories of reports.

THE PARLIAMENTS WORKING PROCEDURES

Most parliamentary business is discussed both in Chamber and in committee.
All items are first considered in **plenary session (or the Chamber),** where the members have an opportunity to discuss them in the Initial Debate, after which almost all business, with the exception of certain kinds of notification, is sent to a **Special Committee** on the advice of the Speakers' Conference. Submissions and motions must always be considered in committee.

The committees may hear experts and their business is always conducted behind closed doors. When a committee has finished an item of business, it presents a **report,** which is then discussed in the **Chamber.**

The committee reports are best viewed as proposals to the Parliament, since all final decisions are taken in the Chamber. If an item relates to international treaties or is a legislative proposal, the decision must be taken only after three separate debates in the Chamber.

The First Debate is an occasion for general discussion. After the First Debate the Parliament decides whether an item should be sent to the **Grand Committee** or not. Eight votes in favour ensures that an item goes to the Grand Committee.
If an item of business is sent to the Grand Committee, it will not be discussed in the Second Debate until the Committee has presented its report on it. If an item is not considered by the Grand Committee, the **Second Debate** takes place immediately. Final decisions on items relating to international treaties and legislative proposals are taken after the **Third Debate.**

Decisions that do not involve legislative proposals or international treaties are taken on the basis of reports from special committees. This is known as a **Single Debate.**
The Parliament takes its decisions as a rule on a majority vote. For cases which relate to the Autonomy Act, a qualified, i.e. a two-thirds majority, is required. In the case of an equal number of votes for and against, the Speaker has the casting vote, except in elections, when the lot decides.
Business which has not been finished when the Parliament is dissolved before an election is dropped from the agenda. There is thus no obligation to consider a specific item of business. In practice, however, all items except a small number of motions are dealt with.

SUPERVISION OF LEGISLATIVE AUTHORITY

When the Parliament has resolved to enact a law for Åland, the resolution must be submitted to **the President of Finland,** who verifies that the Parliament is acting within its authority. Before an act is put before the President, **the Åland Delegation** must report on it.

The Åland Delegation is a board of arbitration which consists of five members, two of whom are chosen by the Council of State and two by the Parliament of Åland. The Governor of Åland acts as chairman. In addition to supervising legislation, the Åland Delegation has certain duties relating to the financial equalisation between Åland and the Finnish State. The President may veto laws enacted by the Parliament of Åland if

1) they exceed the legislative authority of Åland, or
2) they are contrary to the Republic's external or internal security.
Thus the President may not annul an act partly or wholly for reasons of expediency.
Before the President uses his power of veto, he must obtain the opinion of **the Supreme Court** on the act.

According to the Autonomy Act, the President must make his decision within four months. Once this has happened, the Government of Åland may promulgate the act, thereby giving it the force of law.

PARLIAMENTARY ELECTIONS

In accordance with the Åland Autonomy Act, the Parliament represents the population of Åland in matters relating to the autonomy of the Åland Islands. The members of the Parliament are elected by **direct and secret ballot** in which **suffrage is universal and equal.**
In accordance with the Autonomy Act, the Parliament itself has the power to legislate on matters concerning its election. The rules governing Parliamentary elections are stated in the Act of Åland on Parliamentary and local council elections. (39/70).
This information leaflet explains who may vote and who may stand in Parliamentary elections as well as how elections are organized and how the results are calculated.

FRANCHISE AND ELIGIBILITY FOR OFFICE

The franchise in the Parliamentary and local council elections is limited to those persons whose eighteenth birthday falls on or before the election day and who have the rigt of domicile in Åland. The right of domicile is also a necessary condition for eligibility, that is to say, the right to stand as a candidate in elections.
The right of domicile is automatic for persons born in Åland of parents who themselves have this right. The Parliament of Åland may also grant the right of domicile to applicants who have been resident in Åland for five years and who have satisfactory proficiency in the Swedish language.

THE TIMING OF PARLIAMENTARY ELECTIONS

Statutory elections to the Parliament are held every four years on the third Sunday in October.
Local council elections are held simultaneously and not at the same time as elsewhere in Finland. Parliamentary and presidential elections are thus held simultaneously with the rest of Finland.
Advance voting may take place by post or at home in case of infirmity or in hospitals or other institutions.

ELECTORAL ASSOCIATIONS AND ELECTORAL ALLIANCES

A number of electors may join together into an **Electoral Association** and draw up an common list of candidates with one or several names on it. Electoral Associations may in their turn join into **Electoral Alliances.**

Party politics is of fairly recent date in Åland, but during the last few decades the electoral alliances have largely coincided with the political fractions or parties.

THE CALCULATION OF ELECTION RESULTS

In Parliamentary elections each candidate has his or her own numer. Voters write their candidate's number on the ballot paper. In contrast to the procedure in many other countries, voters do not cast their votes for party lists.

In the Parliamentary elections in Åland votes are cast both for individual candidates and for lists. The principle underlyling the election system is proportional representation and the result is calculated according to the so-called d'Hondt Method.
The distribution of the thirty seats in the Parliament is done proportionally on the basis of the total number of votes cast for the electoral alliances, that is to say, the total number of votes cast for all the candidates of an electoral alliance. In this sense a vote for a candidate also benefits an electoral alliance or party.

The number of votes cast for each individual candidate decides which candidates have been elected.

If the candidates of an electoral alliance appear on single-name lists, i.e. if electoral associations put up only one candidate each, the candidate who has received the most votes is given the electoral association's first seat, the candidate with the second most votes is given the second seat etc.

If candidates appear on multi-name lists, they are first awarded a comparative number on the list according to the number of votes cast for eache of them. The candidate with the largest number of votes is given the highest comparative number etc. The seats are then distributed according to the comparative numbers.

THE MOST RECENT ELECTION

The most recent Parliamentary election was held in October 2003. The seats in the Parliament were distributed as follows:

Åland Centre, 7 seats
Liberals in Åland, 7 seats
Åland Social Democrats, 6 seats
Moderates ("Frisinnad Samverkan"), 3 seats
Independents, 3 seats
The Future of Åland, 2 seats
The Åland Progressive Group, 1 seat

ALAND AND FINLAND

REPORT COMPLETED ON THE IMPORTANCE FOR THE PROVINCE OF ÅLAND OF WORK ON THE FUTURE OF EUROPE

In the EU Convention on the Future of Europe and the subsequent Inter-Governmental Conference, Finland must strive for treaty formulation which retains the existing legal effects of the Åland Protocol in both EU law and Finnish legislation. Potential for augmenting the Act on the Autonomy of Åland with provisions enabling the administrative organs of the province to make their views known to the Finnish Parliament should be explored.

These are the recommendations made in the report "EU competence and Åland" (in Finnish and Swedish), submitted by Government Counsellor Niilo Jääskinen to the Prime Minister's Office. Jääskinen had been appointed to study how changes in the division of powers between the EU and its Member States that may arise in the Convention and the next Inter-Governmental Conference could affect the sphere of competence of the Province of Åland. He was further required to investigate how any changes made in EU competences and decision-making procedures could affect the position of Åland in Finnish EU policy.

In terms of safeguarding Åland's position, Jääskinen reports that the implications of the EU's being a legal person should be studied separately. He also recommends that, in future negotiations, the Government should argue for the inclusion of general provisions regarding the status of regions in a future constitutional treaty on the EU, thus safeguarding the position of Åland. The report focuses separately on areas of policy in which the Finnish Government should give particular attention to Åland's interests.

Jääskinen considers that there is no need for any further preparation on matters related to Åland's having a representative in the European Parliament, or equation of the Åland Legislative Assembly with the Finnish Parliament in EU rules on the status of national parliaments and in cooperation between national parliaments and the European Parliament.

Further information: Alec Aalto, State Secretary for EU Affairs, Government Secretariat for EU Affairs, tel. +358 9 1602 2180, Counsellor Petri Helander, Government Secretariat for EU Affairs, tel. +358 9 1602 2190 and Sten Palmgren, Senior Advisor, Legislative Affairs, Ministry of Justice, tel. +358 9 1606 7745

ALAND PEACE INSTITUTE

The Åland Islands Peace Institute belongs to a network of researchers and institutes that are focused on new challenges in peace research. The Peace Institute conducts research on minority rights and autonomy. It relates to the notion that “democratic participation” of minority groups and persons belonging to minorities can prevent conflicts in multicultural societies and safeguard their cultural identity.

RESEARCH PROGRAMME ON DEMOCRATIC PARTICIPATION

One of the most pressing demands on modern constitutionalism is to meet the demands of minorities, indigenous peoples and immigrants for political representation. Minority groups demand some kind of representation in parliaments, indigenous peoples require power over their lands and resources that they traditionally use and immigrants claim partaking in the political debate. In some cases these demands leads to conflicts with other groups in the society. In either way, the constitution-makers can either ignore these requests or find a way to meet with them. Everything indicates, however, that the former is not a durable strategy; instead, history shows that the demands are not disappearing, but keep on repeating themselves. Besides, it is questionable whether it is democratic to ignore demands for political representation; it might be that the circle of those participating in the public deliberations must be enlarged and include not only the cultural majority in the state, but also cultural subgroups, non-citizens and other communities in a permanent minority position.

In current legal, philosophical and political science the issue of democratic exclusion is debated. It is inter alia said that modern democracy tends to exclude certain groups from public deliberations, despite the fact that the democratic processes in general are inclusive and relies on equal suffrage. How is this possible; how can democracy be both including and excluding? And how does participation in democratic processes and law-making help preventing ethnic conflicts? The answer to that question can be found in the following argumentation.

Democracy presupposes and probably works best in a community of people who knows each other and who have a sense of belonging together. The members of the group have the same basic preferences, but can have different experiences and thereby also separate opinions in certain everyday matters. Occasionally, and as a consequence, a member of the sometimes community belongs to the political majority and sometimes to the political minority. This varies and is balanced over time. The members of the group are therefore generally accepting the basic premises of the public deliberations and sense that they are fair; people are thus confident in the democratic process and in the laws.

For diverse reasons, however, some individuals are not allowed to or able to participate in the community and in the public deliberations held in it. Instead there are subtle rules on who can participate in and with what they can contribute to in the deliberations. People who have or are considered to have deviant experiences and interest can categorically be excluded from the community. In this context, scientists differentiate between two kinds of exclusion, the external and the internal. External exclusion is that which is codified in the legislation. So are, for example, immigrants often denied suffrage, at least on parliamentary level, because they are non-citizens of the country they live in. They can also be refused employment by public authorities for the same reasons as citizenship often is a requirement for holding public office as it is for voting rights. Another example is children who are kept out by legal means, in spite of them being citizens. Most states have an age limit for the right to vote.

Internal exclusion has another character. In these cases it is not the laws that prevent people from participating, but more subtle structures and expectations concerning behavioural patterns. Knowledge of certain rhetoric a certain social behaviour and of what issues are addressed and what the political "non-issues" are, are required for membership in the community. The experiences and interests of women and immigrants can belong to these non-issues. For example, it has long been accepted that what happens behind the closed doors of the home, where women traditionally have found their occupation, belongs to the private domain and should not be politicised. For that reason important experiences and interests has been kept back from the political agenda. In many European states women have a formal possibility to participate in the political sphere, but are often prevented from being elected to higher posts in decision-making bodies or from addressing certain matters. It is not part of the common conception of femininity to engage in politics and for them to try to gain power over political matters. That is why also socio-psychological obstacles work against women participating. Common is furthermore that cultural, gender and social exclusion works together. Women who belong to minorities can both be excluded from the community and from the political deliberations because of cultural and also because of social reasons.

It is however not necessarily so, which should be emphasised in this context, that the political elite does not address these groups, minorities, women or immigrants, and their situation at all. On the contrary, it may well speak about these groups, but seldom with them on their own conditions. People belonging to these excluded groups rarely have the access themselves to define their specific problems and interests in the public fora. In that respect they lack legal means of participating in public deliberations and are democratically excluded.

Consequences of exclusion

Political representation matters to the long-term democratic development and also for the prevention of conflicts. Democracy relies on the fact that people experience themselves as implicated in the decisions and that they have the same chance to belong to the democratic majority as anyone else. What consequences, then, does exclusion have for persons belonging to so called permanent minorities, i.e. for these individuals who are more permanently are left out from the public dialogue?

According to some researchers exclusion has the consequence that people loose their trust in democracy and in the laws, exactly because they lack the chance to influence democratic decisions and the content of legal statutes. This in turn involves a risk that the situation of the permanent minorities becomes static, and that the democratic system therefore to some degree can loose its legitimacy. It can furthermore affect the legal system: groups of persons who do not trust the legal system can find it an eligible option to establish and withhold private norm structures. These non-official norms function as the public legal order and can even consist of sanction mechanisms which are applied in case of breaches of the informal rules. One illustrative however extreme example of this is the so called Mafia in Italy. Since the laws are not always perceived by them as "valid", it relies on informal norm structures with its own sanction mechanisms. Because of this the state law is partly fragmentized. Thus, if in a state more than one subgroup relies on informal norms the legal order is at risk of being shattered. When adding nationalism to this equation, the political and legal exclusion can easily lead to the mobilization of ethnic tension and conflicts between the excluded groups and the state, or between the excluded group and other groups in the society. Ethnic mobilization is often a question of a power imbalance between different groups who identity themselves in ethnic terms. It can be perceived as, and rightly so, injustice that one cultural group systematically receives the cultural goods that the state distributes, whereas the other cultural groups are referred to the private sphere and to private funding.

For these reasons, to avoid fragmentisation of the legal order, a democratic deficit and ethnic conflicts, it is essential that the state guarantees all citizens, and even non-citizens, representation in the democratic processes. Democratic and legal marginalisation is a direct threat to democracy, regardless of whether it concerns groups that typically do not have any influence, as women victims of trafficking, or men who are seen as representatives for a permanent minority. How, then, is it possible to decrease or prevent the risks of democratic exclusion, or in other words, how can the circle of participants in public deliberations be extended?

The research at the Åland Island Peace Institute

The research of the Åland Islands Peace Institute concerns minority rights, autonomy and other forms of democratic participation that could have an impact on democratic development. Democratic inclusion is viewed not only as a value in itself but as a guarantee for conflict prevention. The research therefore and in this respect aims at contributing to the current peace and conflict research. Currently the Institute's research concerns the Nordic Autonomies. The research project involves the autonomies in the Nordic states, i.e. Finland, Norway, Sweden and Denmark. These states encompass inter alia the Åland Islands, Greenland, the Sami Parliaments and Svalbard. It is investigated how the different forms of local or regional self-government of cultural minorities is legally formulated. It is then taken into account how some minority groups are granted "group rights" of this particular kind while others are not. Not all cultural minority communities in the Nordic countries have access to their own self-determination institutions and the motives behind that differentiation is examined. Moreover, the competences of the autonomous units in these countries vary. For example, the Åland Islands autonomy is probably the strongest whereas the Sami Parliament in Sweden has a comparatively week self-government. The reason behind these differences is searched for. Another comparison that is made is that between the Nordic autonomies and the international law standards concerning this type of "internal self-determination". To the treaties that are particularly studied in this context belongs the ILO Convention No 169. The research results in a report that is presented at the end of 2003.

STRATEGIC INFORMATION FOR BUSINESS AND INVESTMENTS

INVESTMENT AND BUSINESS CLIMATE

Åland's economy is heavily dominated by shipping, trade and tourism. Shipping represents about 40% of the economy, with several international carriers owned and operated off Åland. Most companies aside from shipping are small, with fewer than ten employees. Farming and fishing are important in combination with the food industry. A few high-profile technology companies contribute to a prosperous economy.

The main ports are Mariehamn (south), Berghamn (west) and Långnäs on the eastern shore of the Main Island.

Mariehamn was the base for the last large oceanic commercial sailing ships in the world. Their final tasks were bringing Australian wheat to Great Britain, on which Åland shipowner Erikson kept going until after WW2, 1947 being his last year. The ships latterly made only one round-trip from South Australia to Britain per year, after each marathon voyage going back to Mariehamn to lay up for a few months. The ship *Pommern*, now a museum in Mariehamn, was one of these last vessels.

The abolition of tax-free sales on ferry boats travelling between destinations within the European Union made Finland demand an exception for the Åland Islands on EU's VAT rules. The exception allows for maintained tax-free sales on the ferries between Sweden and Finland (provided they stop at Mariehamn or Långnäs) and at the airport, but has also made Åland a different tax-zone, meaning that tariffs must be levied on goods brought to the islands. Unemployment is well below that of surrounding regions, 1.8%

The Finnish State collects taxes, duties and fees also in Åland. In return, the Finnish Government places a sum of money at the disposal of the Åland Parliament. The sum is 0.45 per cent of total Government income, excluding Government loans. In 2006, the sum was about 182 million EUR.

According to Eurostat, in 2006 Åland was the 20th wealthiest of the EU's 268 regions, and the wealthiest in Finland, with a GDP per inhabitant 47 percent above the EU mean. Åland enjoys the largest state subsidies of any Finnish region (maakunta/landskap), totalling annually about 4,000 EUR per inhabitant more than the Ålanders pay in state taxes (2006 figures). While the official currency is the euro, the Swedish krona also circulates freely in Åland.

Åland has an open economy and welcomes new influences. There is a strong entrepreneurial spirit within the Ålandic business community. Foreign investors have discovered the growing potential in several smaller Ålandic businesses.
Åland has become increasingly successful in attracting labour force. The maritime industry gives the business community an international character. Several Ålandic companies can offer attractive career opportunities.

1. COMPETITIVE ECONOMY

The Åland Islands has long-standing shipping traditions and it permeates the entire society. Åland is very much a service economy and competence is one of the key traits associated with the business community. This competence has been built during a long period of time, and spin offs from the shipping industry have helped to discover new business concepts. The business sector has proven to be resilient despite the global financial crisis. According to statistics from Eurostat, in 2006 Åland was the 20th wealthiest region in the European Union.

2. STRATEGIC LOCATION

Excellent sea, air and road links make Åland an important business hub with easy access to the rest of Scandinavia. The prime location in the heart of Scandinavia, near dynamic cities like Stockholm, Turku, Helsinki and Tallinn has really benefited the Åland economy. Åland has over the years developed an expertise in logistics management. A combination of strategic location, excellent infrastructure and competence has made the logistics industry grow rapidly.

3. INTERNATIONAL BUSINESS ENVIRONMENT

An international outlook and openness is firmly ingrained in the Ålandic culture. Åland is not an isolated island in the periphery. The economy is surprisingly wide and cross trading is part of everyday life. The international business community is a strong reason why most of the population is bilingual or multilingual.

The business community of Åland is often described as an arena wherein innovations happens trough imitation. It is a community distinguished by traveling seamen who come home with new ideas that are then adapted to the Scandinavian conditions. This had been and still is a success factory within the corporate community of Åland.

With 2,300 companies per a population of 28,000, it is safe to say that Åland have a good business climate with a strong enterprising spirit. Åland is like "a country of its own". This is reflected in the local business community, which includes almost every branch imaginable, from shipping to finance, insurance, IT enterprises, telecommunication, hi-tech plastic industry, advertising and other knowledge-intensive business services.

INVESTMENT AND BUSINESS OPPORTUNITIES

SHIPPING

Shipping has historically been the dominant industry on Åland, and it has very much contributed to today's prosperity. The ferry traffic is strong and has been a premise for an expansive tourism sector. A significant part of the Åland fleet is engaged in cross-trading. For example is the fleet carrying oil from the Middle East to Europe and wood between European countries. The Åland fleet has successively been renewed and the passenger ferries have grown bigger and more luxurious. It is estimated that shipping accounts for about 30 percent of Åland's GDP, indirectly for nearly 50 percent.

LEADING COMPANIES

Viking Line is the largest employer on the island. The shipping company has seven vessels, which sail between Sweden, Åland and Finland as well as between Finland and Estonia. Operations include passenger services, recreation and cargo carrier services. Their subsidiary, Viking Line bus also operates bus services on the island.

Rederiaktiebolaget Eckerö is a group divided into five subsidiaries; Eckerö Line, Eckerölinjen, Birka Cruises, Birka Cargo and Williams bus. These subsidiaries are engaged in various activities such as passenger traffic between Åland and Sweden, cruise traffic between Finland and Estonia, freight traffic between Scandinavia and the continent as well as bus services in Åland.

Three large cargo shipping companies are headquartering in Åland. Lundqvistrederierna are specialized in oil transports and has eight tankers sailing in the North Sea, Baltic Sea and Mediterranean. Rederi Ab Lillgaard fleet mainly consisted of dry-cargo vessels in the smaller size and roro-vessels. Their shipping routes are mainly in Scandinavia. Godby Shipping is a shipping company who offers sea transportation for the forest industry. They manage seven ships and sail between Finland and Southern Europe.

Bore Ltd is a ship-owner. Bore is a part of the Rettig Group with an office in Mariehamn.

ASP Ship Management is a global third party ship manager providing a complete range of integrated marine services. Their Scandinavian office is located in Mariehamn.

BANK AND INSURANCE

When the shipping industry advanced, the need for banking and insurance services came up. Åland host a core competence of bank and insurance services around shipping.

LEADING COMPANIES

The Alandia Group is an insurance group with strong emphasis on the marine sector. They are specialists of maritime insurance and maritime laws. The Alandia Group has costumers all over Scandinavia and is market leaders in both Sweden and Finland.

Ålands Ömsesidiga Försäkringsbolag are specialist on insurance services on land. The insurance products are property insurance for homes and businesses, car and motor insurance and statutory accident insurance. The company was founded in 1866, making it one of the oldest companies on the island.

The Bank of Åland was established in 1919 by forward-looking farmers and sea captains. In that time, the world's largest fleet of Windjammers had its seat in Åland

and the need for banking services was large. Today, the Bank of Åland has offices in both Sweden and Finland. They have a large competence around shipping finance and private banking.

INFORMATION TECHNOLOGY

The fastest growing sector these days are information technology. Åland have always struggle to reduce the consequence of their insular location. New technique has made that happen and lower the costs. The information business does not depend on freight costs and ferry timetables. Åland has a strong information technology infrastructure, with a number of projects in place to increase broadband standard in the region.

The knowledge exchange between Åland and other regions are intensive. The domestic information technology companies operate both local and global.

LEADING COMPANIES

Crosskey Banking Solutions provides innovative banking solutions for a wide range of industries. They develop, deliver and manage financial banking solutions. Crosskey have its roots in banking and is a subsidiary to the Bank of Åland.
Carus PBS can be described as a modern extension of the shipping cluster. Carus PBS has been supplying reservation and check-in systems, managed services and e-commerce applications to the cruise and ferry industry. They are most famous for developing a booking- and check-in system. Their clients can be found around Europe, the United States, Australia and Africa.
The PAF Group operates gaming activities on Åland, onboard ferries in the Baltic Sea region and on the Internet. The e-gaming division is fast growing and today the PAF Group has customers and partners throughout whole Europe.

HI-TECH PLASTIC INDUSTRY

Åland has a growing high-tech plastic industry with worldwide exports.

Optinova is a leading manufacturer specializing in fluoropolymer medical tubing. Optinova's 5800 m² manufacturing plant and headquarter is located on Åland.

ScanTube is a world-wide producer of high quality tubing, profiles and packing cord. Their products are mainly used in chemical, pharmaceutical, medical and electronic industries. ScanTube have sales offices in USA, Germany and Sweden. The manufacturing plants are located in Thailand and Åland.

Colorant Chromatics is the world's leading specialist in the enhancement of high performance polymers, particularly Fluoropolymers. Colorant Chromatics has manufacturing plants in Åland, USA, China and a distribution center in Germany.

TRAVEL AND TOURISM

Back then, it was about fishing. Today, it is about ferry traffic. About 2 million passengers travel true Åland waters every year. The travelers enjoy Tax-free shopping, relaxation, and good food onboard. To travel by air have become more and more popular. Air Åland provide frequent flights to Stockholm/Arlanda and Helsinki.

AN ATTRACTIVE TOURIST DESTINATION

The service sector is growing, were tourism play a substantial part. More than 540 000 tourists visit Åland each year. The high tourist season is between May and September. The common knowledge is that the population is nearly 250 000 under the summer season.

Exclusive tourism is on the rise. The unspoiled nature and safe society is a great resource. Havsvidden hotel, resort and conference are a good example of that. They offer high standard living in a beautiful environment. Another good example is Silverskär, a unique meeting place in the northern archipelago. A high standard conference center and living in a old farming environment.

There are several interesting spots in downtown Mariehamn. One of them is the Alandica Culture & Congress Centre. Alandica is a dynamic arena for meetings, cultural events, concerts and seminars. Another one is the Paf Casino. The casino offers all types of gaming, from slot machines to poker tournaments. The casino is located in the Hotel Arkipelag, which also provides the liveliest nightclub in Mariehamn. There are also several trendy bars, restaurants and hotels crowded in the same district. Near this hectic district is the Eastern harbour, one of Scandinavia's liveliest guest harbours. The Eastern Harbour also contains the Sea Quarter. The Quarter is a living marine centre with a boat-building yard, a seafarers' chapel, a smithy and other traditional handicrafts.

FOOD PROCESSING

Agriculture has always been a visible sight in the Åland landscape. Today, the primary sector comprising agriculture and fishery only accounts for a small part of total employment. However, the sector forms indirectly the basis for a considerable part of production and employment. Local delicacies are very appreciated by tourists. The small-scale agriculture has created local delicacies such as mustard, cheese, sausage beer and wine.

LEADING COMPANIES

Many successful companies have their roots in agriculture and fishing. The food processing industry dominates by small companies. The largest food processing company is the Chips Group. They are market leader in snacks in Finland, Sweden, Norway, Denmark and Latvia. Chips headquarter along with their flagship factory is located in rural areas in the Saltvik municipality. The Chips Group is since 2006 a part of the Orkla Group.

Chipsters are a food processing company who supply their products to catering firms. Headquarter as well as a processing plant is located on Åland. They export most of their products to Finland.

TAXATION LAWS

TAXES AND FEES

Taxes and fees to the Province

Email a Landskapsskattelag (1993:58)

§ 1. Scope

On the income tax payable to the landscape (landscape taxes).

With the earned income provided such income under the provisions of the Income Tax Act (FFS1535/1992) or are considered earned.

With landscapes tax provided additional tax on earned income.

See Sk 101 SF.

§ 2. Taxable

Liable to pay tax landscape are natural persons and estates under municipal Act (1993:37) for the Åland Islands are liable to pay council tax, but not limited tax liability.

See E 5, Kommunalskattelag (1993:37).

§ 3. (2002/43) calculated by the tax only earned income

The taxable income beräknaspå same basis as taxable income for municipal taxation is calculated under the provisions of municipal law for the province of Åland.

If the taxable income somfastställs for a taxpayer under 10 million the tax is not charged.

See E 5, Kommunalskattelag (1993:37).

§ 4. Loss Remedies

Loss Compensation referred to in § 131 Income Tax Act shall be deducted from landscapes tax under this section if a portion of underskottsgottgörelsen be deducted from municipal taxes under § 133 of that law. The remuneration shall, if so, after deductions under 132 § said Act have been allocated among the respective taxes enumerated in 133 § nämndalag in relation to those amounts, however, so that the landscape of tax and municipal tax amounts adderasnär the part of underskottsgottgörelsen to be deducted from the local tax rate under 133 § said lagräknas out. The share of the compensation to be avdrasfrån municipal tax under § 133 of that law divided between landscape and tax kommunalskatteni relation to these amounts.

See Sk 101 SF.

§ 5. (2002/43) Tax rate The tax rate for landscape purposes is 3.5.

§ 5a. Repealed (2002/43). § 6. Taxation Procedure

The determination of the landscape because of earned income each year based on landscape treasure in stödav this Act and the tax levying and uppbördverkställs mutatis mutandis as thereon ärstadgat of tax on income payable to the municipality in the Act on Assessment Procedure (FFS1558/1995) and the Regulation on Assessment Procedure (FFS 1579/1995) and in bestämmelsersom issued under the Act or Regulation. (1997/39)

The in subsection 1. aforementioned statutes and regulations issued thereunder shall be applied in the landscape as they obey when this Act comes into force. Thereafter changes to statutes or regulations issued thereunder, the amended provisions apply in the landscape from the time of their entry into force of the kingdom.

Mom. 3 repealed (2002/60).

Mom. 4 repealed (2002/60).

See Sk 301 and 302 (FFS 763/1998) SF.

§ 7. Prepayment

For the collection of landscapes tax effected during the tax year Prepayment mutatis mutandis enligtvad thereon is provided on the tax under the Act prompted cat tion procedure shall be charged to a com Act on Prepayment (FFS 1118/1996) and the Regulation on Prepayment (FFS 1124/1996) and in rules issued under the Act or Regulation. (1997/35)

The in subsection 1. aforementioned statutes and regulations issued thereunder shall be applied in the landscape as they obey when this Act comes into force. Thereafter changes to statutes or regulations issued thereunder, the amended provisions apply in the landscape from the time of their entry into force of the kingdom.

See Sk 201 and 202 SF.

§ 8. Tax collection

Collection, recovery and refund of the landscape taxes and advances, other payments and withholding tax paid by förskottsuppbördskall enforced in relevant part as thereon Charter of municipal and advances, other payments and withholding tax paid by the Prepayment of the Act on tax collection (FFS 611/1978) and in Regulation on tax collection (FFS 903/1978) and provisions utfärdatsmed under the Act or Regulation.

The in subsection 1. aforementioned statutes and regulations issued thereunder shall be applied in the landscape as they obey when this Act comes into force. Thereafter changes to statutes or regulations issued thereunder, the amended provisions apply in the landscape from the time of their entry into force of the kingdom.

See Act for tax collection (FFS 609/2005), Sk 604 SF.

§ 9. Management tasks

The management information according to those in § 6 subsection 1., § 7 subsection 1. and § 8 subsection 1. these statutes is for the state agencies or officials in the province administered by the [Provincial Government] for the under 23 § Autonomy Act is for the landscape.

See A 1, Autonomy (1991:71).

§ 9a. Penalty Sanctions

For failure to timely pay the province tax is charged interest on late payments and the residual charge mediakttagande mutatis mutandis to the provisions omförsummelse to timely pay municipal taxes in the law on penalties and penalty interest (FFS1556/1995). (1997/30)

The in subsection 1. said Act shall apply in the landscape as it reads when this Act comes into kraft.Sker then changes to the Act, the amended rules apply in the landscape from the time of completion served effect in the kingdom.

See Sk 606 SF.

§ 10. Loss of tax

If the limitation of the tax landscape for what ompreskription of tax is in accordance with national legislation. See Pr 608 FL I.

§ 11. Appeals

If the right of appeal by rectification, tax objection and appeal, to appeal and the appeal procedure, way to make rectification and fiscal note required by [tax law], the Act on Prepayment and engaged on tax collection.

See Sk 201 and 604 SF.

§ 12. Coming into force provisions

This Act takes effect immediately. By landscape type is determined when the landscape of first-time tax to be levied. (1998/116)

This Act repeals the Landscape Act (1958:18) on 9 July 1958 concerning the collection of taxes to the province of Åland.

E 2 Landscape Act (1993:27) on the Charge to the Province

§ 1. Scope of application

This Act regulates the general principles of närlandskapsregeringens and subordinate agencies function shall be chargeable and the amount of the fees collected for such performance.

This Act does not apply to landscape business or funds.

§ 2. Toll performance

The following performances will be charged:

1) goods produced or marketed;

2) services provided by request or otherwise on behalf of someone,

3) examination of the application and

4) other activities, when performance is undertaken as a result of an action by the recipient.

§ 3. Exemption performance

The following achievements should be free of charge:

1) subject matter which can not be considered directly utfördaför an individual or an individual company or otherwise for a clearly defined group,

2) performance whose purpose is to provide benefits in some seeds backs of the individual's livelihood and

3) advice, instructions, guidance and information if they pose only a low cost.

§ 4. Fees for public performances

Fees for public performance must be calculated so that full cost recovery is achieved.

If there is evidence of causes somhänför to health care, welfare facilities, environmental, educational activities and public cultural activities or causes that can be compared meddessa can provincial government determine that a fee is generally charged to full cost recovery is not achieved or that the fee not be collected.

If there is reason to provincial government determine that a fee that would otherwise be determined as attfull cost recovery is achieved, set at a higher rate or to an achievement that must be avgiftsfribeläggs with fee.

The costs are based at a fee determined shall not be higher than what an appropriate level of quality required.

§ 5. The price of the other performances

Prices for other achievement than those mentioned i4 § determined on commercial grounds.

§ 6. Decision-making authority

Landscape government decides what prestationersom is a charge and determines the level of contributions.

Police: ÅLRB (2005:24) and ÅLRB (2007/12)

Landscape government's public administration: ÅLRB (2007:100)

§ 7. Collection of fees for public performances

Fee must be paid in connection with the order or the application is filed. Unless this happens, the customer or applicant required to pay the fee within a certain time. At the same time, the customer or applicant notified that the order is carried out or attansökan processed only if the fee is paid within the prescribed time. Otherwise, the fee paid vidöverlämnande performance or by billing immediately when performance is completed.

Landscape government may waive the requirement that the fee payable in connection with the order or when the application is filed.

Payment of a fee shall be at least 14dagar reckoned from the time the bill was posted or transmitted by other suitable means. (2007/24)

If the fee is not paid by the due date, the steps necessary for obtaining payment. On an unpaid amounts charged interest at the Interest Act (FFS 633/1982). (2007/24)

Refundable fee in time shall refuse the application or order is not executed.

Landscape The Government may, there is some special reason, to repay all or part of the fee bow performance.

See 410 Ci FL I.

§ 8. Collection of charges

Fees for public performance may Indri-vase under the Law on Collection of Taxes and Charges through Execution (FFS 367/1961).

The recovery of claims relating to other performance observed what is decided about the recovery of civil and commercial claims.

See Law on execution of taxes and fees (FFS 706/2007),

Pr 608 FL I.

§ 9. Effective date and transition provisions

This Act comes into force on 1 July 1993.

The provisions for fees and stamp duty ideal solution in terms of support

1) Landscape Act (1952:27) concerning the fees that shall be paid for specific Åland administration subordinate authorities expeditioneroch service ordinances,

2) 1 § 2 and 3 above. Landscape Act (1971:10) ompolisverksamheten,

3) 17 and 47 § § Landscape Act (1977:37) ombrand and rescue services;

4) § 10 and § 26 subsection 3. Landscape Act (1977:41) on nature conservation,

5) 24 and 34 § § Electricity Act (1982:38) for the province of Åland,

6) § 3 subsection 1. Landscape Act (1971:12) on the application of Åland of certain national regulations relating to hazardous substances;

7) Landscape Act (1977:73) on stamp duty and

8) § 15 Landscape Act (1975:9) on the motor vehicle agency

applied and supported by them issued regulations that apply in the landscape of this Act träderi force, shall apply in the province until the provincial government by virtue of this Law determines otherwise.

E 3 Landscape Act (1947:6) on pharmacy fee of Åland

§ 1. For pharmacies operating in the province of Åland holders pay an annual fee, as determined in accordance with pharmacy sales.

§ 2. Pharmacy fee paid under the pharmacy's turnover, since VAT is deducted from this, as follows (2002/44):

Pharmacy Pharmacy sales - Fee

percent fee for

the sales turnover

tion ne as above

less than the limit

The lower limit

ago

€ €

741367-864515 - 6,00

864515-1111640 7389 7.00

1111640-1358487 24 688 8.00

1358487-1730129 44 435 9.00

1730129-2223276 77 883 9.50

2223276-2717796124 732 10.00

2717796-3212042174 184 10.25

3212042-4077381224 844 10.50

4077381-5312169315 705 10.75

5312169-448445 11.00

The amounts under ÅLRB (2007:114)

From the turnover of the branch pharmacy sales deducted in their entirety, if it represents more than 50,500 euros, or one-third of sales, with a minimum 50.500euro if it exceeds 50,500 euros before branch pharmacy sales are consolidated with the pharmacy's turnover for the determination of the pharmacy fee. (2002/44)

Pharmacy Charges set out in the whole euro. (2002/44)

Pharmacy fee of less than 5 euros is charged not. (2002/44)

The amounts in the table in subsection 1. for pharmacy sales and pharmacy fee for the lower limit may be adjusted annually by the [Provincial Government] under iriket statutory grounds.

§ 3. For the determination of the pharmacy operating circulation, pharmacy owner of [the Åland Board] shall submit notification of the movement inkomsteroch expenses in each calendar year by 1 April the following year. [Landscape Board] may, however, in special circumstances grant a pharmacy owner may also later submit the said notification. Notification must be prepared in accordance with instructions issued and in form, somfastställts of [landscape Board].

§ 4. Based on the notification pharmacies holder Rein left the sets [landscape Board] the pharmacy fee, payable for pharmacy operations.

Neglects pharmacy owners within the stipulated tidtillställa [landscape Board] in § 3 Board anmälanoch submits nor such after being requested or it is obvious that a smaller circulation than denverkliga stated, owns [landscape Board] authority to establish pharmacy fee as one of the same estimated market turnover.

[Landscape Board] decisions regarding pharmacy fee shall be imparted to the person thus, to them itjänsteväg to be an extract therefrom, provided with qualified teaching problems and note on the service.

§ 5. Has the pharmacy during the year, for which the fee must be paid, transferred to another holder, it shall be for the calendar year estimated fee distributed among the holders in proportion to the size of everyone's sales.

§ 6. (1952/28) [provincial government] takes a year to decide, whether the payment of the pharmacy fee is payable in one or more lots, and determine the times when the pharmacy fee shall be paid to [landskapsstyrelsenskamreraravdelning].

§ 7. (1966/39) Pharmacy fee not been paid on time, may be seized without a court order or ruling såsomdärom is provided.

See Law and Regulation on the enforcement of taxes and fees;

Pr 608 and 609 FL I.

§ 8. Exempt from payment of fee pharmacies are pharmacies, established in hospitals and sanatoriums.

Where special circumstances exist, the [landscape Board] free pharmacy owner from the payment avapoteksavgift either in whole or in part.

§ 9. Pharmacy has to observe at the records, what about it is the kingdom decided.

See the Accounting Act and Regulation, Ft 301, and 302 FL I.

§ 10. Pharmacy Marketing is the responsibility of the person, so by [landscape Board] appointed, orally or in writing give the additional information and inquiries, which the pharmacy fee determination are avnöden, and present his business books and related inventory and stock lists, contracts ochskuldsedlar, bills, receipts and correspondence, and AS WELL AS other documents demonstrating his stock.

§ 11. Everyone is obliged to keep secret, what he's on duty or in public office learned about pharmacy movement's financial condition or business conditions.

§ 12. The decision, in support of this landscape type barrel-lished by [landscape Board], may be appealed hoshögsta Administrative Court by means of written complaints, which come with the application of the contested decision no later than 12 noon on the thirtieth day after the decision delfående, shall be submitted to the Supreme Administrative Court's Registry but yesterday the decision, however, regardless of symptoms immediately in effect.

§ 13. (1966/39) has the highest förvaltningsdomstolenavlyftat pharmacy fee or reduced it, the [Provincial Government kamreraravdelning] återbetaladet too much amount paid plus six percent annual interest thereon from the date of payment to the date föråterbetalningen.

Has the pharmacy fee otherwise paid in addition to the fixed amount, it must be too much the amount paid, plus interest, calculated as in subsection 1. is mentioned, påansökan be refunded to the person of [landscape Board kamreraravdelning].

Has the pharmacy fee due to the turnover reported incorrectly set too low, the fee amount corrected and pharmacy owner ordered to pay the supplement, not later than the fifth calendar year after the end of the year when the fee, to be corrected, charged, or should have charged.

§ 14. (1966/39) neglected the payment of the pharmacy fee on time, be on the amount due iavgiftstillägg paid twelve percent annual rate, calculated from the date on which fee was last paid off, until the payment date.

§ 15. Where, in violation of the provisions of this landscape type or under similar provisions issued, punished, unless the act or omission elsewhere in the law more severe penalty is provided, with a fine.

E 4 Landscape Act (1974:83) on the traveling fee

Chapter 1. General

§ 1. Adherents of scheduled passenger traffic by sea between ports except port and in the Åland Islands are required to provide the landscape such as trade tax to pay travel tax as of this statute. (1975/46)

Traffic is considered to be regular, on schedule for the same publication.

In subsection 1. intended trafikidkare named in this lagredare.

§ 2. (1975/46) Traveling fee is set at maximum per passenger, which, making use of redarentillhörigt or of him upphyrt ships arriving from ports other than the countryside to the port in the province during the time the fee under § 3 are collected.

For passengers in transit through åländskhamn payable no travel fee. Nor to pay fees for passengers on ships between landscape and the kingdom of the ship owners, the landscape or the state.

§ 3. Traveling fee will be charged for the time and to detbelopp, who had no special decision fastställermed observance of the time be located mid March 31 and October 1 and to levy ejöverstiger 34 cents per passenger. (2002/45)

[County Council] decision concerning the collection of passenger fees will take effect no earlier than the ninetieth day efterdet such a decision.

Chapter 2. Collection

§ 4. Since the [county] in § 3 that decision enters into force takes owner for each calendar month avgiftenuppbäres by the end of the subsequent calendar month to the [Provincial Government] shall notify antaletav in § 2 for passengers.

Based on the in subsection 1. said notification sets [Provincial Government] traveling fee for Denman notification relates. Thereafter, the fee shall be paid within thirty days of the owner received part of the [Provincial Government] decisions.

§ 5. Neglects owners within the stipulated time to make [Provincial Government] in § 4 Board notification and submit non such after being requested or is it obvious tatt a small number of passengers than the actual haruppgivits, owns [Provincial Government] the power to fix passenger fee to an estimated number of passengers.

[Provincial government] decisions on the collection of passenger charge to be imparted thus to the owner with a receipt tillställes protocol excerpt provided medbehörig inconvenience teachings.

Chapter 3. The use of through travel charges influences utna funds

§ 6. In virtue of this Act shall be collected funds in the manner [county] in connection with the adoption of the [individual] årsstat closer Decision may be used mainly for environmental protection and the promotion of tourism or for beviljandeav landscape contribution to the municipality for such purposes.

Chapter 4. Special Provisions

§ 7. In [Provincial Government] in support of this law decisions can be appealed to the Supreme Administrative Court no later than 12 o'clock dentrettionde days after receiving notice.

The decision is nevertheless appealed immediately iverkställighet.

§ 8. Has the Supreme Administrative Court waived travel fee or reduced to it shall be [Provincial Government] to repay the excessive amount paid plus six percent annual interest thereon from the date of payment to the date of repayment.

Has traveling fee otherwise paid in addition to the fixed amount, the amount paid too much, plus interest, calculated as in subsection 1. is mentioned, påansökan be returned to the owner.

Has traveling fee, because the number of passengers reported incorrectly set too low, the fee amount be corrected and the owner be required to pay the supplement, not later than the fifth calendar year after the end of the year when the fee to be corrected, charged or should have been charged .

§ 9. If payment is not traveling fee on time, skallpå the amount due on fees additional paid twelve percent annual interest, from the date when the last fee should have been paid to the date of payment.

If cancellation of travel fees it [Provincial Government].

§ 10. A person who violates the provisions of this landscape type or under similar provisions issued punished by a fine, unless the act or omission elsewhere in the law more severe punishment is provided.

§ 11. Further provisions concerning the Application Enoch enforcement of this Act shall, if necessary through landscape regulation.

Taxes and fees to local governments

E 5 Kommunalskattelag (1993:37) for the Åland Islands

§ 1. Scope of application

On earned income and the incomes of samfundoch collective benefits to be paid tax to the municipality and allowed loss relief in municipal taxation in accordance with what that effect is föreskriveti Income Tax Act (FFS 1535/1992) and regulation of tax on income (FFS 1551/1992), announced Except as provided in of this Act and special provisions. In addition, the law on the elimination of international double taxation (FFS1552/1995) in the landscape as it is the issue of inkomstsom acquired in a foreign state, unless otherwise specified in this Act. (2001/24)

The in subsection 1. abovementioned provisions shall be applied in the landscape as they obey this Act träderi force. Thereafter amended the said provisions, the amended rules apply in the landscape from the time of their entry into force of riket.Ändringar of rules on which this Act provided for deviations shall not apply shore landscape.

See Sk 101 and 102 SF. While Sk 143 SF.

§ 1a. (1994/62) Provisions shall not tillämpasvid municipal taxation

The provisions of § 154 Income Tax Act shall not apply to municipal taxation.

§ 1b. (1995/14) Law Corporate tax

Liable to pay council tax on income ärsamfund who is domiciled in the Province of inkomstsom acquired in the province and elsewhere, and corporations domiciled in the country and foreign corporations for income acquired in the landscape.

§ 2. Other provisions of the Income Tax

If the calculation results of näringsverksamhetoch agriculture, withholding tax on interest income, and asked to cat-accession process, Advance tax and tax collection are special provisions.

On the taxation of nonresident income applicable provincial law on municipal förbegränsat taxpayer (1973:12). (2004/48)

See E 13, Landscape Act (1973:12) on the municipal tax for limited

satellite taxable.

§ 3. The application of the references in the Income Tax Act

Cited in the in § 1 subsection 1. those statutes to the provisions of national law which owns the equivalent of landscape law shall be deemed to refer to the provisions of the landscape law thus is in question. Förutombestämmelserna in landscape legislation, references, however, with regard to support and allowances mentioned in the references, deemed to apply to their counterparts in national legislation in so far as regards aroma tax liability for income and deductions for the production of income.

§ 4. (2004/48) Municipal tax rate for corporations and collective benefits

Communities and collective benefits, the taxable income pay 5.7278% of council tax.

§ 4a. Repealed (2002/78)

§ 5. (2002 / 6) The reporting of municipal tax revenues to communities

Local taxes referred to in 4 and 4a § § this lagoch paid by the corporation and collective benefits are reported to local authorities under the Act on tax accounting (FFS 532/1998), except as provided by this Act and special provisions.

See Sk 607 SF.

§ 5a. (2003/85) The distribution between the individual municipalities

A municipality's share of municipal tax revenues of the corporation and collective benefits down taxes annually as a relative percentage of the total amount of municipal units. Proportion The size is determined relative to the sum of the tax under subsection 2-4. recalculated each municipality as a whole.

The basis for calculating a municipality's share of the data in the last three completed fiscal centers as well as those in the offi cial Enterprises and statistics for these years. For each of the three years the council tax as a corporation charged credited to the individual municipalities pursuant to subsection 3 and 4. (2004/48)

If a corporation during the year has had an establishment, only in a municipality included community tax the municipality as a whole. If the community has had an establishment iflera municipalities include community tax these municipalities benefit in proportion to the number of employees vidsamfundets establishments by municipality. Taxes församfund standing in group relationship under provincial law (1989:23) on the group in municipal taxation the same count and räknasde municipalities concerned to benefit in proportion to the number of employees at the Group denominated government establishments by municipality.

If a corporation with an establishment, in others you municipalities also have staff on board the ship, its skattmed deviation from the provisions of subsection 3. counts municipalities benefit in relation to the number of employees at the community's permanent establishments per kommun.Samfundets employed on board ships shall dockhänföras to the municipality that is the community's home on the community in question has at least one employee of a permanent establishment in the municipality.

The official's Business statistics for the three years that form the basis for calculations under this section refers to the statistics as it looks like January 1st of the year in which the distribution relates. Landscape The government sets for each tax year the individual municipal units by the end of March. Before the shares of the tax year has been set is an interim report to the municipalities through the application of the previous fiscal year's allocation, which is then adjusted subsequently. Shares down to eight decimal places. Before a decision is taken, the fixing of Åland municipalities kf heard.

Approved the distribution of communities and collective förmåners council tax between the various municipalities under § 5 subsection 6. regarding 2004, [ÅLSB] (2004:12) for 2005, ÅLRB (2005:17) for 2006, ÅLRB (2006:27) for 2007, ÅLRB (2007:17) for 2008, ÅLRB (2008:69)

5 § 5 and 6 subsections. repealed 1 January 2009. (ÅFS 2008/96)

§ 5b. (2008/96) Determination of the distribution

Landscape The government sets for each individual skatteårde municipal units by the end avmars months. If the data used to calculate the basic division between the municipalities down proportions changed again in September.

Before the shares of the tax year has been set is an interim report to the municipalities through the application of the previous fiscal year's allocation, which is then adjusted subsequently. If the proportions changed in September also adjusted the taxes reported for fiscal years after the fact.

Shares down to eight decimal places. Before a decision is taken, the fixing of Åland municipalities kf heard.

§ 6. Landscape and Ålands Penningautomatförening charge

If the province's obligation to pay council tax will apply to what the State's obligation to pay income tax to the municipality is written in it in a § subsection 1. said Act.

Åland's Slot Machine Association is under no obligation attbetala council tax.

§ 7. VAT for funding from the province's resources

Subject to the provisions of § 3 Skalli respect of VAT for funding from the province's resources apply as in § 1 subsection 1. aforementioned provisions are prescribed for aid on grounds beviljasav considered equal to the state.

§ 7a. (2007/13) General deductions

A taxpayer physical person is entitled to municipal taxation do a general deduction of five percent of earned income. The deduction is made after all other deductions in municipal taxation hargjorts, but before the basic deduction.

With the income referred to in subsection 1. Net earnings in municipal taxation desserts all deductions in municipal taxation, förutomgrundavdraget, has been made.

See D 10, Landscape Act (2007:14) on compensation for loss

of tax revenues.

§ 8. (2006/102) Travel Cost Reductions

In § 93 Income Tax Act intended deductions may vidkommunalbeskattningen made for the cost of travel between home and work with allmäntfortskaffningsmedel and for the cost of travel between home and work with different kind avfortskaffningsmedel. Costs may be deducted an amount not exceeding 6 000 and only to the partial defini during the tax year exceeds EUR 340. If more than half of the net eligible costs utgörsav cost of travel by public transportation, may also be the part of the cost of less than 340 euros are deducted. The costs of resormed other type of conveyance than the general conveyance calculated according to the pleas tax board determines pursuant to 93 § 2 mom.inkomstskattelagen.

As in subsection 1. for expenses shall also be deemed taxable costs incurred by atthan or her because of communication conditions had to rent a house elsewhere ashore vicinity of place of work. With such communication relationships between workplace Enoch residence in municipality provided the services of free-range ferry or travel time under normal conditions is longer than three hours round trip.

If not the actual costs are lower rental costs may be deductible to a maximum of 6 EUR and 90 cents per square foot per month and to dendel the leased property size does not exceed 30kvadratmeter.

Tax Board's decision on the size of the travel expense deduction for tax purposes for 2007 (FFS 969/2007)

§ 8 has been changed, the previously applicable section is:

§ 8. Travel Cost Reductions

In 93 § Income Tax Act intended deductions may be in municipal taxation be made for the cost of travel between home and work by bus or other conveyance which is a scheduled service as well, calculated according to the principles [Provincial Government] established annually, the cost of travel between home and work with other types of vehicles. Costs may be deducted only to the extent they exceed EUR 340 during the tax year. If more than half of the net eligible costs consist of expenses for travel by bus or other conveyance which is in uninterrupted service, but also the part of the cost of less than 340 euros are deducted. (2002/46)

As in subsection 1. for expenses shall also be deemed taxable costs incurred by him because of communication conditions had to rent a house elsewhere in the province. The costs are calculated according to the principles provincial government annually sets.

For the past 8 § and also for previous § 4 of the landscape types (1993:41) on the municipal tax for the farm was on taxation grounds following: 2003; [ÅLSB] (2003:81), 2004; ÅLRB (2004:43) in 2005; ÅLRB (2005:62) 2006; ÅLRB (2006:105)

For the past 8 § 2 subsection. the basis for calculating the rent covered by the travel expense deduction related to the following: 2003; [ÅLSB] (2002:77), 2004; [ÅLSB] (2003:82) in 2005; ÅLRB (2004:44) in 2006; ÅLRB (2005:63)

§ 9. (2001/24) Seafarer's income

In § 74 subsection 1. Income Tax Act intended seafarer's income is at the municipal taxation löneinkomsti money or money's worth of work on board ships with a gross tonnage of 100 register tons, if the work performed in connection with vessel traffic ki employment with the shipowner, or any jämställbarav tax board approved employer in charge of vessel traffic and the

1) the ship is in international voyages or during the tax year mainly in coastal, 2) the vessel is under the Maritime Board and used in sea or OM3) the vessel is under the Aland landskapsregeringoch is another ship than ferry.

§ 10. Illness Cost Reductions

Taxpayer is entitled to municipal taxation in full deductions from earned income for own and family members illness costs in excess of 84 euros. For husbands, however, that deductions from earned income may be made försjukdomskostnader aggregating more than 168euro. (2002/46)

For the cost of illness as a result of hospitalization outside the European Economic Area, unless the admission occurred on grundav domestic physician referral, the taxpayer the right attvid municipal taxation deductions from earned income with a maximum of 300 euros, spouses, however, a total of more than 600 euros. If the taxpayer during the tax year supplied the children before the tax year, the input does not turn 17 years old, in this subsection intended amount increased by EUR 70 for each such child. (2006/102)

Deductions may be made for travel expenses for doctors, hospitals or hospitals with a comparable institution outside the European Economic Area for the treatment of disease, whether it is made without referral or prescription from local doctors. (2006/102)

Deductions may be made for costs reimbursed because of insurance or any other reason. § 10 subsections 2 and 3. has changed, the earlier version is: For illness expenses incurred for hospitalization outside Finland and Sweden, unless admission was due to domestic physician referral, the taxpayer's right to municipal taxation deductions from earned income with a maximum of 300 euros, spouses, however, combined with maximum 600 euros. If the taxpayer during the tax year supplied the children before taxes of year does not turn 17 years old to be in this subsection intended amount increased by EUR 70 for each such child. (2002/46) Deductions may be made for travel expenses for doctors, hospitals or hospitals with a comparable institution outside Finland or Sweden for the treatment of disease, whether it is made without referral or prescription from local doctors.

§ 11. (2006/102) Tuition Deduction

The taxpayer is entitled to municipal taxation is deducted from net earnings, förutomde deduction referred to in § 105 Income Tax Act, 340euro for each semester during which he received instruction at the elementary level or conducted studies somhuvudsyssla at a college or other educational institution ilandet or abroad.

§ 11 has been changed, the earlier version are:

§ 11. (2002/46) Tuition Deduction

The taxpayer is entitled to municipal taxation is deducted from net earnings, in addition to the deductions provided in 105 § Income Tax Act, EUR 340 for each semester during which he received regular and full instruction in an educational institution at the primary, secondary or university level or in a comparable training institute.

11 a §. (1993/59) Reductions in loss compensation from the municipal tax

Compensation referred to in 133 § Income Tax Act, after deductions under 132 § said Act hargjorts divided between the respective taxes enumerated in 133 § said Act in relation to these amounts, however, so that landscapes tax and municipal tax amount added when the part of the indemnity to be deducted from the municipal tax enligt133 § said Act is calculated. The part of gottgörelsensom be deducted from the local tax under § 133 of that law shall be allocated among municipal Enoch landscapes tax in relation to these amounts.

Entry into Force Provision (1993/37):

This Act comes into force on 1 July 1993 and applied for the first time at the municipal taxing somskall enforced for 1993.

This Act repeals

1) municipal Act (1988:70) for the province of Åland,

2) Landscape Act (1969:33) on förlustutjämningvid municipal taxation and

3) Landscape Act (1989:14) on tax out positions and bonds.

Notwithstanding the provisions of this Act shall, vidbeskattningen for 1993 in terms of tax förinkomst collected or benefit enjoyed before this Act comes into force, previously applicable provisions shall apply if the income or privilege intevar taxable under the earlier provisions.

Entry into Force Provision (2002/78):

This Act comes into force on 1 January 2003.

Entry into Force Provision (2003/88):

This Act comes into force on 1 January 2004.

Entry into Force Provision (2004/48):

This Act comes into force on 1 January 2005 and to apply the first time in the taxation for the year 2005samt on statements relating to fiscal year 2005.

Entry into Force Provision (2006/102):

This Act comes into force on 1 January 2007 and to apply the first time when the taxes are implemented for 2007.

Entry into Force Provision (2007/13):

This Act comes into force on 1 April 2007 and to apply the first time in the taxation of fiscal year 2007.

Entry into Force Provision (2008/96):

This Act comes into force on 1 January 2009.

E 6 Landscape Act (1993:42) on the municipal tax on business

§ 1. The result of the economic activity is expected in the municipal taxation in accordance with what that effect is written in the law on taxation of business income (FFS 360/1968) with The derogations provided by this Act and special provisions.

The in subsection 1. said Act shall apply in the landscape as it reads when this Act comes into kraft.Sker then changes to that law, the amended rules apply in the landscape from tidpunktenför their effect in the kingdom. Changes to the rules on which this Act provided for deviations shall not be applied in the landscape.

See Sk 112 SF.

§ 2. Refer to it in § 1 subsection 1. the said Act to the provisions of national law which owns counterpart in landscape law shall be deemed to refer to the provisions of landskapslagstiftningensom thus is in question.

E 7 Landscape Act (1993:41) came on munalskatt for farm

§ 1. The outcome of Agriculture estimated in municipal taxation and net income from forestry is expected in municipal taxation for the years 19932005, in accordance with what that effect is written in the Income Tax Act for the farm (FFS 543/1967), and forest tax regulation (FFS 1208/1991), with deundantag conferred by this Act and special provisions .

The in § 1 subsection 1. these statutes is to be followed in the landscape as they obey when put raids in force. Thereafter amended the said provisions, the amended rules apply in the landscape from the time of their entry into force iriket. Changes to the rules on which this Act provided for deviations shall not be applied in the landscape.

See Sk 115 SF and 116 SF 2006th

§ 2. Cited in the in § 1 subsection 1. those statutes to the provisions of national law which owns the equivalent of landscape law shall be deemed to refer to the provisions of the landscape law thus is in question.

§ 3. In the case of tax for the support of landscape resources and the deduction for property taxes paid to the municipality in the province shall be as in § 1 1 mom.nämnda regulations prescribed for aid påjämställbara grounds granted by the state andon deduction for property taxes paid to the municipality in the country .

§ 4. Repealed (2006/104).

The previous wording is:

§ 4. Deductible expenses for the production of income and impulses becoming entrenched

tion is in addition to the expenses shown in § 1 subsection 1. said

regulations also costs for rental of furnished rooms in the taxpayer's dwelling or in connection therewith premises with or without full board. These costs are calculated according to the grounds [Provincial Government] for each of fiscal years shall determine, unless the actual cost of the size investigated.

For previous tax bases; See E 5, Kommunalskattelag (1993:37), in previous § 8.

§ 5. Repealed (1998/114).

§ 6. In § 9 subsection 2. A point of the ITA forecourt use intended depreciation of the local taxation even for recreational building that is used exclusively in the rental business.

§ 7. (1994/24) in § 10 subsection 1. Income Tax Act forecourt use intended depreciation may in municipal taxation shall not exceed 20 percent of utgiftsrestenom not a higher depreciation rate for certain utility or some utilities are permitted under § 10 Income Tax Act for the farm. As the acquisition cost is also considered renovation spending förtäckdiken, bridges, dams and other such facilities.

§ 8. Landscape The government should provide tax certificate on the conditions for relief set out in 14 and 14 a § § Income Tax Act for the farm.

Landscape The government must provide the taxpayer and the tax records of expenditure referred to in § 13 subsection 1. 2-5 paragraphs Income Tax Act for the farm and on the conditions under which expenses may be deducted.

Entry into Force Provision (1994/24):

This Act comes into force on 1 April 1994 and applied the first time at the kommunalbeskattningsom be enforced for 1994.

This law applies to the depreciation of such goods which have been obtained for the Prevention of Water and Air Pollution January 1, 1994 or later. On the depreciation of the corresponding nyttighetersom acquired before 1 January 1994 are applicable § 7 Landscape Law on local taxes for the farm as it reads before this Act comes into force.

Entry into Force Provision (2006/104):

This Act comes into force on 1 January 2007 and to apply the first time when the taxes are implemented for 2007.

E 8 Fastighetsskattelag (1993:15) for the Åland Islands

§ 1. Property tax to be paid yearly to communicate according to what that effect is written in the property tax law (FFS 654/1992) and by virtue of the provisions issued, except as provided by this Act.

Change of property tax law and with the support avden issued provisions shall apply in the landscape from the time of their entry into force of the kingdom, såvittinte Subject to what provisions of this Act.

See Sk 407 SF.

§ 2. The property tax law § § 11-14 that tax rates may be less than 0.00% and in § 13 subsection 1. that percentage can be determined as attden is more than 0.90 percentage points higher than the tax rate for buildings used huvudsakligenför permanent residents, up 0.90%.

The tax rate provided in the property tax law § 13 subsection 1. does not apply to second homes used exclusively for rental.

§ 3. This Act first apply for the tax to be implemented for fiscal year 1993.

When the taxes are implemented for fiscal year 1993 refers to a property owner who owns the property on 1 April 1993 and with such innehavaresom treated as the owner on 1 April 1993uppfyller in property tax law § 5 subsection 2. the requirements.

Before the Act comes into force by the invitation recipes referred to in § 16 property tax law is given.

By 31 March 1993, kommunfullmäktigeför fiscal year 1993 to determine the in § § 11-14 property tax law that tax rates.

E 9 Landscape Act (1981:77) on the dog tax

Chapter 1. Tax liability and tax

§ 1. For a dog to be in accordance with this statutory paid annual dog tax to the kommundär dog owner had his actual home and residence (domicile) at the end of the preceding calendar year (fiscal year). Dog Tax shall be paid annually to an amount not exceeding EUR 25 in accordance with the City Council decides. (2002/47)

The City Council may decide that the dog tax not be levied.

§ 2. The person at the tax year end had a dog in his possession is liable to pay dog tax.

What this Act is provided for dog owners also applies to minor children's guardian if the dog is ibarnets possession.

§ 3. Dog Tax is not payable:

1) for the dog at tax year end is less than five months;

2) for dogs owned by the province or state, or whose maintenance costs paid by the province or state funds;

3) for disabled or handicapped person's assistance or guide dog;

4) for dogs who are trained for the tasks of civil protection and civil defense and for which signed undertaking that the dog shall be available for these tasks;

5) for dogs who are trained for tracking injured deer and for which concluded connection to the dog if necessary shall be made to the police authority's disposal, and

6) for dogs owned by the person in the province serving in the foreign state Consulate, headed by consuls, or member of his family, or private servants, if they are not f other manufacturers and citizens.

Chapter 2. Reporting obligations and taxation procedure

§ 4. Whoever during the tax year has been a dog in his ägoär bound to within the month of February the following year, notify the matter to the local municipality of their residence.

The notification, which shall be made on form as the City has established for that purpose, shall contain information on the dog's previous and current owner's name and domicile of the dog's name, characteristics, race and birth date. Municipal board shall annually in January through public service, as provided for in the Administrative Procedure Act for Åland, provide information on each notification shall be submitted and where forms for this purpose can be obtained. (2008/34)

§ 5. Dog owners must make notification of changes, if during the tax year moved to another municipality or the dog has died.

Change Notification shall during the month of February of the year following the tax year made to the City Council who have received in § 4 intended notification. Do dog owners previously failed to notify the change notification shall be submitted to the City of the place, where the notification should have been made before the change.

§ 6. Regarding dog for any dog tax paid to the City annually print out a tax debit note on the record is:

1) the owner's name and address;

2) the dog's name, characteristics, race and date of birth, and

3) amount of tax, payment and payment type.

For the 3 and 16 § § for dogs for which tax not paid print out a check note on the recorded data on the dog owner, dog and the reason for tax exemption. If the City Council adopted in § 1 subsection 2. intended decision discharged not control bill.

The municipal tax shall send the debit note or verification note to dog owners during the last majmånad years after the tax year.

§ 7. Has the dog owner is not within the time reported a dog on which tax is paid, can the City for the fiscal year for which notification should have been raising a dog tax to more than double the amount.

Has the dog tax to in subsection 1. intended cause could not be established for the fiscal year, the City påförahundägaren tax plus interest corresponding to the stipulated interest on the missed payment of taxes and raising taxes to double the amount. Fastställandetav dog tax shall be made no later than the fifth year after the end of the fiscal year and the dog owner shall be given an opportunity to make the communication.

§ 8. (2002/47) Does the dog owner neglected to make notification of changes to the transfer to another locality or sign confided tax-dog, can the City impose on him a default fee of 10 euros. The fee shall be charged later in the fifth year following the year for which notification should have been done. Subject neglect charge for the rest of what the dog tax is enacted.

§ 9. Do dog owners have become involuntarily escaped the imposition of dog tax, the City shall determine that the dog owner shall pay the tax later underdet third year after fiscal year end.

§ 10. Anyone who has been charged dog tax may hoskommunstyrelsen make written claim to the right. The claim shall be submitted within three årräknat from the beginning of the year in which tax was imposed.

Dog Tax is payable even if the amendment has söktsi decision on the imposition of tax.

§ 11. Anyone who is dissatisfied with the Municipality Board decides on the basis of the claims are entitled to within 30dagar after he received the decision over written appeal to the [county board].

The decision establishing the dog tax may not be appealed until correction of the tax harsökts the way in § 10 states.

Chapter 3. Specific provisions

§ 12. In addition to the 16 § staid task can the matters under this Act is for kommunstyrelseni as stated in [§ 37 subsection 5. Local Government Act (1980:5) for the Åland Islands] is written in the instructions instruct official.

§ 13. Dog owners are required to keep the tax debit note or verification form and to show this led municipal authorities who supervise taxation.

§ 14. Municipal Executive shall keep records of entered dogs.

§ 15. Of notification containing information on the dog's former owner, and a change notice on the owner's relocation to another municipality to City Council for the supervision of taxation send transcript to the City Council has jurisdiction medhänsyn to the dog's previous, current or nyaägares address.

§ 16. Municipal board may for special reasons to total or partial grant exemption from the dog tax.

§ 17. Detailed rules for the enforcement ochtillämpningen of this Act shall, if necessary through landscape regulation.

§ 18. This Act first apply for tax for 1981.

This Act repeals the Regulation on 14december 1894 on constituting the tax for dogs ochdäri latter being those changes, however, so that its provisions apply to the dog tax somutgår for the year 1980 or prior years, therefore.

E 10 Landscape Act (1989:23) on the group of municipal taxation

§ 1. This Act contains provisions on how the group should be treated in municipal taxation.

With the group referred to different rate than capital investment as a commercial company or co-pays to another company or cooperative for its motion, if the contribution is not avdrasenligt landscapes Act (1993:42) on kommunalskattför business. (1993/43)

§ 2. If a domestic corporation or cooperative (parent corporation) owns at least nine tenths of the share capital or voting rights in another domestic corporation or cooperative (subsidiary corporations), the parent community frånsin taxable business income deduct a group contribution paid to the sub community. Group contribution is regarded as taxable business income will slow otter community. (1993/43)

As the daughter communities may also be limited liability companies or cooperatives in which the parent community to the blacksmith one or more subsidiary corporations owning at least nine tenths of the shares or units.

As in subsection 1. is provided on the group from the parent corporation to subsidiary corporations shall apply påmotsvarande way when the subsidiary corporation pays to the parent group or community to another of the parent community's daughter communities.

§ 3. Group represents the cost of principal and income to the recipient during the fiscal year for which the allowance harbetalats.

§ 4. Group contributions may be deducted as an expense only omöverensstämmande expenditure and revenue records made in the donor's and recipient's accounts.

§ 5. (1993/43) A group may not be less than the present job loss before deduction for group contribution.

§ 6. In addition to the above is provided shall be for a refund to be considered as group following conditions must be met:

1) in § 2 above group relationship between donor and recipient must have continued during the entire tax year;

2) the donor and recipient fiscal periods shall have expired at the same time, if not bokföringsnämndenbeviljat exemption under Chapter 11. § 10 of the Companies Act (FFS 734/1978), and

3) (1993/43) the donor or recipient may not be the depositary bank, credit institution, insurance or pension provider referred to in Landscape Law omkommunalskatt for business.

E 11 Landscape Act (1984:45) came about

munalbeskattning of the shipping companies and

Owner

§ 1. The provisions of this Act apply to the municipal taxation of shipping companies and ship owners, dåbolaget formed by corporations engaged in business and the company's assets include a single vessel used in commercial shipping and that is recorded in the ship registry in Finland.

§ 2. Where the taxable income is determined by the way thence company established by corporations engaged in business, not deducted acquisition and renovation costs of the ship from the shipping company's income. Transfer Price or otherwise the ship erhålletvederlag regarded not as the shipping company income. That expenditure and income behandlasvid taxation of shipowners in relation to their ship tickets.

§ 3. One of the shipowner's ships castles corresponding part of the acquisition and renovation costs for ships in this Act shipping companies acquired, as well as on the ship related part of the acquisition cost of vessels castle owners acquired inämnda company, is deducted from the owner's income in detsätt as provided in [§ 30 Landscape Act (1969:32) omkommunalskatt for business], which lagiakttas even otherwise, mutatis mutandis, the ship ticket is non-current asset in the business that the owner carries.

Owners who can not do in subsection 1. intended deduction fåravdra expenditure during the fiscal year in which the ship or ship ticket has been assigned.

§ 4. A lot of ships corresponding part of the transfer price of the vessel and the other for the ship and the ship erhålletvederlag castle consideration received represents the owner's taxable income, regardless of hurlänge vessel or vessels owned lot.

§ 5. This Act applies to the shipping company, formed avsamfund engaged in business, where the company formed and the company belonging to the ship entered ifartygsregistret in shipowners' name in 1984 or later.

E 12 Landscape Act (2003:15) came about

munalbeskattning of communities in

connection to the tonnage tax

§ 1. At the municipal taxation of a corporation approved by tonnage required under medtonnageskattelagen (FFS 476/2002) is income from tonnage taxed activities are not taxable. Omgodkännandet withdrawn, however, such income taxed at the municipal taxation in the same way as in state taxation.

See Sk 125 SF.

§ 2. The provisions of other inkomstbeskattningän tonnage tax in the Tonnage Tax Act shall be applied in municipal taxation in the same way as in state taxation. The rules are applied as they are subject when this Act comes into kraft.Sker then change to the amended rules apply from the date of their ikraftträdandei kingdom.

To the parts they in subsection 1. intended provisions include references to provisions in other national legislation, the references in municipal taxation refer to the corresponding provisions ashore lation.

§ 3. This Act comes into force on 1 March 2003 and to apply the first time when the taxes are implemented for the fiscal year beginning during kalenderåret2002.

E 13 Landscape Act (1973:12) came on munalskatt for nonresident

§ 1. Anyone under municipal Act (1993:37) for the Åland Islands are nonresident skallpå of Åland acquired dividend, interest, royalties, salaries, pensions and other payments under provincial law (1997:32) on the application of Åland of national legislation on Prepayment subject withholding pay council tax on the grounds and in the manner provided in the Act on the taxation of nonresident for income and wealth (FFS 627/1978). (1997/33)

Occurs in the future change in that legislation, barking changed the provisions apply in the landscape from the time of their entry into force of the kingdom.

E 14 Regulation (1978:66) on the application

the law on taxation of limited

subject to taxation on income and wealth

hot in respect of council tax in

Åland

(FFS 1048/1978)

§ 1. Then in the Åland legislation issued regulations referred to in § 23 subsection 3. Act prompted cat tion of nonresident for income ochförmögenhet (627/1978), the said Act apply also in respect of council tax in the province, starting on 1 January 1979.

See Sk 132 SF.

§ 2. Municipalities in the Province of Åland will be such as municipal tax share of 40 percent avavkastningen of it in § 3 Tax Act avbegränsat taxable for income and förmögenhetavsedda withholding tax levied on income somförvärvats in the municipality in the province.

The provincial legislation provided distribution avkommunalskattens share between municipalities in the province enforce the [Abo Tax Office] who pay to municipalities the share of each semester to them, in the following September ochmars months in relation to population enligtmantalsskrivningen for the previous year.

§ 3. Does the county tax office decision, by which harförordnats the amount of withholding tax levied förmycket be refunded to the taxpayer or by which uppbördsskyldig imposed erläggaskatt as non-recovered or tax imposed on the taxpayer, or [administrative court], or the Supreme Administrative Court's ruling, by which someone declared taxable or which the amount of taxes raised or lowered, or through which beskattningenannars communication, tax on income that harförvärvats the municipality within the province, the avskriftav decision or ruling be sent to [Abo Tax].

E 15 Landscape Act (1995:54) came about

munalbeskattning shareholder of

foreign CFC

§ 1. Scope

A share of a foreign CFC income is taxable income for a general taxpayer ikommunalbeskattningen as specified in this Act.

§ 2. Foreign CFC

With a foreign CFC referred to in this team's community in which one or more of municipal taxation generally, taxpayers have discretion and for which the real level påinkomstbeskattningen the community's state of residence ärlägre than 3 / 5 of the level of taxation in the province of ettmotsvarande community resident here.

Notwithstanding the provisions of subsection 1. is not considered a foreign CFC

A) an entity whose income is under investigation mainly has been received by the industrial production activities, or shipping operations as community engaged in the State of residence or from the performance betaldaav such communities within the same group that provided in [Chapter 1. § 2 of the Companies Act (FFS734/1978)] which is domiciled in this State and where pray-run industrial production activities or

2) a corporation with the State of residence of Finland, the entry of an agreement to avoid double taxation, the rules become effective in the landscape through the approval of added nothing to the entry into force the Constitution, omsamfundet under the contract shall be deemed to be domiciled in this State and the contract shall apply to income community will receive, subject to taxation of communities in the state in question can be considered comparable to the taxation of corporations that are made in the province.

The states in which the taxation of corporations considered to correspond to the conditions specified in subsection 2. Two punk-ten is determined by landscape regulation.

See Companies Act (FFS 624/2006), Ft 103 FL I.

§ 3. Discretion

Authority referred to in § 2 subsection 1. in a foreign CFC is deemed to exist if one or fl era in municipal taxation generally taxable persons directly or indirectly holds at least 50 percent of community capital or total voting power of shares of community causes. Authority is also considered to exist if one or more of municipal taxation generally taxable persons are entitled to at least 50 percent avavkastningen of community wealth.

§ 4. Taxable income

Taxable income is the portion of a utländsktbassamfunds income that corresponds to the taxpayer's direct and foreign indirect share ownership ellermot his status as a beneficiary, if's cat person alone or together with persons within the same sphere of influence takes at least 10 percent avsamfundets capital or as förmånstagareär entitled to a share of least 10 percent of the proceeds of the community's wealth.

Dividend or other distribution of profits as delägaresom referred to in subsection 1. received from a foreign CFC taxable income only to the Delden exceeds the amount over the same skatteåreller the five previous tax years pursuant to subsection 1. harräknats as taxable income of the shareholder.

§ 5. Deduction of losses

A member referred to in § 4 subsection 1. may deduct, fråndelägarens under this Act, taxable andelav the foreign bassamfundets income, co-owner of sandalwood same denominational loss during the five fiscal years following the loss year as received rooster will.

§ 6. Deduction of foreign tax

From the municipal tax on income that is taxed under this act set off the amount of state income taxes that the foreign bassamfundet paid on the same income to the extent that the amount has not been offset by other taxes on income.

If the foreign community residing in a country with which Finland has in force an agreement to avoid double taxation, the provisions of which have become gällandei landscape through approval of added nothing to the entry into force the Constitution, deducted pursuant to subsection 1. the taxes under the agreement would offset the benefit was taxable if it had paid them. Medstöd of this subsection, no deduction of tax to be deducted under the contract, to the extent that denöverskrider the actual amount of tax bassamfundet paid.

§ 7. Obligation to provide information on foreign CFC

A taxpayer that is such member or beneficiaries referred to in § 4 subsection 1. is to merge its tax

1) a list of direct and indirect foreign share ownership in the foreign CFC,

2) an account of the taxpayer's ställningsom beneficiaries in a non-CFC and

3) an account of other information that behövsför calculation of income that are taxed under dennalag and the payout from the CFC, the accounting loss and in § 6 for skattersom community has paid.

If a foreign CFC is a subsidiary undertaking of a taxpayer referred to in [22 a § Accounting (FFS 655/1973)] or an interest in enterprise-provided in [22 c § Accounting Act] shall be the taxpayer's tax return attach a certified copy of the statement and balance sheets of the foreign community as well as accounting ävenav balance sheet for the previous räkenskapsperiodeller of the corresponding financial statements. Of a document in a language other than Swedish shall also påanmodan made a Swedish translation somgjorts by a sworn translator or another competent person.

In cases other than those referred to in subsection 2. should the taxpayer provide the documents referred to in 2 mom.på request, unless the taxpayer shows it is likely that it is not possible to obtain the document.

§ 8. Entry into force

This Act comes into force on September 1, 1995 ochtillämpas first time at the municipal taxation to be implemented for fiscal year 1995.

Income referred to in § 4 subsection 1. and baseraspå an accounting period or a calendar utgåttföre this Act comes into force shall not be considered taxable income.

E 16 Landscape Ordinance (1995:88) on the

States referred to in § 2 subsection 3. country

Community law on municipal taxation

shareholder of foreign CFC

§ 1. The States referred to in § 2 subsection 3. provincial law on municipal taxation of shareholders in utländskabassamfund are:

Australia, Belgium, Brazil, Bulgaria, Canada, Denmark and the Faroe Islands, Egypt, Estonia, Philippines, France, the United States, Greece, India, Indonesia, Iceland, Israel, Italy, Japan, China, Croatia, Latvia, Lithuania, Luxembourg, Morocco , Netherlands, Norway, New Zealand, Poland, Republic of Korea, Romania, Russia, Slovenia, Spain, Sri Lanka, United Kingdom, Sweden, Tanzania, Thailand, Czech Republic, Turkey, Germany, Ukraine, Hungary, Zambia and Austria.

See E 15, Landscape Act (1995:54) on the municipal tax

partner in foreign CFC.

§ 2. This Regulation shall enter into force on 1 november1995 and applied the first time at the municipal taxation to be implemented for fiscal year 1995.

E 17 Landscape Act (1987:44) on residential

husreservering at kommunalbeskatt

tion

§ 1. (1993/39) Association referred to in § 3 Income Tax Act (FFS 1535/1992) may, at the municipal taxation of their income deduct a reserveringsom formed for those at the municipal tax deductible expenses occasioned by the construction, operation, maintenance, repair and improvement avsamfundet belonging to residential and underhålloch use of land adjacent to such residential (housing provision).

A corporation can deduct a residential reservation only from other income other than income from business or farming. A corporation whose main line operations is based on ownership and possession to the real estate or rental business based påågande of property may deduct a residential reservation even from their taxable business income of community has a basis of [landscapes Act (1982:14) on support for housing, Landscape Act (1982:13) on support for home improvement or landscaping Act (1982:17) on räntestödslånför acquisition of rental housing] granted loans or interest subsidies for the construction, reconstruction or acquisition of housing. (1995/41)

The laws (1982:14) (1982:13) and (1982:17) has been repealed by G 4, Landscape Act (1999:40) on housing.

§ 2. In this Act, a residential building ivilken least half of the apartments' area at fiscal year end permanently used as a residence. As residential buildings under this Act is not considered a byggnadsom part of a trader's current assets. (1995/41)

An apartment in a residential building is considered to be varaktigtanvänd as a residence if it is essentially avseddför this purpose and not in other use. Enbyggnad has begun to be built to permanently användassom housing is also considered to be permanently used as a residence. (1995/41)

With residential building area means the surface under the outer dimensions of all floors, basement and attic insulated. The area does not include balconies ochskärmtak nor spaces whose free height is less than 160 cm.

§ 3. (2002/48) A residential provision shall be made isamfunds records later in the determination of the financial statements. The maximum amount of the reservation is during the tax year 68 euros per square meter of residential building area.Om residential provision refers to a surface understiger200 square or on the reservation is less than

Euro 3500 is not deductible for tax purposes.

§ 4. A residential provision will be used disguised the expenditures referred to in § 1, within ten fiscal years following the end of the fiscal year for which the reservation is made. A previous residential provision should be used prior to a subsequent reservation made. (1995/41)

Expenses covered with a bostadshusreserveringär not deductible for tax purposes.

If a residential provision has been used to cover the expenditure for tax purposes would avdrasgenom annual depreciation, amortization is approved only for the difference between the cost ochdet amount of residential provision använtsför its cover.

§ 5. The formation and use of a residential provision will be explored sufficiently specified in the tax return.

§ 6. A residential provision has not been used underden period provided in § 4 subsection 1. counted as inkomstför the fiscal year in which the reservation last should have been used. (1992/16)

Dissolution of community or own is no longer any residential dwelling counts reservation as community income for the fiscal year in which winding community is taken or at the end of which community no longer owns any homes. (1992/16)

If residential buildings destroyed include residential provision as community income for the fiscal vidvars starting community no longer owns the destroyed building or other residential buildings.

§ 7. (1995/41) A residential provision considered intesom deduction in determining the loss in accordance with municipal Act (1993:37) for the Province of Åland.

§ 8. Detailed rules for the enforcement ochtillämpningen of this Act shall, if necessary through landscape regulation.

Entry into Force Provision (2002/48):

This Act takes effect immediately and apply the first time in the taxation to be implemented for fiscal year 2002.

E18 Landscape Act (1994:50) on tax relief

costs for the promotion of production

and tourism activities

§ 1. The law's purpose

For the promotion of productive activity and tourism activities in the province of Åland beviljasvid municipal taxation tax credits in enlighetmed what of this Act.

§ 2. Investments eligible for tax relief

Taxpayer engaged in business activities ochunder years 1994 - 1997

1) based new production facility or new tourism businesses or

2) expands its production facility or its tourism or renews its machinery, equipment or fixtures so that

a) the establishment of production capacity or production refinement significantly increases or

b) the tourism company's capacity significantly increases or its quality level substantially below

may deduct the acquisition cost of the fixed assets acquired for the new production facility or the new tourism business or for extension or renewal of a production facility or tourism business in the manner prescribed in this Act.

The provisions of subsection 1. also applied to small ochmedelstora company engaged näringsverksamhetoch that during fiscal years 1998-1999, under the conditions specified in subsection 1. founded a new production facility or a new tourism or utvidgarsin production facility or its tourism. Enhöjd depreciation may be made only if företagetvid end of the fiscal year is a small or medium enterprise. The provisions of this subsection does not apply to companies in the following industries:

1) processing of agricultural products;

2) manufacture of steel or steel tube;

3) the production of konstfi spreads,

4) manufacture of cars or car parts or

5) making or repairing ships. (2003/19)

§ 2a. (1998/42) Small and Medium Business

With small and medium-sized enterprises are corporations

1) which has fewer than 250 employees;

2) having a turnover of more than 120 million or a balance sheet of more than 60 million and

3) where one or more undertakings which are not small or medium-sized enterprises in total hold less than 25 percent of its capital or the votes carried by the shares involved.

In calculating the amounts referred to in subsection 1. also takes into account the number of employees, turnover and balance sheet in such a company where the company's share capital or the votes of the shares, whether directly or indirectly at least 25 percent.

§ 3. Definition of the production facility and tourism

In this Act the production facility

1) establishment of industrial manufacturing or processing the products and

2) labor movement that mainly produce or process products. (2003/19)

In this Act with tourism

1) hotels, motels, guesthouses, cottages motion, motion camping, hostels, guesthouses and other comparable accommodation, movement,

2) catering business as owner of a hosting business carried on in connection therewith, and

3) hosting a business carried on in connection with agriculture, if the activity constitutes an agricultural stand-alone business.

§ 4. Fixed assets tax credit applies

In this Act produktionsinrättnings assets subject to wear loose, plant and equipment and building and konstruktionsom used as a factory, workshop, power station or warehouse, or for any other purpose that directly connects addressed to produktionsinrättningens activity.

In this Act with the tourism company assets subject to wear loose, plant and equipment, and building or construction somanvänds for purposes that directly connects to the tourist company's operations.

§ 5. Height depreciation

With deviation from what is stated in 30 and 34 § § Act on Taxation of business income (FFS 360/1968), which according to province Act (1993:42) on the municipal tax on business activity shall be applied in the calculation of results for business in the municipal taxation, the taxable from the acquisition cost of such assets within the meaning of § 2 for tax fördet fiscal year during which the assets entry into service and for the two following tax years deducting högstdet a 50 percent increase in the amount of maximiavskrivningen under the provisions of the country, encapsulating the council tax for business.

Depreciation provided in subsection 1. may not be påanskaffningsutgiften for such anläggningstillgångarför which depreciation has been made pursuant to [Landscape Act (1993:110) on a temporary rise in depreciation ikommunalbeskattningen on productive investment].

See Sk 112 SF and E 6, Landscape Act (1993:42) on municipal

tax on business.

§ 6. (1996/52) Business Transfer

Taxpayer, for which activities have been transferred in accordance with 52d § Law on Taxation of Income avnäringsverksamhet under § 1 Landscape Law omkommunalskatt of business shall apply when calculating the results of näringsverksamhetvid municipal taxation and continue business as the parent community previously conducted, the vidbeskattningen deduct the acquisition cost of fixed assets belonging to the business transferred to the taxpayer to conduct yourself as if taxpayer had made an in § 2 board investering.Med parent corporation referred to what is the parent corporation in accordance with § 2 subsection 1 or 2. Landscape Act (1989:23) on the group contribution for tax purposes.

See E 10, Landscape Act (1989:23) on the group communication

nalbeskattningen.

§ 7. Accounting provisions and making declarations

In order to depreciation under this Act shall be deducted for tax purposes must be the acquisition cost of fixed assets have been deducted as depreciation in the same way in the taxpayer's records. The acquisition cost of fixed assets for tax credit and the depreciation incurred on the cost shall be specified as clearly in the records to be easily distinguished from other expenditures. For the enforcement of taxation, the taxpayer make such investigations as necessary förbeviljande of the tax credit.

§ 8. Coming into force provisions

This Act comes into force on 1 July 1994.

This Act applies at kommunalbeskattningenför fiscal years 1994-2003. (2003/19)

E 19 Landscape Act (1982:18) concerning

application at kommunalbeskatt

tion of the law on tax

for shipping

§ 1. Act June 18, 1981 on tax försjöfarten (FFS 433/1981) and with the support of densammautfärdade provisions shall, except in lagens12 § is compulsory, as in this Act take observance, at the municipal taxation in the province of Åland. Deductions for isavgiftsklass may, with the deviation from what the law § 6 is prescribed, made even dåfråga is about in the paragraph intended vessels ordered abroad as well, with special authorization by the [Provincial Government], in the case of the section is intended fartygsom purchased used and whose age when it was collected did not exceed ten years. From the acquisition cost of used ships and vessels ordered during the years 1994 - 1998, that deduction shall be made over the years dåfartyget in use and during the subsequent interesting cat years. (1997/62)

Taxpayer is entitled to annually from the income of the shipping business deduct funds set aside for the classification of ships with a net tonnage of at least 19registerton, however, does not exceed the amount of what can reasonably be assumed to be required at the annual provision förnämnda purposes and subject to the classification provisions not used to cover avklassificeringsutgifter be recorded as income during the tax year when the classification was performed, the abil-get transferred or loss of the ship was found (classified ceringsreservering). (1993/44)

§ 1a. Taxpayer is entitled to the income from shipping business to deduct the amount of provision which hangjort in their financial statements for the years 1994 - 1998 (ship replacement reserve). (1997/62)

Vessel replacement reserve referred to in subsection 1. or part thereof shall be used to cover the acquisition cost of vessels of less than 19 GRT or, for that matter, the acquisition price has not been used to cover the acquisition cost of vessels, recorded as income by the fifth tax year following the tax year when the reservation was made. With the provision covered acquisition cost of the vessel or part of such acquisition cost is not deductible expense.

Taxpayer pursuant to subsection 2. used the vessel replacement reserve for the purchase of a vessel, to join its tax utredningom ship acquisition reserve ring use to cover the acquisition cost of the ship, amortization of acquisition costs of the tax year and on the undepreciated acquisition cost of the ship in the fiscal year end.

§ 2. The administrative functions under the Act omskattelättnader for shipping is for the Treasury and the County Tax Office will then issue is whether municipal taxation administered by the [Provincial Government]. (1986/39)

The reference in the Act, § 2 to § 30 Act on the taxation of business income (FFS360/1968) in the landscape relate to § 30 Landscape Law on local taxes for business.

§ 3. The law on tax breaks for shipping and medstöd of the same provisions issued is to be followed in the landscape as they obey when put raids in force. Thereafter changes to the above provisions, the amended rules apply in the landscape from the time of their entry into force iriket. Changes to the rules on which this Act provided for deviations shall not be applied in the landscape.

§ 4. This Act applies at the kommunalbeskattningar executed for the years 1981-1995. Nevertheless, to apply § 6 Act on tax breaks for shipping ävenvid the kommunalbeskattningar executed for the years 1996-1999 and in the case of vessels acquired used or new vessels ordered in åren1994-2000 even at the kommunalbeskattningar somverkställs for the years 2000-2005 and the provisions of the the said Act, § § 7-11 at the kommunalbeskattningar executed for the years 1996-1998, with the deviations provided by this Act and the provisions of § 1 of this Act at the kommunalbeskattningarsom executed for the years 1996-2003. (2003/20)

A classification provisions that have not used before the end of 1995 is considered as taxable income for 1995. A ship replacement reserve, which has not been used before the end of 1998anses as taxable income for 1998, dockså in § 1a board ship replacement reserve, which has not been used before the end of 2003 is considered as taxable income for 2003.

E 20 Landscape Act (1977:19) on tax relief

costs at the municipal taxation of

public corporation engaged in

socially important activity

§ 1. Income under municipal Act (1993:37) for the province of Åland is taxable undertake public benefit corporation engaged in socially meaningful activities can be declared fully or partially tax-free in municipal taxation in enlighetmed what of this Act. For income tax exemption of fastighetfår granted only in the case provided for i2 subsection. (1993/40)

Income from property which, according to in subsection 1. angivnalag is taxable can be declared tax-free only in detfall that the property is primarily used for general or public utility purposes.

§ 2. Tax relief under this Act is granted by the [Provincial Government] for a maximum of five fiscal years at a time. Tax relief may be granted only if relief can be justified in respect to the advantage of community activities pose to society. Further, it considered whether the granting of tax relief for vissav community does business is detrimental not call for traders bedrivermotsvarande activity. (1990/38)

If need be, the [Provincial Government] set conditions which must be taken to the relevant communities will retain their entitlement to tax relief.

§ 3. Public benefit corporation may be deemed to be socially important activity of its egentligasyftemål is to promote political, social or other activities that fill major needs in the community, unless this activity covers the entire landscape, or is otherwise of substantial nature and won the staid forms and is persistent.

Is the work of the organization, which is formed by the communities which should be considered as special taxpayers, socially significant at the 1 mom.avsett way, when examining whether the conditions förbeviljande of tax credit for each samfundbeaktas entire organization, if with regard to organization's character and community's position in the organization is warranted.

§ 4. Tax relief under this Act shall be filed in writing within four months from the end of the fiscal year for which exemption is sought. The application shall be accompanied by the required investigation. It is also skyldigatt on demand, provide the additional information and reports to the adventure is required. (1990/38)

Before deciding on the application for relief shall be the municipal council of the applicant's domicile opportunity that providing advice on the application. Is an essential part of the applicant's business located in another municipality than the municipality, also stand that municipal governments be given the opportunity to GIVE statement.

The application for relief shall be treated as urgent and, if possible, be settled within six months from the date it was filed.

§ 5. [Provincial government], shall, from the date it determines, in full or partial recapture tax relief granted to communities

1) if it is found that the community's character changed so that it no longer can be considered in this Act avsettallmännyttigt communities,

2) the nature of the business community ask-driver amended to allow tax relief, therefore, can not be granted under this Act, or

3) if the community failed to observe the 2 § 2 mom.angivna conditions.

Before the decision on withdrawal of tax relief to make the affected community an opportunity to yttrasig the matter.

§ 6. By virtue of this Act granted relief pray-woo not corporations from making declarations that detutan relief would be in accordance with the [tax law (FFS 482/1958)].

Communities granted tax relief under dennalag, is required to so structure their accounts, attdärav shows the income, for which skattelättnadbeviljats.

§ 7. For the purposes of this Act, the [tax law] penal provisions and provisions on confidentiality, and where applicable further provisions of [tax law] observed.

§ 8. Further provisions on the enforcement Enoch purposes of this Act shall, if necessary through landscape regulation.

§ 9. This Act first apply the tax to be enforced for 1976.

Notwithstanding the provisions of the statutes in § 4 subsection 1. can tax for the fiscal year, starting in the year 1976 be sought before the end of March 1977.

E 21 Landscape Act (1984:4) on deduction of

municipal taxation for amortization

ring on student loans

§ 1. Taxable natural person who is permanently resident in the province are entitled to in accordance with Vadi this law is written from their taxable income only in municipal taxation do a avdragför repayments on student loans (student loan deductions).

With student loans under this Act by kreditinrättningbeviljat loans for which the Åland Labour ochstudieservicemyndighet, provincial government or student committee appointed by landskapsstyrelsenbeviljat landscape bond and interest rate support under provincial law (1972:48) for study or landscape bail under provincial law (1995:94) on Student and raised in studies opened before On 1 August 2005. (2006/103)

§ 2. As student loan deductions may be deducted from the amount which the taxpayer to the credit institution has paid the mortgage on student loans. The deduction may not exceed 500 per calendar year. (2002/49)

Student loan deduction may be made for amortization somerlagts during the calendar year in which the capitalization of the interest has ceased and over the next four calendar years when repayments are made. The deduction may be made from taxable income the year in which principal paid. Studielåneavdragetbeviljas for up to five years for a single taxpayer. (2006/103)

§ 3. (2002/49) On application by a municipality, provincial government, the municipality has a low tax base, lowering the upper limit of the in § 2 above deduction to lägst250 euros.

§ 4. The Government of Åland shall issue more detailed instructions regarding the application of this Act.

§ 5. This Act first apply for the tax to be enforced for 1983.

Those who before this Act comes into force påbörjatamortering on student loans may make in the law intended deductions exceeding five years less the number of years over which repayments made before the entry into force.

Entry into Force Provision (2006/103):

This Act comes into force on 1 January 2007 and to apply the first time when the taxes are implemented for 2007.

E 22 Landscape Act (1997:38) on the application

tion in the Åland Islands of rikslagstift

tion on taxation procedure

§ 1. Scope

Act on Assessment Procedure (FFS 1558/1995) and the Regulation on Assessment Procedure (FFS1579/1995) and with the support of these provisions shall be issued in the province during the execution of municipal taxation and the fastställandetav forest management fee, considering the avvikelseroch specific provisions provided by this Act .

The in subsection 1. said statutes and the medstöd of them issued provisions shall apply such they are subject when this Act comes into force. Thereafter changes in statutes or in the regulations issued thereunder, the amended rules apply in the landscape from the time of completion served effect in the kingdom. Changes to the rules on which this Act provided for deviations shall not apply in the province.

See Sk 301 and 302 (FFS 763/1998) SF.

§ 2. The management of administrative functions

The administrative functions under the Act and the Regulation on Assessment Procedure or pursuant to regulations issued thereunder is for the state authorities in the region of hand-held by [Provincial Government], if these data enligt23 § Autonomy Act is for the landscape.

§ 3. Skattetagarkommun

Council tax, as nonresident must pay on income derived from the landscape, is paid to the municipality where the taxpayer förvärvatstörsta part of their income.

Council tax as taxable corporations ochsamfällda benefits payable divided between the municipalities under municipal Act (1993:37) förlandskapet Åland.

See E 5, Kommunalskattelag (1993:37) for the Province of Åland.

§ 4. Double taxation

Income derived by taxpayer resident in the province acquired in the kingdom, and income taxpayer resident in the kingdom acquired the province and which is taxed in the municipal taxation there, [Provincial Government] on the application and conditions [Provincial Government] decides wholly or partly exempt from council tax charged on corresponding income here, after the competent national authority in whole or in part, has denied relief from the corresponding tax charged on the profits of the kingdom.

If the above in subsection 1. said double harkonstaterats can [Provincial Government] on the application ochpå the conditions [Provincial Government] decides to grant deferment of payment of council tax.

A decision taken under this section may not be appealed.

§ 5. Declaration of Obligation for the corporation with domicile in the country

Taxable entities that are domiciled in the realm of the tax return must disclose the taxable income derived from the landscape and the deductible expenditure on revenue acquisition.

§ 6. The costs of enforcement of municipal taxation

Municipalities are required to pay kostnadernaför enforcement of municipal taxation to denmyndighet which enforces the municipal taxation on the grounds the law on tax administration (FFS1557/1995) indicates the municipality.

See Sk 308 SF.

§ 7. Act came into force and application

This Act takes effect immediately and apply the first time at the municipal taxation to be implemented for fiscal year 1996.

This Act repeals the Landscape Act (1959:21) on the application of tax law on land landscape of Åland.

Except as provided in subsection 1.

1), as in Landscape Act tillämpningav taxation law of the Province of Åland stadgatsom tax classification, appeal of tax classification and identification of revenue bases förskogsbruk exercised in the taxation to be implemented for fiscal years 1996 and later,

2) community interest calculated at the beskattningsom be enforced for tax year 1996, in derogation from the provisions of § 41 Act on Assessment Procedure, the earliest from 1 November 1996;

3), 2 and chapter 3. and § 33, § 36, § 49, 65 och87 § § Act on Assessment Procedure applicable range of taxation to be implemented for fiscal years 1995 and

4) may be in decisions about the loss determined for tax year 1995 or prior fiscal years in the order somanges of the Act on tax procedure applied for modification 31 December 2000.

Cited in the landscape law to tax law, the corresponding provisions of lagenom taxation procedure shall apply.

E 23 Regulation (1997:72) on the execution

of municipal taxation in

Åland

(FFS 860/1997)

§ 1. The administrative functions under the law on taxation procedure and legislation omförskottsuppbörd is for Åland [Provincial Government] shall be administered by the Reich tax.

See E 22, Landscape Act (1997:38) on the application of rikslag

law on taxation procedure and E 24, Landscape Impact

(1997:32) on the application of national legislation on förskottsupp

gestations.

§ 2. Municipalities of Åland take part in the costs of enforcement of taxation on the sättsom out in landscape types.

The landscape is responsible for the costs orsakasav characteristics of the legislation on kommunalbeskattningi landscape in accordance with the [Provincial Government] and the tax board agree. An agreement must be concluded annually on the landscape for costs during calendar year thereafter.

§ 3. This Regulation shall enter into force on 1 oktober1997.

Agreement on the costs of enforcement of municipal taxation for 1997 ingasi connection with the agreement on the costs of taxation for 1998.

E 24 Landscape Act (1997:32) on the application

tion in the Åland Islands of rikslagstift

tion on Prepayment

§ 1. Scope

Act on Prepayment (FFS 1118/1996) and Regulation on Prepayment (FFS 1124/1996) and with the support of those issued rules to be applied in the landscape to the enforcement of municipal taxation with regard to the avvikelseroch specific provisions provided by this Act. (2008 / 95)

The in subsection 1. said statutes and the medstöd of them issued provisions shall apply such they are subject when this Act comes into force. Thereafter changes in statutes or in the regulations issued thereunder, the amended rules apply in the landscape from the time of completion served effect in the kingdom. Changes to the rules on which this Act provided for deviations shall not apply in the province.

See Sk 201 and 202 SF.

1 § 1 subsection. has changed. The previous wording is:

Act on Prepayment (FFS 1118/1996) and Decree

Prepayment (FFS 1124/1996) and under them out

traveled provisions shall apply in the province of executive

tion of municipal taxation with regard to the deviations

and special provisions provided by this Act. In addition,

the Act on temporary exemption from the payment of advances

withholding tax incurred by the seafarer's income from certain pas

sagerarfartyg (FFS 625/2004) the execution of the withholding

position in the landscape. (2004/53)

§ 2. The management of administrative functions

The administrative functions under the Act and the Regulation on Prepayment or under regulations issued thereunder is for the state authorities in the province operated avlandskapsregeringen, if these data according to § 23 Autonomy Act is for the landscape.

§ 3. Act on Assessment Procedure

Accrued on advances applicable provisions of the Act on Assessment Procedure (FFS1558/1995).

See Sk 301 SF.

§ 4. Entry into force and application

This Act comes into force on 1 April 1997.

This Act repeals the Landscape Act (1959:27) of 16 December 1959 on the application completed on Prepayment of Åland.

The provisions concerning the employer's declaration obligation of the former Act on Prepayment (FFS 418/1959) in 1997, the 1996 Prepayment. The previous Act's provisions regarding the issuance of withholding evidence and fogande of the tax return to apply to taxation are for 1996 and 1997.

The provisions of § 39 subsection 3. Act on Prepayment first apply to the charging decisions 1998th Based on previous similar decisions refundable tax withholding if necessary after application.

Tax Increase in accordance with § 44 subsection 4. Act on Prepayment may be applied by reason of the omission of the declaration requirement which occurred after the law comes into force.

Rectification according to § 48 Act on Prepayment must be made even when the change is sought in a beslutsom taken before entry into force. Request for rectification shall not be made if a decision has already been delivered on the occasion of rectification or hassle.

The provisions of 56 and 57 § § Act on Prepayment shall also apply to interest ochrestavgift referred to in the law on late payments ochrestavgift.

Cited in another province relating to the former Act on Prepayment of the corresponding provisions of the Act on Prepayment applied.

Entry into Force Provision (2004/53):

This Act comes into force on 1 January 2005 and to apply the first time in the förskottsinnehållningsom execution of remuneration paid in 2005.

Entry into Force Provision (2008/95):

This Act comes into force on 1 August 2008.

E 25 Landscape Act (1996:50) on the application of Åland to the law on penalties and penalty interest

§ 1. For failure to timely pay municipal taxes or forestry fee or advances thereof shall, in this Act specified deviations, the Act of 18 December 1995 on penalties and penalty interest (FFS 1556/1995) shall be applicable in the Province of Åland.

If in subsection 1. the said Act be amended to apply the changes in the landscape from the time the requested entry into force of the kingdom, unless otherwise provided in this Act.

See Sk 606 SF.

§ 2. Refer to it in § 1 above the law of the provisions of national law, which owns counterpart ashore lation, shall be deemed to refer to the provisions of law landscape.

§ 3. Detailed rules for the enforcement ochtillämpningen of this Act shall, if necessary through landscape regulation.

§ 4. This Act comes into force on 1 July 1996.

This act repeals the landscape Act (1977:11) on 4 March 1977 on the application of Åland of law on late payments and restavgiftpå tax.

E 26 Landscape Act (2007:23) on the grounds

for contributions to the Åland health care

care

§ 1. Scope

This Act regulates grounds for the charges somuppbärs of Åland's health. The Act does not apply to contributions in environmental health, nor the price of services Åland Health sells.

§ 2. The maximum fee

The fee for a service may be up as much as the cost of production of the service.

§ 3. Toll-free service

The following services are free of charge:

1) visits in psychiatric outpatient care,

2) school health, child and maternity care and cervical cancer screening;

3) visits to the doctor to assess if the patient is barking up for care regardless of his or her will;

4) home visits that take place entirely on the doctor or nursing staff initiative,

5) examinations and treatment of public health hazard my diseases and HIV infection, gonorrhea and chlamydia infection that is transmitted sexually.

The Åland Government can decide on grounds offended a service under this Act is chargeable shall be free of charge to the user.

§ 4. High-cost

As high-cost case that a person sub rett calendar year pays fees to a maximum of 300 euros in total (cost limits) for services somomfattas of protection. For people under 18 years ochöver 65 is the price ceiling EUR 125 for one calendar year. The lower cost ceiling will apply to and including the calendar year in which the person reaches 18 years and from ochmed the calendar year following the year the person reaches the age of 65.

Cost ceiling includes patient charges föröppenvårdsbesök, day surgery, short-term institutional care, rehabilitation and Physiatrics and the hire of borrowed filed aids. With regard to day duties omfattasdock only additional part of the cost ceiling, menlandskapsregeringen may decide that neither the basic allowance shall be payable after the price ceiling is exceeded. Fees for certificates and statements may also be subject to the cost ceiling as landscape Government.

If a person during the calendar year have contributed to an amount exceeding kostnadstakethar he or she is entitled to recover the excess. If recovery has not been made before the end of the calendar year following the year of kostnadstaketöverskreds person is deprived of his right to a refund. If, on account of an agency's authorizing rett insurance decisions or because of a change request becomes clear only after follow-up years on charges covered by the high cost threshold or not, the demand for repayment made within one year fråndet decision has been issued or any decision anledningav appeal is final .

§ 5. Long-term institutional care

Institutional care, which is expected to last or has pågåttlängre than three months are considered long-term institutional care.

The fee for long-term institutional care (long term care fees) according to the patient's ability to pay. The fee shall not exceed an amount equal to 80 percent of the patient månadsinkomst.Patienten must always be at his disposal haminst 80 euros per month.

If a person who is in long-term institutional care immediately before institutionalization initiated has lived in the same household in the marriage or marriage-like relationship and his or her monthly income is greater than the spouse's or spouse's monthly income, provides long-term care fee of basisav couple's combined monthly income. The fee shall not exceed an amount equal to 40 percent of the aggregate månadsinkomsten.Den receiving institutional care must always be at his disposal at least 80 euros per month. If both spouses referred to in this subsection is in long-term institutional care set fee as specified i2 subsection.

Long-term care fee charged from the first full calendar month that the patient is in long-term institutional care. The fees shall be on. It shall be adjusted on the solvency has been changed significantly, it is clear that the relationship densom be taken into account when setting the charges have changed or if the fee is found to be incorrect. A fee determined on the basis of obviously erroneous data the user can be corrected retroactively for up to one year.

§ 6. Fee based income

Long-term care contributions are determined by monthly income as a basis. Varies monthly earnings set fee to the average monthly income in the previous year as a basis. As the revenue account the income after taxes withheld ochför shots payments and tax-free income as provided in this section.

In addition to earned income taken into account pensions and meddem comparable benefits, annuities and benefits payable in money and in connection with the transfer of a property has been reserved for a fixed period or for life (life annuity), and other ongoing personal income and net capital income and other property, such as interest, dividend and rental income.

As income also takes into account income-ochför acquisition income shares of the agricultural and economic activities as established in the last completed tax and taxpayer's share of a same-circuit income. That revenue may, in comparison with the income that the last completed taxation shows, adjusted by the percentages tax determined annually in its decision deninkomst to be the basis for the imprest.

As the income not taken into account:

1) child benefit,

2) child disability allowance under the legislation on child care support,

3) allowance for pensioners who are paid in connection with the state pension,

4) child increase payable in connection with public pension

5) housing,

6) Disability,

7) the payment of accident insurance in respect of medical and investigative costs,

8) benefits paid by reason of the performance of civil or military conscription,

9) Front top-up payments related to pension,

10) study,

11) support for rehabilitation, including employment, money and travel expenses paid somutkomststöd,

12) aid payable in connection with the selection tilloch participation in employment promotion training,

13) scholarships and other benefits paid feasibility studies, training or other skills-enhancing activities,

14) alimony or maintenance paid to a minor child to the patient or if the fee is determined based on the couple's combined income, to a minor child to the patient's spouse;

15) in pensions and similar incomes depth increases due to dependents or

16) other similar benefits or compensation for the costs of family care or support for care avbarn in the home.

§ 7. Deductions from revenue

Before long-term care component is fixed to the patient's income is deducted:

1) the required maintenance to be paid by him or her;

2) other similar costs resulting from his or her actual family relations and

3) The benefit of him or her shall be paid in money and in connection with the transfer of enfastighet has been reserved for a fixed period or for life (life annuity).

Deduction under subsection 1. A point is not whether the person is a recipient of child support is the spouse of the person who pays child support ochmakarna has lived in the same household immediately before institutionalization began.

§ 8. Fee according to ability to pay

The Government of Åland may order any charges other than long term care fees be levied under the user's ability to pay. Contributions are determined under which the grounds specified in § 5 2 and 4 mom.samt 6 and 7, § §. The Government of Åland may därutöverbesluta that the fee shall be determined with regard to PM the party concerned are living in the same household in the marriage or marriage-like relationship, attdet's minor children in the same household, andraav person's actual family situation-dependent factors that affect the ability to pay or denunderhållsskyldighet referred to in the Act on underhållför children (FFS 704/1975).

§ 9. Fee for failure to visit

Landscape government may decide that a special fee shall be collected by the pre reserveratmottagningstid but without an acceptable reason underlåtitatt come to the clinic on the reservation tiden.Avgiften can be recovered even in the case of a service that would otherwise be free of charge.

§ 10. Waiver and reduction of the fee

Åland's health may decide that a fee be waived or reduced to the delförutsättningarna for the patient or his family responsibilities, or the realization of the patient's legal dependents compromised by the fee Moventas out. The Authority may also decide that a fee be waived or reduced if warranted having regard to the treatment observations.

§ 11. Charges for care reimbursed under the statutory accident insurance and motor insurance

The determination of fees förvård whose costs are reimbursed within the framework of the accident and motor insurance is the law omklientavgifter in Welfare and Health (FFS734/1992). Such fees are not covered by the cost ceiling.

See 713 So FL II.

§ 12. (2007/78) fee for anyone who does not reside in the landscape

Fees and allowances received by the person who is not domiciled in Aland can be established on grounds other than those specified in this Act, unless otherwise provided by international agreements that are bindandeför landscape. In determining the applicable provincial law (1993:27) on the Charge to the landscape, however, so that the fee for a service may be more than equal to the cost of production avtjänsten.

See E 2, Landscape Act (1993:27) on the Basis of Payment

the landscape.

§ 13. Appealing

An appeal against a decision of an officeholder may not be appealed. If the debtor is dissatisfied with such a decision can be male ller she seek correction of the decision in line by 14 § subsection 1. Landscape Act (1993:60) on health ochsjukvården.

A decision taken in respect of rectification is sought by appealing to the Åland Administrative Court within 30 days from the receipt. Besvärkan within the said period also submitted to the Åland health care, which sends them to the Administrative Court. In the Åland Administrative Court ruling fårändring not be appealed.

See K 1, Landscape Act (1993:60) on health care.

§ 14. Collection and recovery of charges

Regarding collection and recovery of avgiftersom purposes of this Act applies 7 and 8, § § Landscape Act (1993:27) on the Charge to the landscape.

See E 2, Landscape Act (1993:27) on the Basis of Payment

the landscape.

§ 15. Entry into force

This Act comes into force on 1 January 2008.

E 27 Landscape Act (1974:23) on wastewater charge

§ 1. Municipality has the right to compensation for kostnadernaför diversion and purification of sewage and rainwater collecting sewage charges in line with what contemporary law states.

§ 2. Wastewater fee shall be paid by owners or by the owner equal owners of the property, which is connected to municipal sewage treatment plants.

As in subsection 1. is provided on property owners in the same way private contractors, who supported avtomt or land lease agreement holds the property.

§ 3. Wastewater fee consists of connection charges and service fees.

§ 4. Connection fee is paid to cover the costs of the construction of sewers and to demanslutna facilities for the treatment of wastewater. As construction costs considered only those resources that are already used for the construction of the facility, including the amount that can be expected to be required to put the plant in a condition, that in § 1 above measures effectively execute.

As a basis for determining the connection fee can be taken from the following options:

1) the plot area and floor area;

2) the property is located on the gross floor area;

3) the number of apartments in the buildings on the property and its gross floor area, or

4) other bases, which are comparable to those in paragraphs 1-3 above.

In determining the connection fee is also building production are considered.

Does the size of the subsection 2. estimated rental charge for special reasons manifestly unfair, the fee shall be determined by the use of property is that the wastewater be diverted and treated.

Change the circumstances under which the connection fee established, the fee can be adjusted accordingly.

§ 5. Service fee shall be established by 31 December 2010 due to the amount of water used in the building so that the fee covers kostnadernaför water service. Fees shall be determined for consumption categories industry, agriculture and hushåll.Vid Calculations take into account environmental and resource costs. (2005/56)

If the service fee, as determined in accordance with subsection 1. as a result of drainage water quality or quantity thereof, or any other reason obviously has to be considered too big or too small, or if water can not be measured properly, this and the benefits the property has been the diversion of water beaktasvid determination of service fee.

Municipality that owns the sewage works has the right to the water utilities to obtain information about the property's water consumption, which is connected to the municipal sewer.

With the exception of the requirement in regard to the principle of cost recovery in subsection 1. may force avgifterfortsättningsvis apply if they do not compromise the purposes and carry out the objectives for vattenkvalitetsom provided in Chapter 4. § 1 and 5 kap.1 and § § 2 of the Water Act (1996:61) for the Province of Åland. (2005/56)

The detailed rules for domestic water charges in the landscape Act (1979:29) on the broad waters and sewage. (2005/56)

§ 6. Taxa including detailed grounds for establishing the wastewater charge is approved by the municipal council. Council's decision shall be subject to provincial government for approval.

§ 7. Obligation to pay the sewage charge will be from the property connected to public sewer.

§ 8. Wastewater fee determined and charged by the municipal board. User fees can be charged and also of another in regulations or instructions given municipal authority.

§ 9. (2008/28) Before joining fee down, barked debtor by verifiable notification communicated to the proposed connection fee applies förhonom or her as provided for in the Administrative Procedure Act (2008:9) for the Province of Åland. Comments on the proposal must be submitted to the municipality board within 14 days of notification.

Decision on connection fee shall be served by bevisligdelgivning the debtor under Anything provided in the Administrative Procedure of the Åland Islands.

Proposals and decisions referred to in subsections 1 and 2. fårdelges even so, that the proposal or decision perpost sent by registered mail in the property address or other known address of the property owners or holders.

§ 10. The municipal board sets billing periods for service fee. The Board may also decide, attbruksavgifter which are collected for the calendar year or other period, shall be paid as advance rates in the equivalent of the water consumption during the previous billing period, with the final value determined sedanden actual consumption recorded in the billing period. In this regard, to the debtor promptly refunded the amount paid or else, the lack of specific amount collected.

The municipality shall forward to the pay the debit note, which must show the förbrukadevattenmängden and fee amounts. If bruksavgiftuppbäres by advance installments, shall be of the debit note stated that during the previous billing period, quantity of water consumed and how much of them corresponds to the amount advanced.

Debtor is entitled to seven days efterdet he received the debit note make note Hosien § 8 intended authority. In response to the complaint shall be decided and the final debit note sent to the debtor.

Is applied service fee pursuant to § 5 2 mom.skall proposal containing the grounds for the charge imparted to the debtor, before tax for the first time the property is determined. Regarding notification of proposals and submission of note is what i9 § is provided on the connection fee shall apply accordingly. Changed the basis for the fee later, the same procedure followed.

§ 11. The decision establishing the wastewater fee wanted change by appealing to the [county board] inom30 days.

As regards the decision referred to in § 10 subsection 2. considered the appeal period from the beginning of the period about which states i10 § 3 subsection. or, if the complaint made against the charge, from the receipt of final debit note.

§ 12. The connection fee may be paid in three annual installments. On the rates listed seven per cent interest from the beginning of detkalenderår immediately following the billing avden first årsraten. If delay in payment of the annual accounts, the amount of five percent due to added interest from the beginning of the calendar month following the due date.

Use Fee, notwithstanding complaints raised, erläggasunder the period laid down in the debit note. Pay Use Fee or rat which is not within the time the City decided to be 16 percent annual interest, from the due date, payable on the amount due. (1986/17)

To payment overdue unpaid sewage charge may exquisitely with the debtor in denordning are staid for the recovery of taxes ochavgifter by Execution.

§ 13. Transfer property to a new owner or owners, he is also responsible for such wastewater fee, plus interest, which was not paid a maximum of five years from the start of the calendar year following billing year.

Waived or reduced wastewater charges because of discomfort, the municipality shall reimburse the amount paid, plus interest from the payment date to the redemption date, according to the Bank of Finland Latter Day applying lower discount rate.

§ 14. Notwithstanding the above provisions may municipality decide that joining fee not be paid.

For land or other property entrusted avkommun, the connection fee not paid, if ejrätt to obtain such a charge reserved in the deed of transfer.

The land lease or land contract agreement, by means of which the municipality leased land or other area, shall be mentioned, whether legotagaren owe atterlägga connection fee. Have such an obligation ickeålagts legotagaren, the connection fee non påförashonom.

§ 15. Municipality may, in individual cases agree, that the wastewater fee is determined on other grounds änovan governed. Even in this respect should be foundations be fair and impartial.

The property owner or holder's ability to pay substantially diminished due to illness or accident or other cause, or has he avliditeller is the recovery of fees manifestly unfair Due to the nature of the building destroyed or damage påegendom occurred, the municipality at its discretion grant an application for exemption in whole or in part by payment of a fee. Under the same conditions also stand payment deferrals granted.

§ 16. This Act comes into force on 1 May 1974. Even before the Act came into force may preparatory åtgärdervidtagas and charges approved and established.

Connection fee shall not be paid,

1) for property, for which compensation is paid or payable under provincial law (1956:22), 18 juli1956 the city plan for the City of Mariehamn or under provincial law (1959:29) December 22, 1959 re-regulation of construction or for the recovery of such compensation due in the manner referred to in § 143 subsection 5. of that Act;

2) to plot as the municipality transferred before January 1, 1960 or else left it then, but that under provincial law regulating construction reserve the right to special collection of compensation, and

3) for property on which the agreement before this Act entered into effect on the payment of connection fee or comparable fee.

In the case of private land or area, as kommunutarrenderat before this Act comes into force, the connection fee not paid, unless the subcontract agreement especially reserved the right to compensation for byggandeav public sewer under the provincial law on the regulation of statutory construction principles.

The Municipalities in accordance with § 14 that the connection fee not be paid, should the land ochövriga areas, for which the basis of two and three mom.anslutningsavgift not otherwise ought to be paid, the service charge to be paid only half of the amount under § i6 intended tariff. This relief applies for ten årfrån date of the above intended decision, or, in the event that the property is not yet connected to the public sewer system, ten years from the first. The relief affects not property, that of the decision was connected to public sewage treatment plants for more than ten years.

As in subsection 4. is provided also applies to property, for which under this Act connection fees have been before in § 14 subsection 1. intended decision.

The Municipalities, as adopted in subsection 4. intended decision-and later the connection fee shall be paid, the municipality has the right to receive such a fee only förfastigheter, which after it was taken, is connected to the municipal public sewer. In the case of other properties may regard only such anslutningsavgiftpåföras, as necessitated by the change in förhållandenasom occurred after the decision.

Has the municipality under this Act liable to pay property owners or holders before this Act comes into force agreed service fee for public sewer countries agreed to the following correction.

E 28 Landscape Act (2002:60) on the application

tion of Åland of Chapter 29.

Penal Code

§ 1. The landscape is Chapter 29. straffl Act (FFS 39/1889) for crimes against the public economy are applied in the version when this Act comes into kraft.Ändringar of Chapter 29. Penal Code shall be applied on land exclusion from the coming into force of the kingdom.

With the subsidy under Chapter 29. Criminal Code referred to land landscape landscapes also share or landscape benefit to a municipality or a municipal association.

See St. 101 FL I.

§ 2. This Act comes into force on 1 August 2002.

This Act repeals

1) Chapter 29. Penal Code in the version that was previously in force in the province equal 71 § Autonomy Act and

2) 6 § 3, subsection 4. landscape Tax (1993:58).

INDUSTRIAL SECTOR REGULATIONS

Industries

Performance of the Economy

In a Landscape Act (1996:47) on the right to

exercise nutrition

Chapter 1. General Provisions

§ 1. Scope

This Act contains provisions concerning the right to pursue business in the province of Åland.

Except as provided in this section, the law shall not apply on board vessels registered in the province and mainly travels iinternationell traffic.

The carrying food on a ship referred to i2 subsection. must be of legal age and not be bankrupt.

The initiating nutritional practice on a ship recipes referred to in subsection 2. must notify the [Provincial Government] before starting operations.

§ 2. Nutrient Discharge

With business practice under this Act continued activity of economic acquisition and are independent, consistent with good practice and permitted by law.

Chapter 2. Right to practice nutrition

§ 3. Nutritional right with the law

Age individuals who are not bankrupt and who has homestead rights or uninterrupted harvarit resident in the province for at least five years have been fixed exercise business or profession as an industry in the province.

If minors the right to practice nutrition in some fallstadgas in national legislation.

§ 4. Granted the right nutrition

Age individuals who are not added icon rate but has no homestead right and not continuously resided in the province for at least five årsamt legal personality of the [Provincial Government], the circumstances and after consideration of each case, granted the right to practice nutrition.

Legal persons who are domiciled in the province ochvars all members or styrelsemedlemmarhar homestead right or continuously has resided ashore landscape for at least five years can not without special reasons for being denied the right nutrition.

The right nutrition can refer to a certain time or certain nutrients ochkan granted on conditions [Provincial Government] may deem necessary.

[Provincial government] shall keep a register of approved food dishes.

See A 1, Autonomy (1991:71), § 11.

A company active in construction, which lacked

domicile in Åland, but had to obtain in [§ 4 landscape

Act on the right to carry on a trade in Åland] intended state

erected a prefabricated house for its Executive Director

in one of his leased area in the province. The company was

illegally idkat nutrients in the landscape. HD 1971 II 19.

§ 5. Nutritional self-sufficiency

Notwithstanding what is provided in 3 and 4, § § varoch have a right to exercise nutrition without other assistance than their own spouse or minor children and without the use of business premises, offices or any other particular place.

§ 6. Fisheries and agriculture

Notwithstanding what is provided in 3 and 4, § § harrows and a right to engage in fishing and farming.

§ 7. Trader's branch operations

A business whose primary business fi NNS outside the province, establishing a department or branch in the province shall have the right nutrients referred to in § 4.

Even a business that extends its business to the province so that the product or service motersättning sold to individual consumers or to enväsentlig part produced in the province, but attegentlig department or branch established in the province, shall have the right nutrients referred to in § 4.

If the obligation of a business manager to pårörelsens The answer in the trial resulting Avrora required by national legislation.

Chapter 3. Regulated by the Financial Economy

§ 8. Nutritional status

By landscape types can be a skyldighetatt request authorization from [Provincial Government] förutövande of certain nutrients.

§ 9. Nutrient Application

By countryside regulation can be determined enskyldighet to notify before the exercise of certain nutrients begins.

§ 10. Specific provisions

[Provincial government] can set specific rules for the exercise of certain nutrients.

§ 11. Basic Application

If the obligation for legal persons and individual businessmen to make due notification to the pa-tent and Registration Board before operation inledsstadgas the Trade Register Act (FFS 129/1979).

See Ft 114 FL I.

Chapter 4. Supplementary provisions

§ 12. For instructions on product use and function

A trader is required to ensure that they sell varorhan have clear instructions on product use and function. The instructions must be written in Swedish or obtained in the image.

The obligation referred to in subsection 1. There is inteom it is obvious that information on the product's use or operation is not needed or if it kananses fair to the buyer are satisfied with verbal instructions. In the latter case, nutritional practitioner is obliged to give the necessary instructions.

The provisions of subsections 1 and 2. does not apply pånäringar referred to in 27 and 29 § § Autonomy Act.

Reasonable costs for actions arising from denskyldighet referred to in subsection 1. is replaced by funds granted through the appropriation of the province's budget.

§ 13. (1999/33) Penalties

The carrying food without nutrition right or authorization, carries nutrients without making notification recipes referred to in § 1 subsection 4. or § 9, carries nutrients in violation medsärskilda rules for the exercise of certain nutrients or carrying food on board the vessels referred to in § 1 2 mom.utan to meet the requirements set out in § 1 3 mom.samt who does not fulfill its obligation under 12 § be for breach of the right to practice nutrition to a fine or imprisonment not exceeding six months.

§ 14. Entry into force

This Act comes into force on 1 July 1996.

This Act repeals

1) Landscape Act (1957:11) on 10 April 1957 on the right to conduct business in the province of Åland,

2) Landscape Act (1963:9) April 4, 1963 stirrer trade,

3) Landscape Act (1943:10) 27 February 1943angående trade in open shop with second-hand goods and scrap metal and rags,

4) Landscape Act (1994:67) of 13 September 1994om application of Åland of förordningenom accommodation and catering establishments and

5) Landscape Act (1994:71), 13 september1994 on the application of the Åland Islands of the regulation on real estate agents.

§ 15. Transitional provision

Legal persons, who when this Act comes into force exercises with the assistance of the provincial law on the right attidka Economy of Åland, has the right to fortsättasin business practice under the provisions of the law term.

In two Affärstidslag (1992:40) for the Åland Islands

§ 1. General rule

Professional retail trade may be carried on all dagaroch times during the year unless otherwise prescribed time law.

§ 2. Scope

The rules of professional retail trade contemporary law applies to all professional selling spares directly to consumers except

a) the sale in pharmacies,

b) the sale at the kiosk and comparable trade and commerce through the vending machine,

c) the sale of travelers' needs at the airport, operating funds and in ports in areas that are reserved exclusively for foreign traffic;

d) the sale of gasoline or service station, car repair shops in or on the other with those comparable sales of fuel and lubricants förmotorer, liquefied flammable gas, as well as spare parts, equipment and accessories for vehicles;

e) the sale of flowers,

f) marketing and farmers' markets and

g) the sale of accommodation, or förplägningsrörelser.

§ 3. Exceptions

Professional retail trade may not be conducted

a) Good Friday,

b) Easter Sunday and

c) Christmas Day.

§ 4. Penalty

A person who violates this law shall be sentenced to a fine.

§ 5. Supervision

Police Authority monitors compliance with this Act.

§ 6. Effective Provision

This Act comes into force on 1 August 1992.

This Act repeals

1) Landscape Act (1970:10) April 16, 1970 omminuthandelns business hours,

2) Landscape Act (1970:11) on 16 April 1970 on the kiosk and comparable trading and automated trading, and

3) 4 § subsection 1. 4 point landscapes Act (1990:44) on 28 June 1990 on experiments with frikommuner.

In 3 Landscape Ordinance (1996:49) on

accommodation and entertainment activities

hot

§ 1. Scope

This regulation contains provisions on the exercise of accommodation and trakteringsverksamheti Åland.

§ 2. Definitions

With housing activity provided accommodation tamperproof acquisition purposes by guests in the rooms.

With the entertainment business means serving in trade of food or drink in a local or enplats reserved for this purpose.

§ 3. Exclusions

The regulation does not apply to

a) entertainment activities pursued in sambandmed an institution, association, corporation, or its equivalent, if the activity is only addressed to its own staff or another closed circle,

b) accommodation or entertainment activities in ettprivathem,

c) the accommodation or entertainment activities Somen individual exercises seasonally, if not the number of persons who are accommodated or district served more than 10 people or

d) holiday village consisting of a maximum of four homes adjacent to each other.

§ 4. Title

In an accommodation business can be a name that describes the nature of activities, such as hotels, motels, hostels, guesthouses, guest houses or cottages.

At an entertainment business can use a name that describes the nature of activities, such as restaurant, cafeteria or coffee shop.

§ 5. Notification

The initiating accommodation or entertainment activity shall notify the Åland environmental ochhälsoskyddsmyndighet before starting operations. (2007/143)

The notification must be accompanied

a) an indication of movement, trade name, address and telephone number;

b) an indication of the responsible manager's name, address and telephone number;

c) evidence that the responsible manager ärmyndig and is not bankrupt,

d) specifying the number of rooms and beds, in the case of a housing movement,

e) the number of seats, in the case of an entertainment business,

f) an indication of the time when operations begin and

g) an indication of the intent to give out alcoholic beverages.

If the business will be conducted in multiple facilities or multiple locations, the investigation referred i2 subsection. provided for each site even when a single notification.

If a change occurs to any of the comparatively densom referred to in subsection 2. the amendment shall be notified to the environmental health authority within one month after attändringen occurred. (2007/143)

The exercising accommodation or entertainment business and cease operations shall notify the environmental health authority. (2007/143)

§ 6. (2007/143) Records

Aland environmental health authority for ettregister of accommodation and entertainment movements påÅland.

§ 7. (2007/143) Opening

An entertainment business where alcohol is served must be kept open until two o'clock. Aland environmental ochhälsoskyddsmyndighet be associated with the serving grant also grant permission for extended opening hours under the conditions imposed by the Authority.

§ 8. Manager

An accommodation or entertainment business shall Haen manager.

§ 9. Dispensing and sale of alcoholic beverages

If the dispensing and sale of alkoholdryckerstadgas in national legislation.

Aland environmental health authority grants permission serving of alcoholic beverages. (2007/143)

§ 10. PREFECT

The exercising accommodation or entertainment activities may appoint a prefect responsible attupprätthålla order.

If necessary for the maintenance of ordningenkan police determine that the actor of accommodation and entertainment activities shall appoint a prefect.

In a prefect, the provisions of the prefect at public entertainments applied.

§ 11. Measures for the maintenance of order

The exercising accommodation or entertainment activities, and operating personnel, have the right to reject or remove customers and to refuse to serve mate ller drink if required for maintenance avordningen.

§ 12. Traveling Cards

A Ministry of the Interior established travel card must be completed for every traveler who comes to an accommodation business. Travelers must sign the card.

The operator of accommodation movement to save travel card for at least one year after the date of arrival.

People Short of a foreigner shall be submitted to the police the day after the date of arrival, unless the police to grant more time.

If there is reason to doubt the accuracy of the personal information that a traveler has left, the dettagenast notified police.

Only the police have the right to have a completed passenger card or take advantage of its contents.

§ 13. Departure Notification

For other foreigners than the Danish, Icelandic, Norwegian or Swedish citizens, a departure notification to the police the day after the day of departure, unless the police granted more time.

§ 14. Specific provisions

With regard to design requirements and other technical requirements and requirements concerning the organization and procedures for maintenance of the safety concerns what stadgasi law on building, fire and rescue services and health care.

§ 15. (2007/143) Monitoring

Aland environmental health authority and police monitors compliance with this Regulation.

§ 16. Administrative penalties

The police can give a warning to the actor of accommodation or entertainment business if it fails to comply with this regulation ommissbruk occurred in the operation or whether the activity interfered with the scheme.

If an omission or an offense is serious or repeated despite warnings, the Åland environmental ochhälsoskyddsmyndighet at the request of the police to limit opening hours of business or prohibit the operation or part of it for a fixed period or until further notice. (2007/143)

§ 17. Repealed (2007/143).

§ 18. Entry into force

This Regulation shall enter into force on 1 July 1996.Åtgärder that implementation of this Decree may be taken before it takes effect.

In 4 Landscape Nature (1975:56) of agency operations

§ 1. Conduct-of-agency movement is allowed only medtillstånd the [Provincial Government] and with iakttagandeav provisions of this Act.

§ 2. As practicing of the travel agency business deemed under this Act, the organization, sales and brokerage departures and services in connection therewith and förmedlingav accommodation in holiday homes, when the operation is done for gain.

§ 3. In order to conduct agency business requires a

divorced person to denne1) has the right to carry on a trade in the landscape, 2) age of 25, 3) in control of himself and his property, 4) is solvent; samt5) owns sufficient branschkännedom.Bestämmelsen in § 1 subsection 1. A point is not

individual who is resident in the province, the motion shall be conducted under the conditions somanges in § 11 Autonomy Act (1991:71) for the Aland Islands. (1994/68)

§ 4. To carry on activities of travel agencies are required by association ATT1) the association has the right to carry on a trade in

landscape, 2) the association is solvent, 3) the association of all personally responsible

competent partners and its Executive Director ellermed the equivalent person, and, where applicable, its all Board rules over sigsjälva and their property, and

4) (1994/68) of business under the direction of softening [Provincial Government] approved manager who is resident in the province and meet the in § 3 subsection 1. 2-5 points statutory requirements.

§ 5. (1994/68) Before a license to practice resebyrårörelsebeviljas permit applicant shall lodge security with the [Provincial Government]. The guarantee shall be for ettbelopp as [Provincial Government] in view of the nature and extent determines.

For trips in which the law on package is applicable, adequate security for the repayment softening money paid over and for the repatriation of travelers.

§ 6. Finds [Provincial Government] on the base of ansökanoch OBTAINED investigation that the applicant meets this Act consolidated conditions, the applicant should be granted permission to conduct agency business.

The term agency shall be used only by densom authorized to conduct such business.

[Provincial government] to register as dennalag granted business permit.

§ 7. The person authorized to conduct agency business shall, before starting operations, making the [Landscape Act (1957:11) on the right to carry on a trade in Åland] staid business notification. Regarding the notification to the commercial register of what that effect is specifically provided.

§ 8. Launches that has been authorized to conduct agency business not the business within six months after permission is granted, this has expired, unless [Provincial Government] on application made within the said period extended the deadline.

§ 9. Adherents of the travel agency business shall annually before On 1 April to the [Provincial Government] instill report on its activities for the previous calendar year containing the monitoring information required. The story shall be attached financial statements for the last completed fiscal year.

Adherents of the travel agency business is also required to provide the [Provincial Government] provide requested additional information and statistics and other investigations relating to the business.

Of the travel agency business appointed auditors should at least be of the Central Chamber of Commerce approved public accountant (APA) or approved Fiscal (GRM). In the story, which is delivered annually to the [Provincial Government] shall be attached audit report.

§ 10. Adherents of the travel agency business shall be promptly ochsenast within one month to the [Provincial Government] shall notify the changes that occurred in the conditions which formed the prerequisite for the granting of permits.

When the travel agent movement's domicile or address changes or closures; thereon shall be promptly notified in writing to the [Provincial Government].

§ 11. Has the [Provincial Government], after the trader the opportunity that has given notice, found that the register recorded travel agency business ceased its activities, the movement will be removed from the 6 § 3 mom.avsedda register. If the action, he informed traders.

§ 12. Permission to conduct agency business shall be revoked if it is found that any of those for beviljandeav state statutory prerequisites no longer exist. [Provincial government] may, if it is deemed reasonable, the time limit within which the correction shall be made. Skerej corrected within the time the permit shall be revoked.

§ 13. Dies individual trader of agency operations or put him out of business, matures nutritional status. The death or bankruptcy estate has the right to order the estate to continue operations under the previous state for a period of one year from the date of death or the date of bankruptcy early.

The person or seized resebyråidkaresdödsbo shall, within three months from the date of death of the [Provincial Government] seek the approval avlämplig person as interim manager for the movement.

Trustee of bankruptcy, if applicable, to observe what in subsection 2. is provided in the event that resebyråidkare dies. The time is counted from the date of the creditors decided on the movement continued.

They seized the estate or managing the estate is responsible for operating the operation until interim manager approved.

§ 14. Cover association engaged in travel agency operating in bankruptcy, if applicable, the provisions of § 13 and attention.

§ 15. Dies manager of the shutter travel agency business, he is declared bankrupt, or he leaves his position or he is otherwise permanently unable to care have it, the request omgodkännande of new manager submitted to the [Provincial Government] within three months.

§ 16. Has a private entrepreneur or manager of the shutter travel agency business failed to observe the provisions and regulations applicable to the travel agent industry, abuse ägtrum in the business or has this been carried out in violation of good business practice in the industry, the [Provincial Government] to assign the appropriate warning or some tidförbjuda conduct of the movement.

If neglect or abuse of a serious nature or persists or repeats the above notwithstanding åtgärdervidtagits, can [Provincial Government] withdraw the nutritional status or approval of the responsible manager.

The same applies to the case that the entrepreneur or manager in any other way proved to be unsuitable for his position or the movement's activity is interrupted for longer than three months. Before deciding to vedebörande opportunity that has given notice.

§ 17. It engaged in agency operating without a permit or otherwise violate the provisions of dennalag or by virtue of which provisions issued punished by a fine of not more severe punishment for the crime elsewhere is provided.

§ 18. In [Provincial Government] decisions, thereby warning allocated, the amendment must not be sought. Over another decision by the [Provincial Government] may be appealed to the Supreme Administrative Court within 30 days of receiving notice. An appeal [Provincial Government] under 12 or § 16 announced the decision shall not prevent förverkställighet of the decision.

§ 19. The court shall, if rulings provided for in § § 17 och18 notify the [Provincial Government].

§ 20. The provisions of this Act does not apply to:

1) trafikidkare that sells or arranges services in terms of the kind of traffic they carry, or immediately associated with it;

2) Agents for trafikidkare that sells or arranges travel tickets in case of certain types of traffic;

3) the organization of tours lasting up to ettdygn;

4) hiring of a transport vehicle, nor

5) guidance and information activities in the tourism industry.

Regardless of subsection 1. provided, the provisions of this Act shall apply to the organization, sale and distribution of trips on which the Act applies paketresorär. (1994/68)

§ 21. Compliance with this Act is monitored by the [Provincial Government] and as [Provincial Government] has told the police authorities.

§ 22. The person in this Act comes into force engaged in travel agent business can continue operating without a permit for a period of six months from the date the Act came into force.

§ 23. Detailed rules for the enforcement ochtillämpningen of this Act shall, if necessary through landscape regulation.

The five Landscape Ordinance (1996:48) on real estate

Chapter 1. Preliminary provisions

§ 1. Scope

This regulation contains provisions on the exercise of real estate brokerage in Åland.

§ 2. Definitions real estate brokerage referred to professional

themselves or continuous transmission of

a) property,

b) parts of buildings,

c) buildings or apartments to the right of possession based on ownership of shares,

d) which are common for al your buildings or parts of such areas;

e) the tenancy or lease rights to the areas referred to in A dpunkterna, but not lease the apartments.

With real estate agent means a natural person somutövar real estate brokerage.

Chapter 2. Registration of Realtors

§ 3. Requirements for registration

Real estate brokerage activities may only be exercised avden registered as an estate in provincial government.

§ 4. Conditions for registration

He who is of age and is not placed in konkursoch who have paid real estate broker test may be registered as an estate agent.

§ 5. Procedure for registration

Anyone wishing to become registered as a real estate brokerage boat to apply to a provincial government.

The application shall contain operating name and address and who the responsible manager. The application shall be accompanied by an extract from the Commercial Register if the applicant is a corporation or a foreign organization or foundation registered branch in Finland. Furthermore, the application shall contain an account of the responsible manager meets the requirements of § 4.

Chapter 3. Estate Agents Sample

§ 6. Time of sample

Real Estate Agent Tests shall be conducted at least gångper years, provided there is a need for this.

Landscape Government announces dates for real estate brokerage sample at least 30 days before the test hålls.Meddelandet be through public service published in at least one local newspaper of general circulation ashore exclusion as provided for in the Administrative Procedure Act (2008:9) for the Province of Åland. (2008/50)

§ 7. Skills being tested in the sample

The real estate broker test shall demonstrate that dehar knowledge of the provisions necessary for attutöva real estate brokerage.

Participants must also demonstrate their practical knowledge of real estate brokerage and behärskarde cases that may fall within the real estate business and that they can make up the handlingarsom needed for a real estate brokerage.

The statement of the test indicate the litteraturoch legislative participants should master the test. (2008/50)

Chapter 4. Real Estate Brokerage

§ 8. Title

The term real estate agent or avledningarav this word may be used only by the person registered as an estate agent.

An estate agent shall, at market marketing avsina services using the name "Registered estate agent" or the abbreviation "RFM".

§ 9. Manager

A movement that exercises real estate brokerage activities must have a responsible manager.

The responsible manager must be a registered real estate agents. The manager's task is to directly participate in the management of real estate data, monitor staff activity ochsvara to real estate brokerage activities are lawful.

§ 10. Good property mäklarsed

Estate agents must maintain a high property mäklarsed.

§ 11. Outsourcing

A written contract must be drawn up of all the received real estate brokerage. Assignment Agreement shall be drawn up in duplicate, one of which must be preserved for at least two years of real estate agent and detandra transmitted to the client.

§ 12. Mission Diary

Estate agents must keep a diary of all the received property brokerage. The assignments must be recorded in chronological order and numbered so that enny number series beginning on 1 January each year.

The mission diary shall be recorded

a) the date the assignment was received, b) the nature and object of the order,

c) the name and address;

d) the date an agreement was concluded,

e) buyer's or lessee's name and address;

f) the subject of such contracts;

g) the purchase price or rental amount and

h) real estate brokerage.

If an assignment due, be withdrawn or modified, a note to that effect made in the mission diary.

Mission Diary may be driven with automatic data processing, however, so that it can always be obtained in writing.

Assignment records must be kept for five years or dessert it ended.

§ 13. Information to be provided at the property

Before a real estate brokerage is closing the real estate agent providing both parties with all the information as real estate agent knows or ought to know affect köpslutet. Estate agent must protect both parties' interests.

If the relationship between a fastighetsförmedlareoch a consumer required by national legislation.

Chapter 5. Estate Agents

§ 14. Data

Landscape government appoints four years in Sanders Estate Agents. Their role is attordna the real estate broker test referred to in Chapter 3.

§ 15. Composition

The Board comprises a chairman, a vice-chairman and another member as well as personal ersättareför each. The chairman and vice chairman shall be a graduate law degree or equivalent before graduation and shall not be deemed to represent the estate agents.

§ 16. A quorum (2008/50)

Committee constitutes a quorum when the chairman or vice chairman and at least two other members are present. When voting on a matter is the majority opinion of the Board decision. Falling tie is the view the President advised decision.

Subsection 2. revoked (2008/50).

Chapter 6. Supplementary provisions

§ 17. Monitoring

Landscape government monitors compliance with this Regulation.

§ 18. Disclosure Obligations

Estate agents are obliged to, if necessary, let the provincial government take note of the commission and task diaries and other records necessary for monitoring.

§ 19. Administrative penalties

The police can give a warning to a real estate agent or a manager who does not comply with this regulation or instructions somgivits under it.

If an omission or offense is serious elleruppprepas despite warnings can provincial government at the request of the police stop real estate brokerage business for a fixed period or until further notice.

§ 20. Appeals

An appeal against the legality of the province government's decision may be lodged with the Supreme förvaltningsdomstolen.Landskapsregeringens decisions should also be exercised omdet appeal unless the appellate authority decides otherwise.

Estate Agents Board's decision on the rejection of the real estate broker test may be appealed hoslandskapsregeringen of which failed.

§ 21. Penal provisions

A person who performs real estate brokerage utanatt be registered as an estate agent or stridmed provisions of this Regulation shall predicate of the provisions on real estate to a fine, if not more severe punishment is provided elsewhere.

§ 22. Entry into force

This Regulation shall enter into force on 1 July 1996.

Measures needed to implement this Decree may be taken before it takes effect.

The six Landscape Act (2007:60) on postal services

Chapter 1. General Provisions

§ 1. The law's purpose

The law's purpose is to ensure that postal services idolized quality and special universal services are available on an equal basis across the province.

It is for the provincial government to ensure attsamhällsomfattande services are available in all municipalities in the province.

§ 2. Scope of application

The Act applies to the provision of postal services as otherwise provided below.

This Act does not apply to postal services for

1) newspapers and magazines,

2) correspondence, if the services of the volume is of minor importance with regard to the purpose somanges in § 1,

3) a trader's internal operations, nor

4) correspondence, if the services are based on individual agreements.

§ 3. Definitions

In this Act:

1) postal activities providing posttjänsteroch universal service fee,

2) postal services related to collection, sorting, transport and delivery of mail,

3) Universal Service continually supply of postal services under § 4 for all användarei landscape,

4) access points to the physical facilities, including mailboxes, where postal items may be deposited;

5) collecting operation of collecting postal items deposited at access points;

6) dividends delivery of postal items to their addressees;

7) postal mailing letters and parcels,

8) correspondence in an addressed letter or postkortsom up to two kilos,

9) parcels a self-addressed packets,

10) record companies a license pursuant to § 6,

11) the universal service provider a license referred to in § 6 and somålagts obligation to provide universal service,

12) the sender of a natural or legal person Somen mail shipment originated,

13) the recipient of a postal item recorded the receiver,

14) Use any natural or legal person, which spread as a sender or recipient benefit avatar universal service,

15) registered mail, a service that consists of a flat-rate guarantee against risks of loss, theft or damage

16) insured item a service which also includes insurance to the value of the sender specifies attförsändelsen against loss, theft or damage;

17) receipt of a document in which the recipient acknowledged the receipt of a shipment samtmed

18) cross-border postal mail from Åland to place outside the province, or vice versa.

Chapter 2. Universal service

§ 4. The universal service content

The universal service includes

1) communication addressed to the addressee letter-post items weighing up to two kilograms and postpaketsom up to ten kilos or, in the case of postal packets from destination outside the province, weighing 30kilo, and

2) service for registered and insured items.

The universal service provider shall, in each municipality to have at least one place of business where the provision of universal service.

Each user shall have the option of an entry point which is located a reasonable distance from the user's home or place of business to submit correspondence to be carried by the universal service provider.

At least one collection and at least one delivery shall be made every day. For exceptions to this requirement are contained in § 11.

The universal service includes both mail in the Province as cross-border mail.

§ 5. Quality standards for the universal service

Of the correspondence within the landscape that are intended to reach the addressee by the next business day shall 85procent reach the addressee on the day and the remaining deldärpå following business day.

Cross-border post within the European Community shall be distributed so that at least 85 percent of the transmitters received by the addressee on the third day och97 percent of the items on the fifth day, counted from the filing date.

The universal service provider shall comply with the Community's internal kvalitetsnormerför cross-border mail.

Chapter 3. Postal services

§ 6. Granting of permits, etc.

Post services may be carried out by organizations, agencies, institutions and foundations which beviljatstillstånd of the provincial government.

Permits shall be granted if the applicant has sufficient resources to meet its obligations for a company somutövar postal operations and there is no reason to question the applicant's ability to comply with the provisions concerning postal operations.

Licensing of postal services may be granted for a maximum of 20 years at a time. The licensee has no right to transfer the permit to another person. Transfer between parent and subsidiary is tillåtetmen be reported without delay to the provincial government.

§ 7. Terms and conditions

Permit under § 6 may be subject to conditions

1) on the obligation of the licensee to provide universal service as 4 and 5, § § and

2) regarding the licensee's field of activity, types of correspondence, collection and pricing as well as on other factors that are considered essential to ensure the quality, availability and efficiency.

The conditions for the permit may be modified when a special reason for this exists or if it is necessary försäkerställande of universal service is provided.

§ 8. Applications for permits

A request for authorization of postal operations directed

the provincial government. The application shall contain 1) the name and domicile, 2) the area for which authorization is sought if the application not related to landscape as a whole, 3) the nature of postal services the applicant intends s

invite, 4) terms of delivery of postal services, 5) evidence that the applicant holds in § 6 subsection 2.

assumed resources for the provision of postal services and

6) any other evidence which the applicant considers relevant or that Local Government considers necessary.

The application must include an excerpt of the applicant, the public records of the kind of organization that the applicant, or, if the applicant is not registered in itself, the corresponding investigation of the applicant, and the recently adopted financial statements, if the applicant's obligation to keep books. The applicant shall ocksåförete one to two years prepared comprehensive plan of the denpostverksamhet to be conducted and a financial spreadsheet.

Chapter 4. Post Obligations

§ 9. Receipt of shipments

A record company is required to the relevant contribution received and the receiver communicate brevförsändelseri accordance with permit conditions and delivery terms. The universal service provider is also required to the current fee taemot and the receiver to convey parcels of detslag referred to in § 4 subsection 1. A record company can refuse to receive or convey an item of

1) The shipment contains hazardous substances, objects or products that it is legally prohibited atttransportera or which is otherwise unlawful, or which are obviously causing danger to people or property;

2) shipment of live animals,

3) The contents of the consignment is particularly sensitive to heat or cold;

4) shipment contains liquid substances or objects that can easily break or are broken or if

5) the item is uninsured and includes money, securities or other valuable.

§ 10. Dividend

Correspondence shall be sent to the recipient at his address or delivered in one of mottagandeav mail designed device that is located within ettmed into account the local conditions within a reasonable distance from the address of the recipient states. For the dividend shall be made in a purposeful way, the forms of distribution determined with regard avlokala conditions, the recipient's specific personal needs and other relevant circumstances.

Letters will be distributed at least once every working day, if not an insurmountable obstacle, a provision of law, an interruption of traffic or any other similar circumstance prevents the delivery of mail.

Parcel Post will be distributed in a timely manner. Postpaketoch correspondence to be acknowledged by mail can be distributed on the company's place of business. In such cases, a special arrival will be sent to the recipient.

§ 11. Exceptions to the collection and distribution rules

In the case of postal services to recipients in remote island areas or close to roads that are not generally served with a record company the right to deviate from the collection and distribution density provided for in § 4 subsection 4. and the distribution density prescribed in § 10 subsection 2. Collection and distribution shall be made at least once a week.

If a recipient in respect of which a mom.är applicable is a postal package, an item from the authority or an urgent shipment, the consignee shall, unless the dividend may be made or arrival will be, therefore, before, by the third day frånförsändelsens arrival if possible of pertelefon, e- mail or otherwise that the consignment is to collect the mail company's place of business.

A postal company shall at least once a year inform the provincial government which households affected by the provisions of subsection 1. In response to this notification, the provincial government bestämmaom there are reasons to change the record company's decision as monkey's household to which subsection 1. applied is reduced.

§ 12. Dividend Plan and the distribution agreement

Each record companies to prepare a detailed plan for the distribution under § 10 shall be arranged. A recipient who wishes that the dividend shall be approaching the recipient's home or place of business than the plan requires, have the right to post the company agree on the necessary amendments to the plan to satisfy the desire. Post Company is entitled to charge the beneficiary reindeer reasonable fee for this.

If a receiver and a record company could not agree on the receiver requested changes in the distribution plan and the issue is not settled by ettlagakraftvunnet decision, the record company, on dividends as a result of the dispute could not be done, the right to store the recipient's correspondence on the place of business that is located closest to the recipient adress.Mottagaren have the right to pick which items.

Landscape government has the right to issue further guidance on the placement of devices for receipt and delivery of letter mail.

§ 13. Correspondence; confidentiality

A postal company shall ensure the confidentiality of correspondence.

A person who is employed by a postal companies have not röjavad he or she is at work found out about a client or his affairs, if the disclosure of information may constitute a violation of the provisions of subsection i1. or damage to a business or customer relationship. It said also applies to those who either himself or represented on behalf on the basis of contracts with record company provides services under this Act.

§ 14. Opening of mail

A record company is not entitled to open an end item of correspondence. If there is reason to believe that the mail may pose a risk to health or property shall record company promptly forward the shipment to the provincial government.

A parcel may be opened on

1) the item is damaged and it is necessary attöppna it to be secure or examine its condition, or if

2) there is reason to believe that the mail can utgörafara to health or property.

A record company has the right to forward a postpaketsom referred to in subsection 2. the provincial government in ställetför himself opening the package.

The contents of a mail package that is opened must not be scrutinized to a greater extent than is necessary for the reason that it opens.

Only a person specifically authorized by the provincial government has the right to open a postal packet. At the opening shall be a witness present. On the package, subscribed to the opening and cause åtgärden.Dessutom shall draw up a protocol regarding the opening, which is signed by the person who opened the package and on the witness.

The person authorized to open the parcel is vidutövandet of its mission under official responsibility.

§ 15. Investigation of receivers, etc.

If it is unclear who the recipient of enpostförsändelse likely is intended to be personal, the record company that manages omförsändelsen trying to sort out who is mottagare.Om this is not possible, the item is returned to the sender. If not possible, the record company promptly forward the shipment to the provincial government. If the content is likely HY disturbed, however, the item in its entirety destroyed. The same applies to open or opened item, unless it is obvious that it is impossible to investigate Whether who the recipient is or who the sender.

An item that the recipient does not want to receive should be returned to sender.

A record company has the right to destroy a försändelsesom probably not intended to be personal, omden can not be forwarded to the consignee or omdenne not want to receive it. In the case of this avseddaförsändelser can post a business may agree with the sender if the return of items.

A record company is entitled to the Provincial of the way an item referred to in subsection 3. instead of himself to destroy it.

§ 16. Post Corporate responsibility

A record company is responsible for damage caused to the sender or receiver of a shipment is delayed, lost or damaged. Post Company is exempt from liability if it can prove that the damage caused by a circumstance that the company could not undvikaoch whose consequences it could not prevent.

If a record company or anyone for whose acts the company responsible has caused in subsection 1. avseddskada intentionally or by gross negligence, can detinte exclude his liability under the provisions of subsection 1.

A record company's responsibility begins when the shipper delivered the item to the collection site or otherwise approved by the mail service as submitted to the record company. The responsibility ends when the record company in this Act provided a way or in the agreed way of leaving the consignment to the consignee or his representative. If the record company requires kvitteringpå deed relating to the shipment, hardet right to make this note on the recipient's personal identity and the document in which personal identity verified.

A term to the disadvantage of the sender or receiver differs from ansvarsbestämmelsernai this Act is invalid. If the record company party is not one in chapter 1. 4 § Consumer Protection Act (FFS38/1978) intended consumer's condition, however valid, provided that it is reasonable having regard to contractor status, shipment exceptionellakaraktär or other special circumstances.

A record company and for whose conduct postal company responsible is entitled to invoke in a mom.nämnda discharge bases even in the event that venom composition claims are not based on this law, regarding this has been possible to claim compensation under avdenna law.

The provisions of this Act if a record company liability applies only if the Subject of an international convention which is binding on the landscape.

§ 17. Limitation of a record company's responsibility

To any person harmed by the fact that a shipment has been delayed, in compensation an amount equal to the damage size, a maximum

1) 50 euros for a regular correspondence,

2) 85 euros for a recommended or with a receipt provided item of correspondence and

3) EUR 150 for the second letter, letter mail or parcel post.

For those who suffered damage to an item damaged or lost, in compensation an amount equal to the damage size, a maximum

1) 50 euros for a regular correspondence,

2) the agreed insured value of an insured item;

3) EUR 340 for other items of correspondence and

4) 25 euros per kilo for parcel post.

If a record company or anyone for whose acts the company responsible has caused in subsection 1 or 2. intended harm, either intentionally or through gross negligence, it has no right to limit his liability under the statute.

A record company and for whose conduct postal company responsible is entitled to invoke in subsections 1 and 2. aforementioned limitations of liability in detfall a claim is not based on this law, if it had been possible to claim compensation under this Act.

Damages awarded under this Act kanjämkas according to what is considered reasonable, if the injured party has contributed to the damage or circumstances other than the injurious act harbidragit the damage occurred.

The in subsections 1 and 2. specified monetary amounts kanjusteras through landscape regulation in accordance causes changes in the value of money.

§ 18. Note and limitation

At the risk of entitlement to compensation is lost, a complaint that an item damaged presented to the relevant postal company in enskälig time after the party discovered the injury or should have discovered it. If the recipient is not a i1 Ch. 4 § Consumer Protection Act intended consumer shall note on visible injury framställasnär shipment is received by the recipient or his representative.

The right to compensation is forfeited unless the claim påersättning not made in writing to the postal company within a year or, if the damage was caused intentionally or by gross negligence, within three years

1) from the time the record company's liability under § 16 subsection 3. ceased, the right to compensation based on the item damaged or delayed, and

2) from the time the record company informs the recipient that the mail is lost, the right to compensation based on the fact.

§ 19. Terms

A postal company shall draw up terms of delivery iskriftlig form. They shall be available to users free of charge.

The delivery terms should be clearly stated

1) the customer and post its rights and obligations,

2) what steps the client should take when a shipment has been delayed, damaged or lost or when the service quality standards are not followed,

3) the remedies available to the customer, including the possibility that in some cases begäramyndighets settlement of disputes;

4) fees for the services provided;

5) how customers are informed of fee changes and

6) the basics of securities and other payment guarantees may be required by the customer.

In terms of delivery can be taken other than in subsection 2. specified information about the services somtillhandahålls, including data on various types avpostförsändelser and of the properties they may have and the characteristics of and restrictions on registered and insured mail.

A detailed and clear price list of fees förposttjänsterna be free to be available förkunderna. If bids or contracts for postal services in individual cases, provided or extended, shall be in writing or in electronic form.

Before a record company will introduce such terms and conditions which are intended to be universally applicable, shall detillställas provincial government for approval.

§ 20. Publication of the postal service quality

Each record companies must annually publish data on quality of services, giving particular framgåantalet complaints and how they have been treated.

§ 21. Pricing of Postal Services

The fees that the universal service charge must be reasonable attsamtliga users are given the opportunity to access the award services provided. They must also be clear and transparent and non discriminatory.

The universal service provider shall have a uniform tariff for correspondence within the landscape, with regard to correspondence to be awarded the following business day. This does not prevent individual price agreements with customers.

The fees for postal services shall be based on costs. Any changes in pricing the information will be given at least one month before the change takes effect.

§ 22. Cost Accounting

The universal service provider shall use an accounting of vilketframgår and reasonableness of the fees for the various services, and charges in relation to costs.

The universal service provider shall, in their internal accounting, keep the posts somhör to the universal service separate from other services. The cost of the services related to the universal service uträknasper item types.

The universal service provider shall provide to the provincial government beskrivningarav their accounting systems.

§ 23. Co-Duty

A record company is obliged to ensure that an item submitted to it for mediation forwarded to mediated by another postal operator, if the recipient's address is not within its scope.

A record company is obliged to ensure that försändelsersom forwarded to another mail company for befordrankan awarded to a recipient whose address is located ipostbox or other device as the first record company possesses.

The contractual terms of the agreement between the postal enterprises on the 1 and 2. intended affairs must be non discriminatory and fair. Contracts shall include the transfer conditions and the grounds for prissättningen.Dessutom, the quality requirements prescribed in this Act be followed.

In subsection 3. intended contract shall forthwith communicate to the provincial government for approval. Landscape The Government have approved an agreement if it is not stated otherwise within one month after the date förmottagandet of the agreement. If the provincial government believes that the agreement does not meet the requirements of dennalag, it shall submit a reasonable period within which the Agreement is amended. Before the provincial government approval provided the contract may not apply.

§ 24. Other obligations

A postal operator shall ensure that the postal service works as smoothly as possible, even under exceptional conditions. For this purpose it utarbetaberedskapsplaner and take other appropriate preparatory actions. A competent authority can issue instructions on preparing for emergencies.

The universal service provider shall ensure that statutory notification procedures may be used throughout the landscape. The personsom performing a service procedure related data acting under official responsibility.

Chapter 5. Arrangements for collection and distribution

§ 25. Placement of Mailboxes

A municipality is required to allow mailboxes and modify equipment for the collection or distribution avbrevförsändelser placed on the town plan or building plan designated public areas, unless they tillrimliga costs can be placed in any other förpostföretaget or receiver appropriately. The devices must not be placed in such a way that demedför unnecessary danger to traffic or involves significant inconvenience when using the area in accordance with the city or building plan.

The owner of a property, another property or enbyggnad is required to allow the devices referred to in subsection 1. affixed to a wall, a gate or at ettstaket under the conditions specified in subsection 1.

Further be noted that the equipment is not fårmedföra unreasonable inconvenience to the property or building owners.

Devices referred to in subsection 1. may be placed påsådana side, protection and frisiktsområden as avsesi 40 and 41 § § Landscape Act (1957:23) on public highways in the Åland Islands, on the location of the devices does not cause unnecessary danger to road ken or significant inconvenience to road maintenance.

See M 27, Landscape Act (1957:23) on public roads.

§ 26. Settlement of disputes concerning the placement of mailboxes

If the parties fail to agree on the location softener devices referred to in § 25 subsection 2., Can fråganhänskjutas to the municipal building permits. When the application is considered to be building committee consider both the location in question is used in general and the requirements for proper record activity sets, and the instructions provincial government submitted pursuant to § 12 subsection 3.

But, and damage caused by the devices recipes referred to in § 25 subsection 2. replaced in accordance with the provisions of the Landscape Act (1979:62) on Expropriation of Immovable Property and Special Rights. If the parties have agreed on compensation, the agreement binds ocksåen subsequent owner of the property or building.

See G 8, Landscape Act (1979:62) on Expropriation of immovable property

Judgement and special rights.

Chapter 6. Control and supervision of postal operations

§ 27. General management, development and supervision

The general management and development of postal services is for the provincial government.

The Government of Åland shall supervise attdenna Act and the regulations issued medstöd of compliance. The Government of Åland shall publish a story about how the quality standards specified in § 5 met.

§ 28. Supervision fee for postal services

Postal carriers shall pay an annual supervision fee to the provincial government. The fee shall be used to meet the provincial government costs for the handling of the information under this will cook the provincial government. The supervision fee is 2000 euros.

§ 29. Right to information

Landscape government, notwithstanding another Act contains provisions on the confidentiality of documents, right to the management of the information referred to contemporary law of postal companies have the necessary informationom mail corporate finances and their operations under this Act.

Chapter 7. Duties related to ensuring the delivery of mail

§ 30. Opening of the consignment

Landscape government has the right to open a sealed letter addressed to the provincial government with the support av14 § subsection 1. If there is reason to believe that the mail is not a danger to health or property.

Landscape government has the right to open a sealed letter addressed to the provincial government with the support av15 § subsection 1. If this is necessary to determine iförsta care who the recipient, in the alternative vemsom is the sender.

Landscape government has the right to open a parcel of

1) the item is damaged and it is necessary attöppna it to be secure or examine its condition;

2) there is reason to believe that the mail can utgörafara to health or property or

3) In the case of a consignment which record company neither has been able to adjust the receiver or return to sender.

The person at the provincial government handles the information provided in this section may open a postal item only in the presence of a witness. The contents of an opened item may not be scrutinized to a greater extent than is necessary for the reason that it opens. On consignment shall subscribe to the opening, the cause of the opening, tidoch place of the opening and the provision somåtgärden based. The note shall be signed by the person who executed the opening. Its Except Will it draw up a protocol regarding the opening, which is signed by the person who opened the package and on the witness.

§ 31. Return of an open letter addressed to a postal operator

If an opened item contains information that makes it possible to determine who the recipient or sender, the provincial government returneraförsändelsen together with notes on the opening to the relevant postal company. In order to achieve avbrevhemligheten the consignment shall be closed before it is returned. Post The Company shall also be notified omi item found addresses or other data from which the shipment may be forwarded or returned.

It is up to it in subsection 1. for mail company to send the consignment to the consignee or, if it was only possible to determine the identity of the sender, return it to him.

Postal Companies have the right to charge a fee for new mail forwarding package and for items that are restored under the provisions on distance selling i6 Ch. Consumer Protection Act.

§ 32. Storage and disposal of opened items

If it is in an opened item not switch statement making it possible to determine whether anyone ärmottagare or sender, the provincial government to keep the item in detention for six months, counted from the date of shipment was opened. If detunder this time has not been possible to obtain data that makes it possible to carry the consignment to the consignee or return it to the consignor, the consignment shall be destroyed in an appropriate manner and as far as possible with the preservation of confidentiality of correspondence. If the shipment is in addition to any personal messages contain something that takes economic value, the notice shall be destroyed while the other content can be sold in an appropriate manner.

Funds earned from a sale referred to in subsection 1. goes to the countryside. The same applies pengaroch other valid means of payment available in an item referred to in subsection 1.

A consignment may be destroyed before it in subsection 1. the said period has ended, in the case of

1) an item whose content is likely to have been destroyed;

2) an item whose contents can cause danger to health or property or

3) an item that is clearly not intended to be personal or as that of any other similar reasons, it is obviously unnecessary to store.

§ 33. The concealment of documents and confidentiality

Postal items and documents in the custody of their provincial government under the provisions of this chapter shall be kept secret.

An employee of the provincial government may not be an unauthorized person, information on postal items or their contents, if he or she received them in the performance of tasks referred to in 30-32 § §.

The provisions of subsections 1 and 2. is not hinderför to data from the minutes concerning the opening of mail served a record company, if ärnödvändigt for a shipment to be sent to the recipient or sender.

§ 34. Officials Liability

The provisions relating to official responsibilities, with the exception of the rules on the disposal as a result of dereliction of duty, also apply to a person standing in a different relationship than the service compared to the provincial government when he or honutför information referred to in § 33.

Chapter 8. Penalties, enforcement and appeals

§ 35. Revocation of permit

Licensing of postal services may be revoked by the provincial government

1) if the licensee fails to initiate regular activity within six months from the date dåtillståndsbeslutet become final or

2) if the licensee substantially, or even warning violates this Act, the regulations issued under the Act or mottillståndsvillkor.

§ 36. Warning and coercive

If a record company violates this Act, the regulations issued under the Act or the permit conditions, the provincial government, if the misconduct is so serious that the permit should be revoked, give mail the company a warning and, if warranted, order entry firm to correct the error or neglect.

Decision referred to in subsection 1. may be subject to a fine or penalty of a neglected operation for detförsumliga record company's expense.

The cost of an operation performed in a negligent record company expense paid in advance by the provincial government and the person may apply to the negligent record company be collected without a court order or decision of the ordningsom provisions of the Act on the Recovery of Taxes and Fees by Recovery Proceedings.

§ 37. Unlawful entry operations; violation of professional secrecy

The exercising postal operations without holding time prescribed by law authorized to be for the pursuit of illegal entry activity to a fine or fängelsei up to six months.

Any violators of § 13 subsection 2. prescribed secrecy shall be for breach of professional secrecy to a fine or imprisonment not exceeding six months.

§ 38. Settlement of disputes

Anyone dissatisfied with a distribution plan recipes referred to in § 12 or by mail delivery may appeal to the provincial government. Requests for amendments shall be submitted to the provincial government within 60 days from the date the appellant became aware of the circumstances at issue. A postal company shall on request inform a client about a possible night, apply to the provincial government on crucial here as well designed case.

Landscape government's decision concerning litigation does not include questions relating to agreements between record companies and customers, or a mail carrier liability.

§ 39. Appealing

A decision by the provincial government or a municipal building committee made under avdenna Act may be appealed in the manner particularly prescribed.

If the public interest requires or if the decision by its nature is such that it should be executed immediately, the provincial government appoint attbeslut the provincial government made under this Act to be immediately enforced and be in force for the decision on time, unless an appellate authority shall appoint another .

Chapter 9. Specific provisions

§ 40. Address

A record company has the right to the exercise of postal activities maintain a mailing list of avsändareoch recipients of mail. The register recorded the name and address and social security number or an-nan corresponding identification code.

The universal service provider is entitled to from the population register to personal names, and amendments thereto, data omfödda and deceased persons, information on language and details of the addresses.

The data in a record company mailing användsför carriage of mail and to verify and correct addresses of the sender, which have concluded agreements address services. Name and address in the address register may be disclosed where this is förenligtmed adressregistrets purpose. Social security number or an-nan corresponding identifier must not be left ut.En registered person has the right to prohibit his or her personal data is used to control ochkorrigeringstjänster related addresses.

A statement in an address that is föråldradskall obliterated last ten years from the Dagne a postal companies have learned that the task is no longer corresponds to current conditions.

§ 41. Responses to the postal operations cease

If a record company cease operations, the company shall inform the provincial government on the matter within three months before the operation ceases.

If a record company licensing of postal operations be revoked if the permit is not renewed when it goes on uteller mail the company for any other reason ceases medsin activities, Local Government, if necessary, decide on the measures to be taken to record the activity to be maintained.

Reached, the case referred to in subsection 2., No agreement on the assets necessary for carrying avpostverksamhet transferred to another record company, kanlandskapsregeringen decide on the transfer for consideration. As regards the reasons for and bestämmandetav compensation shall landscapes Act expropriationav real property and special rights apply.

§ 42. Stamp issue, etc.

Landscape government may grant an application for ettpostföretag right to issue stamps to be used somkvitto on payment of carriage of postal items. In the case of stamps designed to användasi cross-border mail is landskapsregeringenvid its licensing into account the provisions somhärvid case.

A decision on the right to issue postage stamps can begränsasi time and ending no later repealed when the relevant record company permission to conduct postal operations cease.

Chapter 10. The entry into force and transitional provisions

§ 43. Entry into force

This Act comes into force on 1 October 2007. Measures for enforcement of the law may be undertaken before the Act comes into force.

44 §. Transitional provisions

The entry in the Åland Islands (item) is entitled to continue sinverksamhet under grandfather rights for six months from the date the Act came into force. If, therefore, before Posten has ansöktom permission for the operation of postal services under this Act, the item entitled under the previously existing provisions continue to operate until the permit application is either approved or rejected by decision becomes final.

The provisions of Chapter 4., Chapter 5., Chapter 7. and 38

- § § 40 shall apply to the delivery business from the date this Act comes into force.

In seven Landscape Act (2006:11) on the employment of other than landscape

§ 1. General

If different landscape plans to pursue employment in Åland requires permission from the provincial government under this Act.

This Act does not apply to the procurement of work for an individual employee, nor intermediate avarbetstagare to an employer, if this happens endasttillfälligt and without charge levied in any form.

§ 2. Application

Applications for permits for placement of employees considered by the provincial government. Permission must be sought in writing.

The applicant for a license shall upon application provide provincial government accurate and sufficient information that the provincial government needs to know to determine the application.

§ 3. Granting of permits

Permission to engage in employment granted by the provincial government for more than five years at a time. The condition can be restricted to employment in a particular sector of employment. The authorization shall specify the conditions under which employment services may be conducted.

Those granted permission to conduct employment shall not make underage labor available for such work that is prohibited by specific provisions.

§ 4. Special conditions

An individual can be granted the right to engage in employment for this

1) may exercise the Economy in the province under provincial law (1996:47) on the right to exercise and nutrition

2) the conditions and characteristics which ensure a regular and efficient management avarbetsförmedlingen.

A legal person can be granted the right to engage in employment for this

1) may exercise the Economy in the landscape and

2) have a manager who meets devillkor specified in subsection 1.

§ 5. Fees

Those granted permission to conduct employment may not charge fees for arbetsförmedlingav sailors.

§ 6. Inspection

Landscape government has the right to have inspekteraarbetsförmedlingsverksamhet for which permission harbeviljats. Landscape The Government Inspector shall be given access to the premises where business is conducted and access to the documents and accounts of summers employment service.

§ 7. Revocation of permit

The Åland Government can revoke permission to placement of employees, if granted the permit has violated law or in the permit conditions imposed or later announced instructions or if missbruki its employment business has disclosed.

§ 8. Penal provisions

The recipient of § 5 prohibits fee shall charge offense to a fine.

Anyone who conducts unlawful employment preceded or someone else's financial gain skallför Employment offense to a fine or imprisonment not exceeding one year. Likewise, on anyone who unlawfully convey or publicly announce that he conveys workers to another country or foreign workers to the province.

The person otherwise engaged in this Act avseddverksamhet without authorization shall be for employment misdemeanor punishable by a fine.

§ 9. Appeals

An appeal against the legality of the province government's decision may be lodged with the Supreme Administrative Court.

§ 10. Entry into force

This Act comes into force on 1 March 2006.

A person who by virtue of § 2 of the Landscape Act (1960:23) on the employment permit was granted attbedriva employment can continue to operate under this Act in accordance with given conditions.

In 8 Landscape Act (2007:98) on the application

tion in the Åland Islands of riksförfatt

tions on safe handling

hazardous chemicals and explosives

§ 1. In order to maintain public safety and prevent and avert damage to the person, environment and property, the law on safety in handling hazardous chemicals and explosives (FFS 390/2005), hereinafter referred to as the Chemical Safety Act, applicable land landscape of Åland with the exceptions resulting avdenna law.

Changes to the Chemical Safety Act shall apply in the province after the coming into force of the kingdom.

Instructions, notes or other information as those in subsection 1. and § 8 for regulations to be included on chemicals and explosives must be written in the landscape, at least in Swedish, unless the provincial government for special reasons, grant exemptions from the requirement.

§ 2. The administrative tasks required by the regulations referred to in 1 and 8, § § is for the state authorities in the province operated by provincial government to the extent that management is based pålandskapets legislative powers.

§ 3. Landscape The government monitors the provisions of the regulations referred to in 1 and 8, § § följs.För monitoring can provincial government anlitariksmyndigheter.

If the monitoring of safety at work are special provisions.

See Occupational Safety and Health Act, Ar 401 FLII.

§ 4. Cited in Chemical Safety Act to other provisions of national law, the references refer to the corresponding provisions of law landscape.

§ 5. The provisions of § 132 chemicals safety law does not apply in the province.

§ 6. Anyone who owns or controls the oil tank of a landed Community Regulation specified design and minimum size shall ensure that the tank be inspected regularly provided the tank is still putting into use. If at besiktningstillfället can note set cistern is in such condition that the risk of oil pollution is the cistern repaired or taken out of bruk.En tank causing immediate danger to be immediately decommissioned.

The provisions of § 55 CSR kind shall be applied for the inspection of oil tanks located above ground.

§ 7. In addition to the penalty provisions of § 125 Chemical Safety Act, the provisions of Chapter 44. § 11 Penal Code (FFS 39/1889) The penalty for violation of the rules on explosives used in the landscape.

Although the provisions of Chapter 44. § 12 in strafflagenom penalties for improper handling of a dangerous chemical or explosive substance or product recipes referred to in Chapter 5. Chemical Safety Act, tillämpasi landscape.

§ 8. The Government of Åland may, within the landscape of competence through landscape decide attförfattningar regulation issued pursuant to the Chemical Safety Act shall apply in Åland are unchanged or with changes landscape Government.

The Government of Åland may, within the province jurisdiction, the landscape regulation of implementation on the landscape of the EU directives concerning matters referred to in this Act.

See Paragraph 9, Landscape Ordinance (2007:99) on the application of the country

Aland landscape of national regulations on chemicals and safety

handling of hazardous chemicals and explosives.

§ 9. This Act comes into force on 1 January 2008.

This Act repeals the Landscape Act (1971:12) on the application of Åland of national regulations on hazardous substances.

Measures needed to enforce the law förutsätterfår undertaken before the Act comes into force.

In 9 Landscape Ordinance (2007:99) on

application of Åland of

National regulations on chemicals and

Safe handling of hazardous chemicals

chemicals and explosives

§ 1. Regulations on chemicals

The following national regulations concerning chemicals shall be applied in the landscape:

A) Government decision on the restriction of the use of PCBs and PCTs (FFS 1071/1989);

2) Government Decision on prohibitions and begränsningarsom certain chemicals that cause hälsoskadaoch products containing these chemicals (FFS489/1992)

3) Chemicals Regulation (FFS 675/1993),

4) regulation on the retail sale of dangerous chemicals (FFS 676/1993),

5) Water and Environmental Board's decision on banned or on the management greatly restricted chemicals (FFS 680/1993),

6) Social Affairs and Health Ministry's decision on the procedure for notification of new substances (FFS1642/1993)

7) Social Affairs and Health Ministry's decision on the assessment of the risks of new substances (SHMb nr57/1994)

8) Repealed (2008/142)

9) Regulation of Pesticides (FFS792/1995)

10) Government decision on the ban pesticides containing certain active substances placed on the market and use (FFS 1361/1996);

11) Agriculture and Forestry Ministry's decision on data requirements and examinations to be submitted with the application for registration of pesticides (JSMb No 98/1996);

12) Government decision on the restriction of the use of hexachloroethane (FFS 961/1997),

13) Government Decision on prohibitions or restrictions on certain chlorinated solvents (FFS1209/1997)

14) Agriculture and Forestry Ministry's Regulation on the labeling of pesticides (JSMf No. 7 / 2005);

15) Prime Minister's decision to prohibit the marketing and use of pentachlorophenol and some difenylmetaner (FFS 143/2000),

16) Social Affairs and Health Decree on packaging and labeling of biocide (FFS 422/2000),

17) Government Decree on the biocide (FFS 466/2000),

18) Ministry of Environment regulation ansökningaroch notifications regarding biocide products and their active substances (FFS 467/2000),

19) Government Decree on the prohibitions and restrictions on the carcinogenic, mutagenic and teratogenic substances (FFS 623/2004),

20) Social Affairs and Health Ministry förordningom RESISTANT the packaging of a hazardous chemical and a warning symbol for the Visually Impaired (FFS 430/2001),

21) Social Affairs and Health Ministry of omens list of dangerous substances (FFS 509/2005),

22) Social Affairs and Health Ministry förordningom bases for classification and labeling avkemikalier (FFS 807/2001),

23) Social Affairs and Health Ministry förordningom safety data sheets (FFS 1202/2001);

24) Agriculture and Forestry Ministry's regulation of pesticides approved active ämnenoch specific rules for their use (JSMf No 50/2004);

25) Social Affairs and Health Ministry regulation on the collection of data on chemicals (FFS374/2002)

26) Government Decree on the restriction of the marketing and use of organic tin compounds (FFS 871/2002),

27) Government Decree on the restriction of the use and marketing of kreosotoch wood treated with creosote (FFS 8 / 2003);

28) Government regulation relating to restrictions on the marketing and use of short chain chlorinated paraffins, and penta-and octabromo (FFS 416/2003),

29) Government Decree on the prohibitions and restrictions on certain azo dyes and products containing them (FFS 694/2003).

30) Government Decree on restrictions somgäller cement and cement-containing brands (FFS 514/2004),

31) Government Decree on restrictions avutsläpp to and use of nonylphenol ochnonylfenoltoxilat (FFS 596/2004),

32) Government Decree on restrictions concerning asbestos (FFS 975/2004),

33) Government Decree on the prohibitions and restrictions concerning toluene and trichlorobenzene (FFS1177/2006) and

34) Government Decree on the Restriction of polycyclic aromatic hydrocarbons iextender oils in automotive and jordbruksmaskiners tires (FFS 550/2007).

35) (2008/71), Ministry of Environment Regulation on the application for approval or registration of biocide and the withdrawal of these from the market and special conditions for them (FFS 20/2008).

§ 2. Provisions concerning safety in the handling of hazardous chemicals and explosives

The following national regulations on hazardous substances shall be applied in the landscape:

1) Regulation on the use of hydrogen or other combustible gas påfyllningsgas for balloons (FFS109/1973)

2) regulation of lighter fluid for charcoal (FFS947/1973)

3) Trade and Industry Ministry's decision on explosives (FFS 130/1980),

4) Trade and Industry Ministry's decision on the periodic inspection of underground oil tanks (FFS344/1983)

5) Trade and Industry Ministry's decision on ammonium nitrate (FFS 172/1984),

6) Trade and Industry Ministry's decision ombrännbara liquids (FFS 313/1985),

7) Trade and Industry Ministry's decision on oil heating equipment (FFS 314/1985),

8) Regulation of explosives (FFS 473/1993),

9) flytgasförordning (FFS 711/1993),

10) Natural Gas Regulation (FFS 1058/1993);

11) Trade and Industry Ministry's decision on the application of natural gas regulation (FFS 1059/1993);

12) Trade and Industry Ministry's decision omgasmonteringar (FFS 1286/1993);

13) aerosolförordning (FFS 1433/1993);

14) Gas appliances Regulation (FFS 1434/1993);

15) Regulation on the verification of explosives with the requirements (FFS 1384/1994);

16) regulation of oil heating equipment (FFS1211/1995)

17) regulation equipment and säkerhetssystemsom intended for hazardous air mixtures (FFS 917/1996),

18) Trade and Industry Ministry's decisions concerning equipment and protective systems intended for hazardous air mixtures (FFS 918/1996),

19) Trade and Industry Ministry's decision omtillämpning of flytgasförordningen (FFS 344/1997) and

20) Government Decree on the Prevention avfara which explosive atmospheres caused workers (FFS576/2003).

§ 3. Provisions relating to both chemicals and safety when handling dangerous chemicals and explosives

The following national regulations on hazardous substances and chemicals shall be applied in the landscape:

1) Trade and Industry Ministry's decision on the handling and storage of petrol (FFS 181/2000),

2) Trade and Industry Ministry's decision on the handling and storage of hazardous chemicals at the distribution station (FFS 415/1998) and

3) Regulation on the Industrial Handling and Storage of Dangerous Chemicals (59/1999 FFS).

§ 4. Exemptions from the provisions of the national provisions referred to in 1, 2 and 3, § §

Trade and Industry Ministry's decision on the periodic inspection of underground oil tanks (FFS344/1983), 'the inspection thereof, shall also apply to tanks above ground whose volume exceeding 2 m3 but so that such tanks should be inspected first time before 25 years have elapsed from the time cistern been initial use. Reservoirs above ground that the inspection found to be undamaged to besiktaspå again within 10 years after besiktningstillfället.

If a metallic tank can not be inspected from the inside as indicated in the inspection decision shall be subjected to such pressure test referred to in § 7 of the decision and inspected visually as possible. If leakage is not observed in the pressure test and significant injuries generally can not be found on the tank shall be inspected again within 5 years after besiktningstillfället.Beslutet shall not apply to double skin oil tanks and comparable oil tanks medläckagevarningssystem.

Regulation of explosives (FFS 473/1993) applies to the person riksmyndighetutfört approval of explosive and verifieringav explosives conformity with specified requirements shall be applicable also in landskapet.Trots provisions of § 33 subsection 2. regulation of explosives can be pyrotechnic articles ärgodkända publicly traded in Sweden and with a maximum charge weight per individual firework does not exceed 1 000 grams approved for general commercial or general use in the landscape.

The regulation on verification the conformity of explosives with the requirements (FFS 1384/1994) skatillämpas so that by the appropriate national authority carried out the approval of the explosive and verification cation conformity of explosives with the established requirements shall be applicable also in the landscape.

The Regulation on equipment and säkerhetssystemsom intended for hazardous air mixtures (FFS 917/1996) shall apply to the competent national authority carried the approval of equipment ochsäkerhetssystem designed for hazardous air mixtures and verification of equipment and protective systems compliance with established requirements shall be applicable also in the landscape .

The prohibition in § 3 of Government Decision on begränsningav use of PCBs and PCTs (FFS 1071/1989) to include PCBs, PCTs and products containing these substances in the country will also apply to the introduction to the landscape.

Trade and Industry Ministry's decision on the handling and storage of hazardous chemicals at the distribution station (FFS 415/1998) is in the landscape also apply to distribution centers in the individual use därcisternernas total volume of 3 m3 or more.

§ 5. Specific provisions

Changes to the national provisions listed in § § 1-3 shall be applied in the landscape from the time they träderi force in the kingdom.

References to provisions of rikslagstiftningeni above provisions shall refer to the corresponding provisions of law landscape.

§ 6. Coming into force provisions

This Regulation shall enter into force on 1 January 2008.

This Regulation repeals Landscape Ordinance (2004:14) on the application of Åland of national regulations on hazardous substances and chemicals.

§ 7. Transitional provisions

Reservoirs, located above ground, which has been in service before January 1, 1986 shall be inspected prior to 1 January 2011. The same applies to storage tanks, located above ground, for which there can not be determined when in use but it can reasonably be assumed that they entered into service before 1 January 1986.

In 10 Landscape Act (1995:92) on the application

tion in the Åland Islands of riksförfatt

tions of alcohol (2007/86)

§ 1. (2007/86) The law's purpose

The objective the control of alcohol consumption prevent the societal, social and medical harm of alcohol beverages shall Alcohol Act (FFS 1143/1994) and regulation of alcoholic beverages and spirits (FFS 1344/1994) tillämpasi landscape, to the extent that they contain bestämmelserom permission to serve alcohol beverages , with the deviations provided by this Act.

Alcohol Law and Regulation alkoholdryckeroch liquor shall apply in the landscape as they lydernär this Act comes into force. Thereafter ändringari alcohol law or regulation alkoholdryckeroch spirits, the amended rules apply on land exclusion from the date of entry into force iriket. Changes to the rules on which this Act provided for deviations shall not be applied in the landscape.

See So 601 and 602 FL II.

§ 2. Application of references

Cited in the regulations listed in § 1 of the provisions of national law which owns counterpart in landscape law shall be deemed to refer to the provisions of landskapslagstiftningensom thus is in question.

§ 3. Authorities

The granting of dispensing, monitoring the serving of alcoholic beverages and other management information as the Alcohol Act and the Regulation on alcoholic beverages and spirits ankommerpå State authorities in the province operated avÅlands environmental health authority on such information under § 23 Autonomy Act is pålandskapet. (2007/127)

The police monitor public order in places where alcoholic beverages are served.

§ 3a. (2007/86) adequate skills for service-call of mild alcoholic beverages

By way of derogation from the provisions of 21 b § in Alcohol Act may, in the case of a serving point where it only serves alcoholic beverages containing more than 22 vol ethyl alcohol, sufficient yrkesskicklighetför the manager and his deputy also noted by one of the restaurant institution issuing the certificate of familiarity with the serving of alcoholic beverages.

Of a certificate referred to in subsection 1. shall state that a test has been completed showing that the person frågaär familiar with the provisions of

1) the conditions for the granting of catering,

2) a prohibition against serving to minors and intoxicated;

3) the order of the dining areas, serving areas, dining times, advertising restrictions and other special obligations of the service,

4) manager and other personnel data and self-supervision and

5) regulatory supervision and sanctions.

§ 3b. (2007/86) personal presence on licensed premises

The manager and his deputy duty to ensure compliance with this Act may be executed even without the personal presence on the licensed premises on

1) the total serving of alcoholic dryckeromräknat in pure ethyl alcohol does not exceed 50 liters per year, but so that the total serving during a single month may not exceed 8 liters,

2) it will be present a person over 20 years, employed by the service center, as designated by the responsible manager to handle the direct supervision and

3) the responsible manager or his deputy may be called to appear on licensed premises within sixty minutes.

§ 4. (2007/127) Appeals

The decision Åland environmental health authority made under this Act may be appealed, when symptoms prohibition does not apply pursuant to § 52 alcohol law, appealed to the Åland administrative court.

Notwithstanding the appeal, the environmental and health protection authority decision taken, if the appellate authority decides otherwise.

§ 5. Penal provisions

Anyone without serving serving alcoholic beverages and the holder of serving ellerden who is employed at a licensed premises and leave the serving received alcoholic beverage to remove from the premises or on the licensed premises or in connection with the offering other than legally to that supplied alcoholic beverages to be for illegal serving of alcoholic beverages be sentenced to fines or fängelsei up to six months.

The holder of a serving or Somara employee of a licensed premises, by any means other than as provided in subsection 1. violates the provisions of the Alcohol Act or regulation omalkoholdrycker and spirit in terms of serving ban on serving times, on serving amounts or the method of payment and the obligation to give account vidserveringen be for alcohol offense be fined. (2007/86)

§ 6. Coming into force provisions

This Act comes into force on 1 December 1995.

This Act repeals, as regards the validity of Åland, the Alcohol Act (FFS 459/1968) and amendments that arose before 1 januari1993 (the old Act).

§ 7. Transitional provisions

By the City Council with the support of the older law given consent to the serving of alcoholic beverages will remain in force.

The right, the permit and the consent somutfärdats on the basis of the old Act and regulations issued under it will remain in effect during the period mentioned in the decision in question. By dennalag repealed, however, the regulations and license conditions issued under the old law, which relate to such rights, permits or consents, and on those applied this law ochvillkor issued under this Act. The special conditions related to the right, permission ochsamtycke, issued under the old law remains in force to the extent that they do not stridmed this Act.

A matter is pending when this Act comes into force consideration and determination under this Act.

In 11 Landscape Act (2007:96) on the application

tion of Åland to the law on

fertilizer products

§ 1. Scope

The law on fertilizer products (FFS 539/2006), hereinafter called fertilizer products law, applied in landskapetmed the abnormalities resulting from this Act. Fertilizer Factory Act shall apply in the landscape as it reads when this Act comes into force. Changes in fertilizer products Act shall apply in the landscape from the time of their entry into force of the kingdom. Changes avbestämmelser on which this Act provided for deviations shall not apply in the province.

Cited in fertilizer products to the law provisions laid down by national legislation, which owns the equivalent of landscape law shall be deemed to refer to the provisions of law landscape.

See La 221 FL II.

§ 2. Provisions not applicable

The landscape does not apply the provisions of the fertilizer products Act

a) 18 § of authorized inspectors and

b) 39 § of the fees and expenses.

If public records and the confidentiality of Landscape officials separately provided.

§ 3. Management tasks

The administrative tasks required by the fertilizer product law is for the national authority on land landscape landscapes managed by the government on these data according to § 23 Autonomy Act is pålandskapet.

§ 4. Determination of the type designations and trade names

Anyone under 6 and 7, § § fertilizer products Act for fertilizer products to the countryside or places or produce such placing on the market before preparation marketed send an indication of the type designation and trade name to the provincial government for approval of them.

§ 5. Marking

If, under § 8 fertilizer products Act or regulations issued pursuant to this Act, information submitted in writing by the person introducing the landscape, markets, manufactures, marketing or transfer of such fertilizer products referred to in fertilizer products law of declaration or otherwise, the data shall be written in Swedish .

§ 6. Penal provisions

Anyone who intentionally or through gross negligence

1) manufactures, technical processes, placing on the market, using, for the landscape or exports fertilizer products or commodities that do not meet the requirements or specific requirements in 5-8 § § fertilizer products Act or the rules and regulations issued under this Act and which refers to the requirements regulated by the said clauses, which are placed on fertilizer products, raw materials tilldem or packing or marking of them,

2) violates a temporary restriction issued under § 9 fertilizer products Act,

3) neglects the notification provided for in § 11 fertilizer products Act or neglects the obligation under § 12 fertilizer products Act to keep records;

4) fails to apply for approval of enanläggning according to § 14 fertilizer products Act,

5) violates an order issued medstöd of § 32 fertilizer products Act or a ban somutfärdats under § 33 fertilizer products Act or

6) violates an order of destruction and dispatches issued under § 35 fertilizer products Act, for violation of provincial law on the application of Åland of fertilizer products law punishable by a fine, if not more severe punishment is prescribed in other legislation.

Anyone who intentionally or through gross negligence neglects the declaration or otherwise provide any written information on the Swedish language as fertilizer products Act or under bestämmelsersom issued under this Act shall be the buyer and the receiver, the offense against language provision be fined.

The Åland Government notifies offenses under this section for consideration of charges. Registration is not required if the offense as a whole can be regarded as obvious call. In such cases, the provincial government to assign the operator who gjortsig committed the offense a written complaint with a request to correct the errors.

§ 7. Landscape Ordinance

The Government of Åland may, within the landscape area of jurisdiction landscape regulation decide to regulations issued by virtue of fertilizer products Act shall apply in the province anti-o one unchanged or with changes landscape Government.

§ 8. Entry into force

This Act comes into force on 1 December 2007.

This Act repeals the Landscape Act (1993:106) on the application of Åland avgödselmedelslagen.

Åland Executive Decision (1996:82) on the application of Åland of national regulations omgödselmedel issued under the repealed Act remains landscapes, to the extent that it is not in conflict with this Act, in force until otherwise provided.

Measures needed to enforce this Act may be undertaken before the Act comes into force.

§ 9. Transitional provisions

An operator, who must notify pursuant to § 11 subsection 1. fertilizer products Act and operating under the law as soon as this Act comes into force, shall Provincial notify according to § 11 subsection 1. within six months after this Act comes into force.

An approval by the provincial government as equivalent to a consent under § 14 fertilizer products Act and by virtue of the by-product regulation to which the Act refers fertilizer products have beviljatsen facility prior to this Act shall remain in force. Other facilities referred to in § 14 fertilizer products Act and operating under § 14 of this Act comes into force shall apply omgodkännande of Local Government within 24 months after this Act comes into force. The Government of Åland shall deal with these applications within four months after the closing date for applications.

In 12 of Åland [provincial government] decisions (1996:82) on the application of Åland of national regulations on fertilizers

§ 1. Scope of the Decision

With the limits set out in this Decision and somföljer of landscapes Act (1993:106) on the application land landscape Aland fertilizer law, the following national provisions applicable in the province of Åland:

1) Agriculture and Forestry Ministry's decision 26 January 1994 on fertilizers (FFS 45/1995);

2) Agriculture and Forestry Ministry's decision 26 January 1994 on some fertilizer products (FFS46/1994)

3) Agriculture and Forestry Ministry's decision 26 January 1994 on the control of fertilizer products (FFS 47/1994).

§ 2. General Provisions

The statutes referred to in § 1 shall apply on land landscape as they obey the implementation of this decision. Thereafter changes in the constitutions barked amended provisions applicable in the province after the coming into force of the kingdom.

Notwithstanding the foregoing, the modifications stool summaries do not apply in the province before the changes published in the Swedish language.

Cited in § 1 of the said constitutions to Implementing Rules of the national legislations which owns the equivalent of landscape law, shall be deemed to refer to the provisions of law landscape.

§ 3. Management tasks

The management information as specified in § 1 regulations is for the kingdom shall landskapethandhas the [Provincial Government], as far as regards aroma tasks that fall within the province's jurisdiction.

§ 4. Entry into force

This Decision shall enter into force immediately.

In 13 Landscape Act (1999:18) on the application of Åland of feed law

§ 1. Purpose

In order to promote the use of safe food makes of good quality and ensure that appropriate data on feed mill-General submitted to the livestock and the quality of animal livsmedeli landscape are safe, feed law (FFS 396/1998) shall apply in the province, with the exceptions resulting from this Act.

Feed Act shall apply in the landscape such denlyder when this Act comes into force. Thereafter changes to the Act, the amended provisions gällai landscape from the time of their ikraftträdandei kingdom. Changes to the rules on which this Act provided for deviations shall not be applied in the landscape.

[Provincial government] may be in the province's jurisdiction to decide the rules on animal feed manufacturers who issued under the Act or other feed rikslag be applied in the landscape either ioförändrad worded or as amended.

See La 220 FL II.

§ 2. Provisions not applicable

The landscape does not apply the provisions of food law

1) § 24 of the control center as a supervisor,

2) § 15 subsection 3., § 25 and § 27 subsection 1. of authorized inspectors and samplers,

3) § 32 of the publication of inspection results;

4) § 33 on disclosure and

5) § 35 of the control charges and fees.

If the confidentiality of Landscape officials and omavgifter for landscape performance is determined separately.

§ 3. The Managing

The management information according to feed the Act is for state authorities in landskapethandhas the [Provincial Government] on such information under § 23 Autonomy Act is for the landscape.

§ 4. Marking

To be under feed law or under bestämmelsersom issued under this Act, information submitted in writing by the person to the province for, produce or place on the market such food brands mentioned in feed law in the declaration ellerpå other way, so must the data be written påsvenska.

§ 5. Recovery of enforcement costs

For the authority's performance under this Act, medundantag for the supervision of medicated feed somutövas by the County, collected fees to the [Provincial Government] under provincial law (1993:27) omgrunderna for contributions to the province, unless otherwise provided by European Community law or international agreement that binds the landscape.

[Provincial government] may issue such rules on the fees in subsection 1. that European Community legislation or an international avtalsom binds landscape requires.

§ 6. Penal provisions

Anyone who intentionally or through gross negligence

1) for the placing on the market produce, place on the market, using, for the landscape or exporting feed manufacturers in violation of 4-12 § § feed the Act or the regulations issued thereunder Of these, or in violation of the restriction referred I13 § feed law,

2) the placing on the market, manufacture, place on the market, uses, or to the landscape feed mills that do not satisfy the feed makes in § 20 feed the Act or the regulations somutfärdats under it;

3) engaged in such misleading marketing that referred to in § 21 food law,

4) fails quality control requirement enligt16 § feed law or neglects to comply with the provisions on self-assessment issued under avden or producing or storing feed manufacturers in breach of the requirements under that provision has been set for production and storage facilities, manufacturing methods, or devices;

5) neglects the notification somnämns in 14 or 19 § § feed law, or determined pursuant to § 30 subsection 3. or 31 § 1 mom.foderlagen,

6) fails to keep records or their duty of disclosure pursuant to § 15 Act or the feed

7) fails to apply for approval enligt17 § fodder Act or registration under § 18 feed law

is the offense against provincial law on the application of Åland of feed law punishable by a fine, if not more severe punishment is prescribed in other legislation.

Anyone who intentionally or through gross negligence neglects the declaration or otherwise provide any written information on the Swedish language sometime thoroughly feed the Act or regulations issued under this Act shall be submitted to the purchaser, shall, for infraction of language provision be fined.

A person who violates a prohibition that has utfärdatsmed support of feed law and who have joined together with a penalty need not be punished for the same offense.

§ 7. Effective date and transition provisions

This Act comes into force on 1 May 1999. This Act repeals the Landscape Act (1993:107) on the application of Åland of feed law.

The decisions [Provincial Government] has made medstöd of the repealed Act remains still the entry, if they do not conflict with this Act.

Measures needed to enforce the law förutsätterfår taken before it takes effect.

In 14 the Åland government's decision

(1999:30) on the application of landscape

Aland of certain national provisions on

feedingstuffs (2006 / 7)

§ 1. Scope of the Decision

With the limits set out in this Decision and somföljer of landscapes Act (1999:18) on the application land landscape of Åland feeds Act, the following provisions apply to the Åland Islands:

1) Agriculture and Forestry Ministry's decision On 1 March 1994 on feed (FFS 180/1994),

2) (2006 / 7) Agriculture and Forestry Ministry's Regulation on the products used in animal feed (JSMF60/2005)

3) Agriculture and Forestry Ministry's decision den26 July 1995 on feedingstuffs for particular nutritional purposes (JSMb No 57/1995);

4) (2006/128) Agriculture and Forestry Ministry regulation on the conduct of activities in the animal feed industry (JSMF 4 / 2006);

5) (2006 / 7) Agriculture and Forestry Ministry's Regulation on feed additives (JSMF 43/2005);

6) (2006/128) Agriculture and Forestry Ministry regulation on the organization of control of the feed (JSMF 3 / 2006);

7) repealed (2001/46),

8) Agriculture and Forestry Ministry's decision on 1 October 1998 concerning the manufacture, prescription, överlåtelseoch import of pharmaceutical feed (JSMb 13/EEO/98)

9) Agriculture and Forestry Ministry's decision on 18 November 1998 on hazardous substances, products ochorganismer in feed (JSMb 163/1998),

10) Agriculture and Forestry Ministry's decision den21 April 1999 on the feed material (JSMb 40/1999);

11) Agriculture and Forestry Ministry's decision on 21 April 1999 on the compound (JSMb 41/1999);

12) Agriculture and Forestry Ministry's decision den28 April 1998 on preservatives in fresh forage (JSMb 48/1999);

13) (2001/12) Agriculture and Forestry Ministry Regulation on 21 December 2000 on animal-proprietary protein and feed plants containing such (JSMF1239/2000).

§ 2. General Provisions

The provisions listed in § 1 shall tillämpasi landscape as they obey when this Decision comes into force. Thereafter changes in regulations, the amended rules applicable in the province after the coming into force of the kingdom.

Notwithstanding the foregoing, amendments stool summaries do not apply in the province before the changes published in the Swedish language.

Cited in § 1 of the said statutes of the provisions of rikslagstifningen which owns motsvarigheti landscape law, shall be deemed to refer to the provisions of law landscape.

§ 3. Exemptions from the provisions of the national provisions referred to § 1

In the countryside, the following deviation from the provisions of Agriculture and Forestry Ministry beslutom feeds:

A) the provisions of 1-4 § §, 6 and 7, § § shall intetillämpas in the landscape.

In the countryside, the following deviation from agriculture ochskogsbruksministeriets regulation on the operation company's operations in the animal feed industry.

1) an application referred to in § 8 shall be sent to the provincial government and

2) an application referred to in § 9 subsections 1 and 2. should be sent to the provincial government and

3) an application referred to in § 11 subsection 1. should be sent to the provincial government and

4) the provisions of § 13 shall not apply in the landscape and

5) the provisions of § 15 shall not apply in the landscape and

6) an application referred to in § 18 subsection 1. shall send to the provincial government

7) a notification referred to in § 19 subsections 2 and 3. shall be communicated to the Local Government (2001/46)

In the countryside, the following deviations from the provisions of Agriculture and Forestry Ministry beslutom feed additives:

1) an application under § 5 must be sent to the provincial government and

2) the provisions of § 8 subsection 3. shall not tillämpasi landscape and,

3) an application referred to in § 11 subsection 1. should be sent to the provincial government.

In the countryside, the following deviations from the provisions of Agriculture and Forestry Ministry of reorganization of oversight of feed manufacturers:

1) a notification referred to in § 3 subsection 1. shall send to the provincial government and

2) a notification referred to in § 4 subsections 1 and 2. should be sent to the provincial government.

In the countryside, the following deviations from the provisions of Agriculture and Forestry Ministry's decision omegenkontroll the manufacture of feed manufacturers:

1) an application referred to in § 5 subsection 1. shall send to the provincial government.

In the countryside, the following deviations from the provisions of Agriculture and Forestry Ministry's decision omskadliga substances and products in feedingstuffs:

1) a notification referred to in § 7 shall be sent to the provincial government.

§ 4. Management tasks

The management information as specified in § 1 provisions is for the Reich authorities Skalli province administered by the provincial government, såvittdet is related to information that falls within the province of competence.

§ 5. Entry into force

This Decision shall take effect immediately.

Decision on declaration of Agriculture and Forestry Ministry's decision (JSMb 48/1999) paragraph 3 and 5 ibilaga 3, however, apply only from 1 January 2000.

In 15 Landscape Act (2001:25) on the application

tion of Åland to the law on

seed trade

§ 1. Purpose

In order to maintain a high quality crop production by promoting the availability and use of seeds that are high quality and appropriate förväxtförhållandena in the landscape, the law on handelmed seed (FFS 728/2000) shall apply in the province, except as provided by this Act.

The law on trade in seed shall be applied in the landscape as it reads when this Act comes into kraft.Sker then changes in the law, the amended provisions apply in the landscape from tidpunktenför their effect in the kingdom. Changes to the rules on which this Act provided for deviations shall not apply in the province.

[Provincial government] may be in the province's jurisdiction to decide the rules utfärdatsmed under the Act on the seed trade to be applied in the landscape either as unchanged as ellermed changes.

See La 211 FL II.

§ 2. Provisions not applicable

The landscape does not apply to the following provisions inserted on the seed trade:

1) § 20 on the inspection plan,

2) § 24 subsection 4. upon personal data,

3) § 25 of the publication of monitoring results;

4) § 26 for disclosure of classified information;

5) § 27 of the Contributions and

6) § 28 of the fees and expenses.

3rd §. The Managing

The administrative functions under the Act on the seed trade is for the state authorities in the province administered by the [Provincial Government], if these data according to § 23 Autonomy Act is for the landscape.

§ 4. Marking

The Act on the seed trade, or provisions issued under dennalag details in writing by the person introducing the landscape, markets, manufactures for promotion or transfer the seeds referred to in lagenom seed trade in the goods declaration or otherwise, so the data be written in Swedish.

§ 5. Approval of checks

[Provincial government] may approve the kontrollersom referred to in § 21 Act on the seed trade sommyndigheterna in other states have conducted.

§ 6. Packing Condition

Operators shall make such underrättelsesom referred to in § 11 subsection 3. Act on the seed trade to the [Provincial Government].

§ 7. Notification requirements

Operators shall make such notification recipes referred to in § 12 subsection 1. Act on the seed trade to the [Provincial Government].

§ 8. Supervision Records

Operators shall provide such meddelandesom referred to in § 24 subsection 3. Act on the seed trade to the [Provincial Government].

§ 9. Appeals

An appeal against the legality of the [Provincial Government] decisions may be lodged with the Supreme Administrative Court.

§ 10. Penal provisions

Anyone who intentionally or through gross negligence

1) produces or markets the seeds in violation med4 or 8 § § Act on Trading in seeds or in stridmed regulations issued thereunder, or who violates a prohibition issued by stödav 7 § Act on the seed trade,

2) promote seed not satisfying the kravsom of this Act and with the support of the issued rules or regulations imposed on seed ellerpå packing or labeling it,

3) package the seed without authorization referred to in § 6,

4) neglects the notification requirements in § 7 or

5) fails to keep records in accordance with § 13 a mom.lagen on the seed trade

the seed trade misdemeanor punishable by a fine, if not more severe punishment is provided elsewhere in law.

Anyone who intentionally or through gross negligence fails to declaration or otherwise provide any written information on the Swedish language sometime written law on the seed trade, or provisions issued under this Act shall be the purchaser, shall, for infraction of language provision be fined.

§ 11. Effective date and transition provisions

This Act comes into force on 1 June 2001. This Act repeals the Landscape Act (1993:108) on 9th December 1993 on the application of Åland passed on the seed trade.

The decisions [Provincial Government] has made medstöd of the repealed Act remains still the entry, if they do not conflict with this Act.

Measures needed to enforce the law förutsätterfår taken before it takes effect.

In 16 the Åland government's decision

(2001:47) on the application of landscape

Aland of certain national provisions on

seed trade (2006 / 6)

§ 1. Scope of the Decision

With the limits set out in this Decision and somföljer of landscapes Act (2001:25) on the application land landscape of Åland to the law on the seed trade, the following national provisions applicable in the province of Åland:

1) Agriculture and Forestry Ministry of omhandel of cereal seed (JSMF 109/2000),

2) Agriculture and Forestry Ministry's Regulation on trade in seed of grass and fodder (JSMF110/2000)

3) Agriculture and Forestry Ministry of omhandel with seed oil and fiber (JSMF111/2000)

4) Agriculture and Forestry Ministry of omhandel with seed potatoes (JSMF 112/2000),

5) Agriculture and Forestry Ministry of omhandel of vegetable seed (JSMF 113/2000),

6) Agriculture and Forestry Ministry of omhandel with beet (JSMF 114/2000),

7) (2006 / 6) Agriculture and Forestry Ministry regulation on a catalog of plant varieties (JSMF51/2004)

8) Agriculture and Forestry Ministry of omutsädesblandningar (JSMF 116/2000),

9) Agriculture and Forestry Ministry of omhandel in seeds of landraces of cereal and forage and fodder crops (JSMF 117/2000),

10) Agriculture and Forestry Ministry of omutförande of cultivation examinations (JSMF 118/2000),

11) Agriculture and Forestry Ministry's Regulation on the Supervision of the seed trade (JSMF 119/2000),

12) (2006 / 6) Agriculture and Forestry Ministry's Regulation Authority supervised sampling ochlaboratorieundersökningar in seed production (JSMF 29/2005).

§ 2. General Provisions

The statutes referred to in § 1 shall apply on land landscape as they obey the implementation of this decision. Thereafter changes in the constitutions barked amended provisions applicable in the province after the coming into force of the kingdom.

Notwithstanding the foregoing, the modifications stool summaries do not apply in the province before the changes published in the Swedish language.

Cited in § 1 of the said constitutions to Implementing Rules of the national legislations which owns the equivalent of landscape law, shall be deemed to refer to the provisions of law landscape.

§ 3. Management tasks

The management information as specified in § 1 regulations is for the kingdom is in the countryside hand-held by provincial government, to the best question is whether the information falls within the province's jurisdiction.

§ 4. Entry into force

This Decision shall enter into force immediately.

This Decision repeals Aland [provincial government] decisions (1996:73) November 19, 1996 omtillämpning of Åland by the National Constitutional aroma seed, as amended.

In 17 Landscape Act (1994:72) on the conditions

tions to the Province of Åland

look for, CLAIM and exploit mining

deposits

§ 1. Anyone under the provisions of [§ 3 Landscape Act (1957:11) on the right to carry on a trade in Åland] will be a general right to engage in business ashore Partner is entitled to the landscape on their own and another area to look for, CLAIM and exploit deposit, which contains the § 2 Mining Act (FFS 503/1965) avseddagruvmineral in compliance with the rest of the provisions of the Mining Act.

Individual and legal entities not subject to the provisions of subsection 1. can the [Provincial Government] be permitted to engage in the moment avseddverksamhet.

§ 2. Notwithstanding the provisions of § 1, the Somara resident in the province the right to look for, CLAIM and make use of the section is intended deposit, if it occurs under the conditions specified in § 11 Autonomy Act (1991:71) for the Aland Islands.

§ 3. This Act comes into force on November 1, 1994 ochgenom Act repealed, as regards the validity of the Åland Islands, a § Mining Act as it existed lydandevid end of 1992.

In 18 Landscape Act (1998:55) on the

application of Åland of Law

the apparatus energieff ektivitet § 1. Introductory provision

Act of 19 December 1997 on energy efficiency appliances (FFS 1241/1997) shall, in this Act specified deviations, applied in the Åland Islands.

LL (1994:72) on ... mineral deposits in 17

Amendments to the Law on energy efficiency appliances shall apply in the province after its entry into force of the kingdom, unless otherwise provided by this Act.

See Ft 706 FL I.

§ 2. Language requirements

Information in accordance with the provisions avsesi 1 and 6 § § given the marketing of anordningarsom fall within the scope of this law Skalli landscape is given in Swedish. [Provincial government] may for special reasons, grant exemptions from the requirement.

§ 3. Management

The administrative tasks required by the regulations referred to in 1 and 6 § § is for the state authorities in the province operated by the [Provincial Government] to the extent that management is based pålandskapets legislative competence in the field.

§ 4. Deviations from the law on energy efficiency appliances

The provisions of § 20 Act on energy efficiency appliances shall not apply in the province.

As in § 5 subsection 2. down on Finland shall apply in the province Åland.

As in § 10 subsection 2. 2 prescribes the f other manufacturers and producers and the importers who place anordningenpå the Finnish market in the countryside apply Aland manufacturers and putting in the device in landskapetoch placed it on the Åland market.

§ 5. Appeals

Determinations made under this Act, an appeal under the provisions of the regulations referred to in 1 and 6 § §, however, that decisions [Provincial Government] made to appeal to the Supreme Administrative Court.

§ 6. Landscape Ordinance

[Provincial government] may be in the province's jurisdiction through landscape decide attförfattningar regulation issued by virtue of the realm right appliances energy efficiency measures applicable in the province of Åland unchanged or with amendments [Provincial Government] prescribes.

[Provincial government] may be in the province's jurisdiction through the landscape regulation of implementation on the landscape of the EU directives concerning matters referred to in this Act.

Detailed rules for the enforcement and application of this Act shall, if necessary through landscape regulation.

In 19 Landscape Ordinance (1998:56) on the apparatus energieff ektivitet

§ 1. Scope of the Regulation

The following provisions shall be nationwide with The derogations provided for in this Regulation shall apply in the landscape:

1) (2004/50) Trade and Industry Ministry Regulation on 21 June 2004 on information to be given to energy labeling of household electric refrigerators, freezers and combinations thereof for domestic purposes (FFS541/2004)

2) Trade and Industry Ministry's decision on 27 mars1996 of information to be given to energy labeling of electrical household machines

(FFS 202/1996),

3) Trade and Industry Ministry's decision on 27th March 1996 on information to be given to energy labeling of household electric tumble dryers for household use (FFS 203/1996),

4) Trade and Industry Ministry of the 9september 1997 on information provided videnergimärkning of combined washer / dryers for household use (FFS 895/1997),

5) Regulation on 30 December 1997 concerning the approval of inspection bodies referred to in the Act on energy efficiency appliances (FFS 1298/1997);

6) (2000/75) Trade and Industry Ministry's decision-December 17, 1998 on energy labeling of household appliances (FFS 1038/1998);

7) (2000/75) Trade and Industry Ministry Regulation on 12 October 2000 on energy efficiency requirements for household electric refrigerators, freezers and kombinationerav those for household use (FFS 854/2000),

8) (2000/75) Trade and Industry Ministry Regulation on 12 October 2000 on the tasks somskall given to energy labeling of household lamps (FFS 859/2000),

9) (2000/83) of Trade and Industry Decree 24 November 2000 on information somskall provided on energy labeling of dishwashers (FFS 1009/2000);

10) (2002/36) of Trade and Industry Decree 17 April 2002 on energy efficiency requirements for ballasts for fluorescent lamps (FFS 318/2002).

§ 2. Exemptions from application of provisions of the

National regulations listed in § 1

For the purposes of the first paragraph stated statutes shall supplier provided equipment supplier in accordance with what is stated in lagenom appliances energy efficiency (FFS 1241/1997).

§ 3. Change in the national constitution

Amendments to the regulations listed in the first paragraph shall apply in the landscape from the deträder into force in the kingdom.

§ 4. Entry into force

This Regulation shall enter into force on 1 July 1998.

In 20 Landscape Act (2005:60) on the application of Åland of national regulations on emissions trading

§ 1. Application of the Emissions Trading Act

Emissions Trading Act (FFS 683/2004) by den30 July 2004 shall apply in the province with the limits set out in this Act. Changes in the Emissions Trading Act applies in the province of the date deträder into force in the kingdom.

See Mi 402a FL II.

§ 2. Application of the references in the Act if the emission

Trade

If the Emissions Trading Act refers to provisions in national legislation and corresponding provisions in the landscape legislation, reference·relate to provisions of law landscape.

§ 3. Management tasks

Management tasks, under the Emissions Trading Act administered by the authorities in the kingdom, skötsi landscape of the provincial government to the extent that management is based on the province's jurisdiction påområdet.

§ 4. Landscape Regulations

The Government of Åland may, within the landscape of competence through landscape regulation decide to regulations issued under the Emissions Trading Act shall apply in Åland unchanged or with changes that provincial government is proposing.

§ 5. Deviations from the provisions of national law

If an operator is required to pay avgiftför overrun allowance shall require substantial payment to the province.

Entry into Force Provision (2005:60):

This Act comes into force on 1 November 2005.Tillstånd to greenhouse gas emissions for the years 2005-2007, for which the application is filed within two months of the law in force, granted retroactively frånoch 1 January 2005.

In 21 Landscape Ordinance (2008:73) on

application of Åland of

some national regulations regarding the

released trade

§ 1. With the tolerances specified in this Regulation, the following provisions apply in Åland:

First Government Decree on Emissions Trading (FFS194/2007)

Second Trade and Industry Decree omövervakning of carbon and on the rapportsom be drawn up on emissions (FFS 647/2007),

Third Trade and Industry Decree omförfarandet for approval of controllers of emissions covered by the scope of lagenom emissions trading and the performance of control (FFS 888/2007).

§ 2. Changes in regulations in § 1 shall apply in the province after the coming into force of the kingdom.

§ 3. The management data that must be handled by government authorities in the constitutions of a § operated in the province of the provincial government.

If the regulations in § 1 refers to the provisions of national legislation and corresponding provisions in the landscape legislation, reference deemed to apply to provisions of law landscape.

§ 4. This Regulation shall enter into force on 1 June 2008.

The 22 President of the Republic Regulation (2006:5) on the management of Åland certain management tasks relating to emissions trading for greenhouse gases

(FFS 87/2006)

§ 1. The regulation provides for the management of Åland of management information relating addressed to emissions trading, and referred to the provincial law on the application of Åland avriksförfattningar the ETS (Åland Statutes 2005:60).

§ 2. Government of Åland shall decide on enförteckning of plants in the landscape and deutsläppsrätter intended to be granted for each softening them with justifications for this. Åland also decides on the allocation and granting of allowances to the operator and for the adjustment, adjustment and cancellation of allowances.

§ 3. The management tasks related to the five och6 Ch. the Emissions Trading Act (683/2004) avseddaregistret and implementation of it, including management information relating to the guard and control of discharges under Chapter 7. the law was shot in the Åland Islands of the Energy Market Authority.

§ 4. Energy Market Authority are reimbursed for the cost of care of in § 3 for management information rörregistret in the Åland Islands in accordance with the Local Government and Energy Market Authority jointly agreed upon.

§ 5. This Regulation shall enter into force on 10 februari2006.

The Regulation applies to emissions trading for greenhouse gases that have taken place in the landscape from 1 January 2005.

Support for business

In 23 Nutritional Support Act (2008:110) of the Åland Islands

Chapter 1. General Provisions

§ 1. Scope of application

With nutritional support under this Act funding for start-up and development or support for the development Avett business environment in accordance with a scheme that provincial government has decided on.

This Act applies both to such nutritional support to business in Åland wholly paid by the province's resources to aid somdelfinansieras with funds from European Community Structural Funds. Nutritional support should be granted with regard to the European Community bestämmelserom state aid to companies.

§ 2. Small, medium and large businesses

In this Act the small business enterprises which meet the conditions enligtEG commission's recommendation regarding re-definition of micro, small and medium enterprises.

Large companies are those companies not specified i1 subsection.

Chapter 2. Adoption and use of nutritional support

§ 3. Companies that are not eligible for nutritional support

Nutritional Support is not granted to

1) companies in the synthetic fibers, shipbuilding and coal and steel industries,

2) companies in the fishing and aquaculture industry or company in primary agricultural production,

3) firms in difficulty within the meaning of the European Community guidelines for undsättningoch restructuring, and

4) companies for export related activities towards third countries or Member States where the aid is directly linked to the quantities exported, to the creation and operation of a distribution network or to other current expenses In connection with the export business.

For the granting of nutritional support, the European Community's sectoral restrictions are observed.

The President has ordered that the law § 4 shall be extinguished.

§ 5. Application

Application for nutritional support should be submitted to the provincial government before action is taken. If there is förenligtmed current eligibility conditions, the applicant may take action before the provincial government made a decision while the leadership of the application.

§ 6. Confidentiality

Anyone dealing with a case under this Act fårinte without permission disclose what he or she is at the handling of the case have been told about a company, an industry organization or individual's financial condition or business or professional secret.

§ 7. Decision-making and disbursement of food aid

Landscape government decides on nutritional support.

Nutritional Support in the form of grants paid in arrears after The beneficiary has presented an adequate account of the expenditure is based only destiny and has fulfilled any conditions of the aid decision. If the actual expenditure is lower than the estimated expenditure was the basis for granting stödetoch of the aid granted exceeds the proportion avutgifterna mentioned in the decision, the aid shall be reduced or component-video equivalent degree.

§ 8. The use of nutritional support

A nutritional support may only be used for the ändamålför which it has been granted under the Provincial-even decision. Except as provided in this Act ochmed under the Act regarding schemes to The beneficiary comply with the conditions imposed by the enskildabeslutet of nutritional support.

A support contractor shall immediately notify the provincial government of any changes affecting the achievement of the purposes for which a nutrition support harbeviljats and the other change that affects pådet granted nutritional aid use.

§ 9. Storage of documents

The beneficiary is obliged to keep all accounting records and other material related to nutritional support in such a way that it is possible attövervaka use of the assistance. The accounts ochdet materials related to the store on detsätt determined in Accounting (FFS 1336/1997). To the extent that it is the issue of funding through the EU sstrukturfonder to records and materials somanknyter to be stored for at least three years from when dentidpunkt The EC Commission has paid slutraten for the current Structural Funds Programme.

See Ft 301, FL I.

Chapter 3. Supervision and recovery

§ 10. Inspection

Landscape government has the right to conduct inspections of The beneficiary to investigate förutsättningarnaför granting and paying support, and to see omvillkoren for granting and paying support has iakttagits.Stödtagaren shall take upon request of the person performing the audit to provide the information necessary to review the be implemented in ettändamålsenligt way and should not be entitled to compensation submit all necessary documents. With the documents referred to data which are produced or stored by means of automatic data processing ellerpå analogy. An inspection can be to the extent that regulatory mandate requiring apply to buildings, facilities, information and documents that are significant in view of the action to support and use of aid. The inspection shall not be carried out in rooms and areas in which to privacy under domestic peace.

The person conducting the examination are entitled to take possession of documents and other materials referred to above, if necessary for the purpose of the audit will be achieved. The documents and other materials shall be promptly returned when no longer needed for conducting the audit.

The provisions relating to inspection of the ändamålsom referred to in subsection 1. also refers to inspectors for the purpose designated by an EU institution and the independent audit firm that performs inspections ienlighet with landscape Government's decision.

§ 11. General provisions for refund avnäringsstöd

Provisions for repayment of aid in the landscape Act (1988:50) on the loan, interest subsidy and understödur landscape resources and landscape of warranty.

Recovery of aid paid under this Act or under regulations issued under this Act may be enforced in the order somgäller for the recovery of taxes in the law on execution of taxes and fees (FFS 706/2007). Återkravkan also enforced by the payment relate to modern granted aid will be deducted an amount to be recovered.

About one in subsection 2. intended claim is less than 3 Eurogas is no need to measure. If a claim is 3 euros or up to 100 euros perstödtagare and support application, Provincial decide that a payment can not be recovered.

See C 39, Landscape Act (1988:50) on loans, interest subsidies and grants

the province's resources and the landscape warranty and Pr 608 FL I.

§ 12. Special provisions for repayment avnäringsstöd

The Government of Åland shall decide that a näringsstödska repaid in whole or in part on The beneficiary

1) on any significant point made false statements in connection with applications for, or utbetalningav support,

2) failed to provide information which substantially would have affected the payment of the aid,

3) refused to provide information, documents or other materials necessary for monitoring or refusing tatt fulfill its obligations or has

4) used the aid for any purpose other than the harbeviljats for.

The Government of Åland shall decide that an investment in whole or in part, to be repaid if The beneficiary in accordance with § 2 is a large company, within five years after the investment has slutförtsoch in use, without justifiable reasons set elleri significantly limited the activities that are the basis for support. For investment into companies that can be defined as SMEs are the corresponding time in three years. Where the investment concerns of plant or equipment which, due to rapid technological obsolescence during that three-or five-year period is required instead that economic activity is retained in the region during the period.

§ 13. Repayment in case of damage

If the assets for which nutritional support harbeviljats destroyed in connection with damage to the provincial government to impose The beneficiary of the insurance amount which may be obtained to the provincial government to pay a portion corresponding to the aid andelav assets at the time of their acquisition. Payment obligation can apply up to an amount equal to the support and considerable damage that has occurred within five years after the aid has been paid to in § 2 meant big business, and within three years after the aid has been disbursed to small and medium enterprises.

Exemption from payment obligation can beviljasom equivalent new assets acquired to replace those destroyed. The conditions placed on aid applies when the new assets.

§ 14. Interest on refund

Landscape government may decide that the person will repay a grant to pay an annual interest rate on the amount of assistance from the date of payment or from the assets have been transferred. The interest rate can not exceed the Bank's base rate ökadmed four percentage points.

At an aid which has been repaid by the due date shall The beneficiary pay overdue interest at the rate provided for in § 4 of the Interest Act (FFS 633/1982).

Chapter 4. Specific provisions

§ 15. Breach of confidentiality

A person who without permission disclose what he or she is in dealing with matters under this Act have been told omett company, an industry organization or individual's financial condition or business or trade secret referred to in § 6 is for breach of confidentiality pursuant to nutritional support Act for Åland sentenced to fines unless more severe punishment is provided elsewhere.

The public prosecutor may not prosecute for crimes recipes referred to in subsection 1. unless the injured party has reported the crime to the prosecution.

§ 16. Subsidy Fraud

Provisions for subsidy fraud, see Chapter 29. Penal Code (FFS 39/1889).

§ 17. Coming into force provisions

This Act comes into force on 1 July 2009.

With the entry into force of this Act repeals

1) Landscape Act (1966:14) on the landscape guarantees for industries and other industries,

2) Landscape Act (1972:58) concerning tillämpningi Åland to the law on state guarantees for companies engaged in shipbuilding or ship owning,

3) Landscape Act (1975:32) concerning holiday pay for small business owners,

4) Landscape Act (1975:45) on investment loans,

5) Landscape Act (1977:29) on interest-subsidized loans for Fisheries,

6) Landscape Act (1977:44) on employment policy to cyclical businesses,

7) Landscape Act (1978:39) on certain interest-subsidized loans granted by credit facility;

8) Landscape Act (1991:43) on the application of Åland to the law on interest rate support for the financing of ship supplies and

9) Economy Support Act (1996:35) for the Province of Åland.

The in subsection 2. repealed provisions tillämpaspå nutrition assistance granted under dem.Dock apply to nutritional support of this law provisions on enforcement and recovery of nutritional support.

Measures needed to enforce this Act may be undertaken before the Act comes into force.

§ 18. Transitional provision

This Act shall apply to an application for assistance to enterprises that are registered with the provincial government when this Act comes into force.

In 24 Landscape Act (1976:43) on the application of the law on export credit in Åland

Act Sept. 14, 1962 on export credit guarantee (FFS 479/1962) and the subsequent changes made therein shall, together with provisions issued hereunder, shall be applicable in the Province of Åland.

The application relating to export credit guarantees for companies domiciled in the province of Åland, the [Provincial Government] statement of the case attached. What is provided here does not apply to companies engaged in such business as provided in [§ 11 subsection 2.] Autonomy Act of Åland.

Occurs in the future change in the in subsection 1. intended constitutions amendments shall apply in the landscape from the time of their entry into force of the kingdom.

In 25 Regulation (1991:67) concerning management of

Åland certain data

under the law on export credit

(FFS 1150/1991)

Extended by (1993/10).

§ 1. Guarantee Board shall perform its duties under the Act on export credit guarantee (479/1962) as defined in [§ 19] Autonomy Act for Åland (670/1951) is for landscape management.

§ 2. This Regulation shall enter into force on 1 september1991.

This Regulation repeals förordningenden July 21, 1977 regarding the handling of the lagenom export credit guarantees for data in Åland (584/1977).

In 26 Landscape Act (1995:46) on the recovery of aid from the province's resources

§ 1. If the Commission has found that support from the province's funds contrary to Article [92 of the Treaty concerning the establishment of the European Economic Community] or rules of the Commission's decision-3855/91/ECSC establishing Community rules for aid to the steel industry, the aid in accordance with Commission Decision fully or partially recovered at the receiver.

Art. 92 matched now by nature. 87th

§ 2. This Act comes into force on 1 July 1995.

AGRICULTURE, FORESTRY AND FISHING SECTOR REGULATIONS

Agriculture, forestry, fishing

H 1 Landscape Act (2007:63) on the financing

ring of rural industries

Chapter 1. General Provisions

§ 1. Purpose

In accordance with the provisions of this Act may be provincial government financial support in syfteatt rural development. Such support will be intended to promote diverse and sustainable business, sustainable use of agricultural and forestry land and practicing sustainable agriculture.

§ 2. Scope

This law applies to the province's national ochmed EU funds co-financed support system within the framework of the European Community's common agricultural policy. For the management of EU funds comply with the provisions thereof in the European Community at all times relevant provisions on support for rural development.

§ 3. Definitions

For the purposes of this Act is the meaning of the following terms and concepts that:

1) Agriculture in landscape pursuit of the cultivation of field crops, greenhouse production, horticulture, cultivation of vegetables in the open, the cultivation of fruit, animal husbandry, beekeeping, and other production activities of the products listed in Annex I to the Treaty establishing the European Community.

2) Farmers are as active in the acquisition, carrying out agriculture in the province.

3) Agriculture's Agriculture and Forestry conducted for profit and the company operates additional business. An agricultural operation device may comprise one or more flats or lägenhetsdelarsom have the same owner or mercenary contractors.

4) rural enterprises are enterprises other than agriculture.

5) support is a financial assistance from the province and the European Community, which has fastställtspå because of some production or action.

6) The beneficiary is a natural or legal persons. Specific provisions on beneficiaries of measures designed to improve the environment and the countryside is in chapter 2.

7) Rural Development Regulation is EGförordningen (EC) No 1698/2005 on support for rural development by European Agricultural Fund for Rural Development (EAFRD).

§ 4. Support

Support may be granted for measures designed to develop rural areas in accordance with a Community approved the rural development program, referred to in Title IV of the Rural Development Regulation.

Except as provided in subsection 1. support may grant such interest subsidy or other national aid enlighetmed landscape Government decision thereon.

§ 5. Agricultural Commission

Landscape government appoints a farm Commission for two years at a time. The Commission consists of five members and two alternates. Agricultural Commission advises the landskapsregeringennär in decisions regarding aid under Article 26i Rural Development Regulation. Agricultural Commission also assists the provincial government vidutvecklande of support systems and provide suggestions for the improvement of support systems. Members of the Commission subject to the confidentiality of the Civil Servants Act (1987:61) for the Province of Åland.

See C 45, civil service (1987:61).

Chapter 2. Support to improve the environment and countryside

§ 6. General

This chapter contains specific provisions on support for measures designed to improve the environment and the countryside referred to in Article 36 of the Rural Development Regulation, which is part of one of the EC kommissionensför landscape of rural development programs.

§ 7. Definitions

In applying the provisions of this chapter is the meaning of the following terms and concepts that:

1) Environmental's agri-environment payments under Article 36 point A IV of the Rural Development Regulation. Environmental aid can be granted as a basic support förobligatoriska and voluntary measures, and in addition dettasom a special support.

2) Compensatory payments are payments to farmers in areas other than mountain areas there are other difficulties, according to Article 36, paragraph A II of the Rural Development Regulation.

3) farms are such a produktionsenhetsom a farmer leads and used for carrying on agriculture, and is formed by one or fl era buildings or parts of buildings or of one or more production buildings plus land. A farm must also be functionally and economically independent, and managed as a whole because Åvägen or lease.

4) Spouses are people who have married medvarandra and in § 7 subsection 3. Income Tax Act (FFS 1535/1992) for people living in marriage-like relationship.

5) Cross-compliance is applicable conditions under artiklarna4 and 5 of Council Regulation (EC) No 1782/2003 omupprättande common rules for direct support schemes under the common agricultural policy and establishing certain support schemes förjordbrukare and amending Regulations (EEC) No 2019 / 93, (EC) No 1452/2001, (EC) No 1453/2001, (EC) No 1454/2001, (EC) No 1868/94, (EC) No 1251/1999, (EC) No 1254/1999, (EC) No 1673/2000, (EEC) No 2358/71 and (EC) No 2529/2001.

6) This instrument is the European Community Regulation (EC) 1974/2006 on the application of Council Regulation EC No 1698/2005om support for rural development from the European Agricultural Fund for Rural Development (EAFRD).

7) control regulation is the European Community Regulation (EC) 1975/2006 on the application of Regulation EC No 1698/2005 as regards controls and cross-compliance in relation to support for rural development.

8) The application is an application for environmental aid basic support, compensatory allowances, environmental support nationellatilläggsdel or an application for compensation grant national additional part, whether the aid is applied påsamma form, and an application for environmental grants special support.

§ 8. Beneficiaries

Support may be granted to farmers who possess engårdsbruksenhet landscape has its hemkommunoch permanent residence in the province and who is

1) a natural person;

2) a legal entity in the form of an association, an estate, a general partnership, limited partnership, ettaktiebolag or a cooperative made up of individuals and engaged in agriculture, provided that the partners in the open company, the general partners in limited partnership or members iandelslaget by themselves participate in the work bedriverjordbruk, in the case of a corporation is assumed that over half of the limited company's voting rights directly held avpersoner which by themselves participate in the work bedriverjordbruk and farmers

3) a municipality, province, state, a church, a foundation, a registered association, an agricultural college or experiment station.

§ 9. General terms and conditions for granting aid

For the grant of environmental or compensatory allowance is assumed that the farmer for a period of time committed to his farm unit shall comply with the villkorsom down for assistance. Of grant also requires that the farmer complies with CC.

Environmental subsidies for agriculture may be granted jordbrukaresom undertake to implement basstödets mandatory measures. Assistance may also be granted for basstödets voluntary measures. Special support may be granted to farmers by contract agree to comply with grant conditions on their farms.

For grant assistance for non-productive investments is assumed that the area was shot at least five years dessert project has been completed in such a way that no new encroachment occurs. It is further required for the granting of aid to support compliance with those conditions in the area supported.

The granting of environmental aid, national additional part is assumed that the farmer complies with the conditions somställs for environmental aid basic support. For the grant avkompensationsbidragets national additional part is assumed that the farmer is complying with the conditions ställsför compensatory allowance. The farmer must ävenuppfylla the general conditions relating to age, the grant approval and the conclusion of the marriage. Pade national supplementary parts, the same reductions and regulatory penalties for compensatory allowances and environmental support.

Landscape government decides on

A) liaison or contract duration,

2) withdrawal from relationships or agreements;

3) change, decay, and transfer to another farmer of relationships or agreements of the gränsersom out in the Rural Development Regulation, the implementing regulation and control regulation,

4) Further provisions on the basic and additional measures imposed in the environmental support for jordbruketoch on the general conditions for them;

5) general conditions for compensatory payments, environmental support base and the special support and support for non productive investments imposed and on the general conditions for granting them;

6) the technical implementation of the farmer's farm unit of the practical measures ingåri mandatory and voluntary measures in environmental grants,

7) the technical implementation of avtalsområdetav the practical measures contained in the various agreements omspecialstöd,

8) the technical implementation in practice of detgäller investments covered by the support for non productive investments and on

9) the basis for determining and granting avmiljöstödets and compensatory grant additional national parts, additional part size and depth of connection of the additional parts.

For 2008, see ÅLRB (2008:62) on environmental support national

additional part of 2008 and ÅLRB (2008:63) on compensation contribute

company's national additional part of 2008.

§ 10. Assumptions relating to the eligibility area and number of animals

Compensatory allowance can be granted to jordbrukaresom possesses at least three hectares of arable land and farmers out of the hold a sufficient number of grazing animals on at least two acres eligible naturbetesmark.Jordbrukare lacking arable land must keep a sufficient number of grazing animals on at least 5 acres eligible natural pasture.

Environmental support basic support can be granted to jordbrukaresom throughout the commitment period uninterruptedly possess at least 3 hectares of eligible land or somodlar garden plants at least 0.5 hectares.

For the conclusion of special support for growing påkänsliga areas, use of manure, priority natural baits, actions focused on natural baits, hävdav wooded meadow and extra-wide buffer zones is assumed attden area covered by the agreement is at least 0.5 hectares. For the conclusion of special support for bevarandeav indigenous breeds is assumed that the contracts concluded for at least four eligible animals.

For the conclusion of contracts for organic production is assumed that the agreement covers at least half of the farms arable land. Grown vegetables, fruits or potatoes can be concluded for a smaller share of a farm area. Contract acreage must be at least 0.5 hectares. Special support for organic livestock production can be granted to a farmer Somper their farms and in their possession throughout the contract period have pets for a number equal to at least one animal unit per hectare covered avekologisk livestock under Council Regulation (EEC) No 2092/91 on organic production of agricultural products and indications referring thereto on agricultural products and foodstuffs.

§ 11. Conditions for aid worker's age

For issuance of marriage or the conclusion of the contract is assumed that the natural person who is a candidate or his or her spouse are 18 years and högst65 is December 31 year relationship and the contract period begins. For grant assistance for non productive investments is assumed that the applicant authorizing dial his or her spouse are 18 years and a maximum 65år December 31 the year before assistance is sought.

A person under the age of 18 can receive aid only if he is married or engaged in agriculture as a joint owner with his parents or either of them or if there are other special reasons to grant aid.

If agriculture is conducted by several farmers elleri form of an association, is assumed for grant assistance to at least one farmer, a member isammanslutningen, partner or a bolagsmanuppfyller age requirement. Age requirement does not apply to public corporations, associations, foundations or the Education Act.

§ 12. Application for support

Aid applications shall be submitted in writing to the provincial government. An application or other document in connection with the application for assistance has lämnatsin by post be deemed to have been filed on time if it is postmarked as directed to Åland by the last day of the scheduled ansökningstiden.Den applying for aid to the provincial government to leave accurate and sufficient information on the conditions for granting and paying support.

§ 13. Conditions for payment of aid

The payment of compensatory allowances and environmental assume that The beneficiary submits annually a written request for payment.

Payment of support for non-productive investment requires the applicant to submit a payment request with details of the actual cost of the investment. Aid paid up for denandel of the eligible costs under ansökanom payment equal to the amount of aid granted.

For payment of aid is assumed that the stödbeloppsom paid for the connection, contract or support years is at least EUR 100 per beneficiary and per each support. If payment covers environmental support or compensation grant additional national shares granted on the basis of a marriage entered into prior år2007 assumed that the amount is less than 84 euros.

§ 14. Reduction of aid and refusing omstöd

Grants are not awarded if the applicant has taken such measures for the change of possession of the eligible land area or equivalent whose residence only intention is to artificially meet the general conditions for granting the aid, or to otherwise påett artificially avoid observing förutsättningarnaför aid is granted. A link or a contract will not be approved if the applicant is in the midst of liaison or contract has been withdrawn from a similar association or equivalent agreement and if there has been two years since the relationship or contract rooster belonged to apply.

The support may be reduced or need not be paid if required by the European Community or on The beneficiary has not complied with the eligibility conditions based on marriage or avtalet.Det amount by which aid is reduced is affected by gravity of, extent of, willful in and the duration for the failure of grant conditions.

Chapter 3. Control, correction, etc.

§ 15. Duty to report

A beneficiary or his successor shall immediately and within ten working days notify the provincial government if such changes are tamper-keeping procedures applicable to the beneficiary, relationship or agreement, a farm, livestock production, production animals or supported activities which may affect the amount or cause the aid to be recovered or withdrawn.

§ 16. Storage of documents

A recipient shall keep documents, notes and certificates to the conditions for assistance under this Act in at least three years of the connection-ochavtalsperioden ceased. Such documents, which refer to non-productive investments must be kept for three years after the last payment date.

§ 17. Inspection Law

Landscape government has the right to conduct inspections of the beneficiary to examine the conditions for granting and paying support, and to see omvillkoren for granting and paying support has iakttagits.Stödmottagaren such inspections are skyldigatt assist landscape officer and without entitlement to compensation at the official request submit all required records and other necessary-acts. With the documents referred to also those needed data, produced or stored Smith using automatic data processing or by analogy. To the extent that supervisory task requires an inspection cover the beneficiary's livestock buildings, crops, production and processing facilities, warehouses, and sales and marketing areas.

An inspection can be to the extent that regulatory mandate requiring apply to buildings, facilities, facts, information and documents that are significant in view of the action stödsoch use of the assistance. The inspection shall not be carried out in rooms and areas in which to privacy under domestic peace.

The provisions relating to inspection of the ändamålsom referred to in subsection 1. also intends

1) inspectors for the purpose designated by enEU institution,

2) certification bodies as referred to in § 5 President of the Republic Regulation (2006:110) concerning the management of the information in the Åland Islands, which belong to the paying agency of the European Agricultural Fund for Rural Development (EAFRD) and

3) independent audit firm to conduct inspections in accordance with the province government's decision.

§ 18. Disclosure and confidentiality of data

On the disclosure and concealment of information to apply provincial law (1977:72) on public records, unless otherwise provided by this Act. Notwithstanding the provisions on confidentiality hardock provincial government the right to the Agriculture and Forestry Ministry provide confidential uppgifterför forwarding to the relevant institution of the European Community, on the behövsför supervision and monitoring of the Community rules have been observed in the European Union co-financing.

§ 19. Additional Payment

An additional payment shall be made without specific application to the person who has received a lower amount than he should have been, if this was due to uppenbaraskrivfel, miscalculation, or other similar errors in the province government administration. If an additional payment is less than 3 euros it gives no cause for action.

§ 20. Rectification

An interested party who is dissatisfied with a decision omstöd the provincial government has taken may, within 21 days from the decision date, in writing, request correction of the provincial government. The rectification, which is the basis for landscape Government for consideration, specifying the decision as desired corrected ochde circumstances rectification based sigpå. A request for rectification shall be treated without delay.

§ 21. Correction

Landscape government has the right to correct obvious clerical mistakes or other comparable klarafel in its decision.

Where aid is paid to an excess or frivolous provincial government can decide attåterbetalningsskyldighet shall be issued to the deldet amount paid exceeded what should hautbetalts.

§ 22. Appeals

An appeal against the legality of the province government's decision under this Act by reason of an appeal may be lodged with the Supreme Administrative Court.

§ 23. Recovery of aid from the beneficiary

Provisions for the recovery in the landscape Act (1988:50) on loans, interest subsidies and grants from the province's resources and the landscape as well as guarantee in Article 73 of EC Regulation (EC) No 796/2004 laying down detailed rules for implementation of cross compliance, modulation and the integrated administration and control system provided for in Council Regulation (EC) No 1782/2003 establishing common rules for direct support schemes under the common agricultural policy and for the establishment of schemes for farmers.

Recovery of aid paid under this Act or under this Act issued the relevant provisions may be enforced in the ordningsom of the recovery of taxes in the Act on Collection of Taxes and Charges through Execution (FFS367/1961). Recovery can also be executed genomatt the payment of subsequent grant support is deducted ettbelopp to be recovered, if the support skallåterkrävas paid for an operation within the same scheme or within the same project.

About one in subsection 2. intended claim is less than 3 Eurogas is no need to measure. If a claim is 3 euros or up to 100 euros perstödmottagare and contribution period as well as aid application can provincial government decide that a payment can not be recovered.

§ 24. Interest and penalty interest on repayable assistance

Landscape government may decide that the somskall refund amount shall pay an annual räntapå any refund in accordance with § 3 Interest Act (FFS633/1982). In case of delay in repayment may be provincial government decide that interest payable under § 4 Interest Act.

No interest is charged on the amount to be recovered as a result of the provincial government has made an overpayment, unless the circumstances are such attdet is reasonable to assume that the beneficiary of detection.

Chapter 4. Specific provisions

§ 25. Violation of the Common Agricultural Policy

Anyone who intentionally or through gross negligence

1) neglects his duty to assist in the control or attge such information as the controls require,

2) fails to provide information or provides incorrect information or

3) otherwise violates the provisions of dengemensamma agricultural policy, is an offense against

CAP fined.

§ 26. The detailed rules

The Government of Åland may, within the landscape jurisdiction to decide on aid provided for in this Act. Unless the matter falls into the realm of law, the provincial government determine in accordance with European Community regulations, adopt the detailed terms and conditions or any information relating

1) beneficiaries, such as the age, education, income, corporate synergy composition and affected property;

2) reporting and implementation of projects or measures, eg regarding the time within which ettprojekt will begin and end;

3) interest subsidies, loans, fixed interest and amortization,

4) the payment or performance of the aid granted,

5) provisions for the transfer of support to other aid recipients,

6) the application and the application process, exempelvisom application forms, content and documents and reports shall be attached to the application and hurdessa ports, application time and mottagningoch processing of applications;

7) Such a relationship or agreement that is the basis for granting aid to improve miljönoch countryside,

8) eligible livestock units and åkerarealeroch other areas as well as other eligibility measures,

9) eligible costs of projects or measures supported, intensity, and maximum and minimum total investment;

10) bases used in calculating dennedre support limit for payment of aid to improve the environment and the countryside and on

11) criteria for depression and denial of support to improve the environment and countryside and it beloppmed which support is reduced to the extent required by the Rural Development Regulation and Control Regulation.

TRAVEL TO ALAND

FAQS

Where can be make our reservations?
Ålands Tourist information does not make reservations for accommodations. Instead you may contact a travel agency or make your reservation directly to the establishment. In Mariehamn you can make reservations with Viking Line, Ålansresor/Eckerö Line, Ålandhotels and Åland Hotel & Konferens.

Is it possible to travel with the archipelago ferries to the Finnish mainland?
Yes it is. The northern route departs from Hummelvik, Vårdö and docks at Torsholma at Brändö. You then must cross Brändö to catch the ferry from Åva to Osnäs in Finland.

The southern route leaves from Långnäs and sails to galtby, korpo in Finland. More information from Ålandstrafiken that also helps with making reservations on the ferries. Skärgårdstrafiken

Are there youth hostels in Åland?
There are no international or national youth hostels in Åland. But there are many Inns and B&B's instead. Stay at B&B

If I want to spend one day in Mariehamn and visit the countryside the next, what should I see?
In Mariehamn there are two museums that are open year round, Ålands museum and Art Museum and the seafaring museum. In the summer you may also want to visit the museum ship Pommern. Walk nice trails around Mariehamn.

You can easily drive all around Åland if you have brought your car with you. The distances are short and there is much to see along the road. The main sights are the castle of Castelholm, the open air museum Jan Karls garden, the ruins of the fortress in Bomarsund, the mountain of Geta, Hunting and fishing museum in Eckerö and the Post and Customs house.

If you have the time and possibility, take the advantage to ride an archipelago ferry. The ferry ride is free if you don't take your car along.

Is Åland closed in the wintertime?
many activities and establishments close in mid August to re-open again in the beginning of June. This doesn't men that you can't visit åland year round! In Mariehamn there are two museum open, you can stroll and shop in the town, you can drive out for excursions to the countryside and you may visit one of the many small islands.

Must I have a fishing license to fish in Åland?
yes, you must. Åland is divided into many fishing license areas and all of them require their own license. Some are sold at the Tourist information, some may be bought from the sport fishing shops and others still are sold at local grocery shops or privately.

Fishing licenses

We have heard of a museum card, what is that?
The museum card costs 7,5 Euro and is valid for four visits to museums of your own choice, usual admission fees are between 2 and 5 euro which means that it pays off to buy the card. The card is valid at most museums, also at the castle of Castelholm and at the museum ship Pommern. the card has no time limit.

Where may I surf the internet?
The Tourist Information has a computer that you may use without extra cost. You may also surf for free at the library and the Åland museum.

MARIA'S TOWN!

The wooden houses are still there in some streets, dating back almost to Maria's days. A tranquil idyll, with gardens and greenery, Maria's town is also a small-scale city, with modern buildings and well-developed services.

A youthful town, Mariehamn was founded in 1861 while Åland and Finland formed part of the mighty Russian Empire. Maria, consort of Tsar Alexander II of Russia gave the town her name.

Mariehamn grew up round the farming village of Övernäs, situated on a peninsula. The harbours built in sheltered bays came to be of great importance. The streets of Mariehamn are wide and straight. Housing sites were large from the beginning, but today they have been divided to provide space for several houses. A distinctive feature is the Esplanade, an avenue of lime trees stretching from west to east, from harbour to harbour.

Mariehamn is a carefree summer town with two large marinas and many hotels and restaurants, most within walking distance. It is also the seat of the highest administration of autonomous Åland, housed in the Self-Government Building.

Mariehamn in brief
10,500 inhabitants, 11.6 km^2
Some 60% of town-dwellers are employed in service industries and the public sector. 20% work in transport and almost 10% in industry.

SHOPS, HOTELS AND RESTAURANTS

Almost 1.5 million people a year come to Åland, most of them arriving by one of the ferries at the Western Harbour of Mariehamn.

Some 260,000 choose to stay for a night or longer and tourism has helped to create a high standard of service in Mariehamn. There are many restaurants, night-clubs and hotels, more than 1,000 hotel beds being available in Mariehamn during the peak season. The town has a large number of shops in relation to its size. In summer an almost Continental atmosphere reigns in Torggatan, the foremost shopping street.

Both the Eastern and Western Harbours have popular marinas with good services. The marina in the Eastern Harbour is one of the largest in Scandinavia with more than 300 berths.

Restaurants are available for most preferences. You can choose pizza or hamburger from a take-away, a salad at an open-air cafeteria or a good dinner of island specialities in marine environment. The choice is extensive.

SHIPPING WITH TRADITIONS

Maritime town is a very suitable name for Mariehamn. Ålanders have always been seafarers and Åland cargo shipping received an impetus after 1850 when Åland ships became larger and larger and their voyages longer and longer.

Many prominent shipowners settled down in the youthful town of Mariehamn. The first of them was Nikolai Sittkoff, a merchant who also engaged in shipping. His ships brought back attractive merchandise from abroad, which was then sold in his shop at Strandgatan. Sittkoff died in 1877, but his name lives on. An arcade with some 20 shops in the town centre is named after him and his statue stands by the main entrance.

August Troberg and Gustaf Erikson are two other prominent shipowners who built up large oceangoing fleets. They were neighbours living in pastel coloured wooden villas, which still stand in the Esplanade. Gustaf Erikson once had the biggest sailing-ship fleet in the world and today one of his windjammers, the Pommern, is amongst Mariehamn's foremost attractions. The Pommern was built in Scotland and 2003 will be her Centenary year. An event worth celebrating in this maritime town!

The Åland Maritime Museum preserves memories of the sailing-ships, one of its exhibits being the red-brown captain's saloon from the fourmasted barque Hertzogen Cecilie, one of Gustaf Erikson's ships. She ran aground off the coast of England in 1936 and before she sank her saloon was salvaged and brought to Åland.

Boat building traditions are kept alive at the Maritime Quarter in the Eastern Harbour. Among the red sheds there is a boatyard and a smithy as well as a boat and shipbuilding museum. Several small ships have been built there, including the galleass Albanus and the schooner Linden. Now work is proceeding on a reconstruction of an open 18th century cargo-ship, which will be over 17 metres long.

Modern shipping flourishes in Mariehamn, where many shipping companies have their offices, specializing in passenger services, carriage of goods and international tanker trade.

Visit places of marine interest!
Åland Maritime Museum, in the Western Harbour. Open 1 May – 30 June and all

August daily 9 am – 5 pm. July daily 9 am –7 pm. Other months daily 10 am – 4 pm. Tel.19930
Museumship Pommern, in the Western Harbour. Open 1 May – 30 June and all August daily 9 am – 5 pm. July daily 9 am –7 pm. 1 September – 31 October daily 10 am – 4 pm.
Maritime Quarter, in the Eastern Harbour. Open 15 June – 15 August daily 10 am – 6 pm. Other times Monday – Thursday 9 – 11 am.

BEACHES NEAR THE TOWN CENTRE

The sea is always close in Mariehamn and three sandy beaches suitable for children – Lilla Holmen, Gröna Udden and Nabben – are situated at a convenient distance from the town centre.

Lilla Holmen, an islet just below the Åland Museum has a jetty and a diving raft. Children enjoy the swings and the 'rustic' ship for climbing on. Lilla Holmen is also a bird island, with colourful peacocks strutting around freely. Various species of small birds have a house of their own and there are rabbits in outdoor cages.

South of Lilla Holmen is Gröna Udden camping ground and beach, with a jetty, raft, climbing frame and seashore sauna.

Nabben, which has the shallowest water of the three beaches is situated in the north of Slemmern bay and can be reached by the bicycle and pedestrian path along the Eastern Harbour.

Between Lilla Holmen and Gröna Udden is Tullarnas Äng Park, a green oasis in Mariehamn with sandy paths for walking or cycling. This park is at its most beautiful in the spring and early summer, when the ground is covered with blue hepatica, white windflowers and yellow cowslips. The sight is just as delightful every year.

A LIBRARY FOR EVERYBODY

Curving forms, light and space and excellent contents. While Mariehamn is waiting for an arts centre, the library overlooking the Eastern Harbour is the town's cultural meeting place.

The Alandica collection contains just about everything that has been written about Åland – both fiction and factual literature. The newspaper room provides more than 300 daily papers and periodicals, free access is available to the Internet, and in a special pavilion music lovers can enjoy both music and the view.

Visitors to Åland can obtain a special borrowers card upon showing proof of identity.

The Åland Museum exhibits the history of Åland from prehistoric times up to the present day. The Åland Art Museum displays pictures by both old and young Åland artists and the Mariehamn Gallery at the Western Harbour has a model of Mariehamn in the 1920s with its wooden houses.

As a festival town Mariehamn has much to offer. Annual events include a jazz festival, an organ festival and an arts festival. During Arts Night in August, musical and other performances may be enjoyed at various places in the town.

The arts in Mariehamn
The Library, open weekdays 10 am – 8 pm, Mondays until 9 pm, newspaper room from 9.am. Saturdays 11 am – 4 pm, newspaper room from 9 am. 1 October – 30 April open Sundays 12 noon – 4 pm. Tel 531441.
E-mail: biblioteket@mariehamn.aland.fi
Åland Museum, Åland Art Museum, open daily 10 am – 4 pm, Tuesday 10 am – 8 pm, 1 September – 30 April closed on Mondays.
Mariehamn Gallery, open daily 1 June – 31 August from 12 noon – 6 pm. 1 September – 31 May, Tuesday – Thursday 6 pm – 8 pm, Saturday and Sunday from 12 noon – 4 pm.

FUN FOR CHILDREN AND ADULTS

Dodgems, merry-go-rounds and cuddly rabbits. A day can easily be spent at Ålandsparken, an amusement park with activities for the whole family. Visit the Sleeping Beauty's Palace, try your ability at climbing and feel the thrill of careering out into the water in the Nautical Jet. Restless youngsters love jumping around in the inflatable castle.

Ålandsparken is just by the Viking Terminal in the Western Harbour.

Mariehamn also offers night entertainment. There are three night-clubs and several restaurants with dancing. Some of the pubs provide entertainment with troubadours or orchestras. In summer a rock festival with many artists is held at the Market Square and sometimes there is dancing on the jetty in the Eastern Harbour.

Read the advertisements in the local newspapers or phone Åland Tourist Information, tel. 24000 to find out what is available in Entertainment Mariehamn.

Opening hours
Ålandsparken, open from middle of May - 30 June and first fortnight in August, weekdays 12 noon – 8 pm, Saturday and Sunday 12 noon - 5 pm. July, daily 12 noon - 9 pm. Last fortnight in August, daily 12 noon – 5 pm.

A WALK IN SONCK'S FOOTSTEPS

The church, the Maritime College, the Town Hall, the yacht Club and several other buildings-

The architect Lars Sonck has left many traces in Mariehamn. An inexpensive way of seeingg the town is to take a walk in Sonck's footsteps.

Professor Lars Sonck was born 1870 and died in 1956. He came to Åland in 1878 when his father became vicar of Finström.

A Sonck walk can start at the church, which was built in 1927. August Troberg, one of the big shipowners of Mariehamn, donated money to have it built. A short way from the church is the Åland Maritime College, a monumental building on a hill. In the adjacent street of Södragatan is a special private house, a brown 'chalet' designed by Sonck in Swiss style.

At the eastern end of Södragatan we reach the Town Hall, opened in 1939, the same year as the Maritime College.

Those who prefer a longer walk can follow the path leading out from the town to the cemetery and its chapel, which was designed by Sonck. A path through the woods leads west to the park of Badhusparken and the Western Harbour. The park contains a building from the beginning of the 20th century when Mariehamn was fashionable spa – a light coloured wooden house where the spa doctors had their consulting rooms. In the harbour is the Customs Warehouse from the end of the 19th century.

The walk can end at the Yacht Club restaurant just below the park. This imaginative red building was designed by Sonck as a summerhouse for one of the spa doctors.

ENJOY SOME EXERCISE!

Being active is easy in Mariehamn. There are several sports halls for various activities.

Baltichallen, in south Mariehamn is suitable for floorball, handball, basketball, volleyball, five-a-side soccer etc. It is open all year round for booked groups and outside the hall are two full-sized soccer pitches and a jogging track along undulating terrain.

Mariehamn has a long indoor ice season, from the end of July to the middle of April. Islandia Ice Rink has fixed times for skating when anyone can skate freely on the rink. At other times it is used by local and visiting ice hockey and rink-bandy clubs.

Islandia, like Baltichallen, is also suitable for fairs, exhibitions and gale performances. For concerts Islandia can house an audience of more than 2,000.

Islandia is situated in Idrottsparken, the foremost sports centre in Mariehamn. It contains several tennis courts, soccer pitches (one grass, one gravel) and a newly renovated athletics area. Close by is Idrottsgården containing swimming baths bowling alley and training facilities. Starting spring 2001 Idrottsgården will undergo extensive renovation lasting approximately 1 year. During this period access to amenities will be restricted.

In the north of Mariehamn is Bollhalla, a hall with tennis and badminton courts. In an area named Backeberg there are two full-size grass pitches for soccer, so Mariehamn has five full-size pitches altogether!

Many teams from Sweden and Finland like to come to Åland and combine a training camp with a mini-vacation. Teams wishing to play against their Åland counterparts can contact sports societies in Mariehamn, the largest being IFK Mariehamn.

Other sports can be practised here too. A boules ground and two minigolf courses are available and for horse-riders Ridklubben Sleipner has facilities with a manege in south Mariehamn.

Mariehamn is excellent for walking and cycling. Worth discovering is the path starting at the Western Harbour and winding along beside the rocky shore to the fishing harbour.

Make bookings at the sports halls
Bookings at **Islandia**, **Baltichallen** and **Idrottsparken** may be made per tel. 531440 or 531441, fax. 23144.
E-mail: jonny.sederstrom@mariehamn.aland.fi or lennart.axelsson@mariehamn.aland.fi
Idrottsgården, tel. 531430 or 531437, fax 15139.
E-mail: carita.facius@mariehamn.aland.fi
Bollhalla, tel. 22950

Mariehamn is a summer town where the sea is always near. Mariehamn is a maritime town with sailing-ships and shipbuilding. Mariehamn is a small-scale city with well-developed services for visitors. A town with a varied sporting and cultural life and pleasant green oases.
Welcome to Maria's town in autonomous Åland

CONTACT INFORMATION

The Municipality of Mariehamn,
PB 5,
AX - 22101 MARIEHAMN
Åland,
Finland.

Tel. + 358 (0)18 5310 (switchboard)
Fax. + 358 (0) 18 531 206
e-mail: info@mariehamn.aland.fi

SUPPLEMENTS

B7 CONTACTS

Bornholm

Bjarne Kristiansen B7 Steering Committee Regional Municipality of Bornholm DK-3700 Rønne, Bornholm tel: +45 5696 6689 mail: Bjarne.Kristiansen@brk.dk	Jørgen Kvist Executive Director B7 Board Regional Municipality of Bornholm DK-3700 Rønne, Bornholm tel: +45 5692 1101 mail: Joergen.Kvist@brk.dk
Jørgen Jespersen Chairman WG Environment tel: +45 5692 2232 fax: +45 5692 1302 mail: Joergen.Jespersen@brk.dk	Henrik Eybye Nielsen WG People to People Regional Municipality of Bornholm DK-3700 Rønne, Bornholm tel: +45 5692 1309 tel: +45 5692 1301 mail: Henrik.Eybye.Nielsen@brk.dk
Bo Dahllöf Chief Executive Officer B7 Board Gotlands kommun Ledningskontoret S-62181 Visby, Gotland tel: +46 498 269 320 fax: +46 498 203 526 mail: bo.dahllof@gotland.se	Ulla Pettersson Director for international affairs B7 Board Gotlands kommun Ledningskontoret S-62181 Visby, Gotland tel: +46 498 269 658 fax: +46 498 269 659 mail: ulla.pettersson@gotland.se
Jan Lundgren County Mayor B7 Steering Committee Gotlands kommun Ledningskontoret S-62181 Visby, Gotland tel: +46 498 269 335 fax: +46 498 215 520 mail: jan.lundgren@gotland.se	Eva Nypelius Deputy County Mayor B7 Steering Committee Gotlands kommun Ledningskontoret S-62181 Visby, Gotland tel: +46 498 269 360 fax: +46 498 215 520 mail: eva.nypelius@gotland.se
Arne Grau-Amnér Head of unit Youth WG People to People	Bengt-Olof Grahn Eco-strategist WG Environment

Gotlands kommun Ledningskontoret S-62181 Visby, Gotland tel: +46 498 269 681 fax: +46 498 269 659 mail: arne.grau_amner@kff.gotland.se	Gotlands kommun Ledningskontoret S-62181 Visby, Gotland tel: +46 498 269 379 fax: +46 498 215 520 mail: bengtolof.grahn@gotland.se
Reet Kokovkin Councellor B7 Board Hiiu County Government Leigri väljak 5, 92401 Kärdla, Hiiumaa tel: +3 724 631 132 fax: +3 724 631 089 mail: reet.kokovkin@mv.hiiumaa.ee	Hannes Maasel County Governor B7 Steering Committee Hiiu County Government Leigri väljak 5, 92401 Kärdla, Hiiumaa tel: +3 724 631 129 fax: +3 724 631 089 mail: hannes.maasel@mv.hiiumaa.ee
Ermo Mäeots Head of the Education and Culture Department WG People to People Hiiu County Government Leigri väljak 5, 92401 Kärdla, Hiiumaa tel: +3 724 631 103 fax: +3 724 631 089 mail: ermo@mv.hiiumaa.ee	Avo Kütt Specialist of plannings WG Environment Hiiu County Government Leigri väljak 5, 92401 Kärdla, Hiiumaa tel: +3 724 631 129 fax: +3 724 631 089 mail: avo.kytt@mv.hiiumaa.ee
Uwe Ahlers Member of County Council Rügen B7 Steering Committee Landkreis Rügen Kreistagsbüro, PF 1343 D-18523 Bergen auf Rügen tel: +49 38391 939 989 fax: +49 38391 939 990 mail: uwe.ahlers.consult@gmx.de	Christian Theel B7 Board Landkreis Rügen Gartenstraße 5 D-18528 Bergen auf Rügen tel: +49 3838 813 353 fax: +49 3838 813 270 mail: christian.theel@landkreis-ruegen.de
Martina Schwinkendorf WG People to People, chairman Landkreis Rügen Amt für Wirtschaft und Kultur Gartenstraße 5 D-18528 Bergen auf Rügen tel: +49 3838 813 292 fax: +49 3838 813 270	Dr. Bodo Noack WG Environment Landkreis Rügen Störtebekerstraße 30 D-18528 Bergen auf Rügen tel: +49 3838 813 296 fax: +49 3838 813 119 mail: bodo.noack@landkreis-ruegen.de

mail: martina.schwinkendorf@landkreis-ruegen.de	
Hans Teiv Acting County Governor B7 Steering Committee County Government Lossi 1 EE-93816 Kuressaare, Saaremaa tel: +3 724 520 500 fax: +3 724 520 503 mail: hans.teiv@saare.ee	Anu Vares Adviser to the County Governor B7 Board Member of the WGE Saaremaa County County Government Lossi 1 EE-93816 Kuressaare, Saaremaa tel: +3 724 520 507 mail: anu.vares@saare.ee
Anne Jakunin WG People to People Saaremaa County County Government Lossi 1 EE-93816 Kuressaare, Saaremaa tel: +3 724 520 516 fax: +3 724 520 503 mail: anne@saare.ee	
Britt Lundberg Minster of Åland Government B7 Steering Committee B7 President 2006 Ålands Landskapsregering PB 1060 22 111 Mariehamn tel: +358 18 25 375 mail: britt.lundberg@ls.aland.fi	Susanne Andersson Legal Adviser – Department of Trade and Industry B7 Board B7 Chairperson 2006 Ålands Landskapsregering PB 1060 22 111 Mariehamn tel: +358 18 25 278 mob: +358 457343 01 78 mail: susanne.andersson@ls.aland.fi
Mikael Wennström WG Environment Ålands Landskapsregering PB 1060 22 111 Mariehamn tel: +358 18 25 455 mail: mikael.wennstrom@ls.aland.fi	Ann Wallskog B7 Secretariat 2006 Ålands Landskapsregering PB 1060 22 111 Mariehamn tel: +358 18 25 277 mob: +358 457 342 53 25 mail: B7@ls.aland.fi
Johan Sjölund B7 website 2006	Jan-Ole Lönnblad WG People to People

Ålands Landskapsregering PB 1060 22 111 Mariehamn tel: +358 18 25 292 mail: johan.sjolund@ls.aland.fi	Ålands Landskapsregering PB 1060 22 111 Mariehamn tel: +358 18 25 375 mail: jan-ole.lonnblad@ls.aland.fi
Gunilla Sanders Media Ålands Landskapsregering PB 1060 22 111 Mariehamn mob: +358 457 343 02 90 mail: gunilla.sanders@ls.aland.fi	
Jörgen Samuelsson Ölands Kommunalförbund B7 Board Ölands Kommunalförbund Box 52 S-387 21 Borgholm, Öland tel: +4 648 588 211 fax: +4 648 512 609 mail: jeurgen.samuelsson@borgholm.se	Tommy Eliasson Ölands Kommunalförbund B7 Steering Committee Trollhättevägen 4 S-380 62 Mörbylånga, Öland mail: tommy.eliasson@morbylanga.se
Anders Nyholm WG People to People Borgholms kommun Box 52, Stadshuset S-38721 Borgholm, Öland tel: +46 485 88 100 fax: +46 485 12 935 mail: anders.nyholm@borgholm.se	Mats Lindahl Head of the Enviromental department, Mörbylånga kommun WG Environment Trollhättevägen 4 S-380 62 Mörbylånga, Öland tel: +46 485 470 60 mail: mats.lindahl@morbylanga.se
Seppo Ekelund WG Environment tel: +46 485 88 019 mail: ekelund@seppo.se	
Ann Wallskog B7 Secretariat 2006 Ålands Landskapsregering PB 1060 22 111 Mariehamn tel: +358 18 25 277	David Hunt B7 Facilitator Regional Municipality of Bornholm DK-3700 Rønne, Bornholm tel: +45 5692 1304 mob: +45 2897 3712

mob: +358 457 342 53 25 mail: B7@ls.aland.fi	fax: +45 5692 2468 mail: david.hunt@brk.dk

IMPORTANT CONTACTS

CHAMBER OF COMMERCE

The Åland Chamber of Commerce is an organisation that represents Åland companies. Our main purpose is to serve our members in areas such as legislation, business contacts, education and training, contacts with governments and authorities etc. We feel it is important to support and assist the starting of new companies and establishing business and contacts between Åland and other regions of interest.

We continuously arrange courses and seminars, and also arrange projects with European Union financing. Furthermore we handle different duties like issuing certificates of origin, supervision of auditors and issuing of ATA-Carnets.

To contact the Åland Chamber of Commerce in a specific matter or to receive more information, here are our contacts. Also you can use the links on the left to know more on the staff and some useful links in English.

POST AND VISIT ADDRESS:

Åland Chamber of Commerce
Nygatan 6, II
AX-22 100 Mariehamn
Åland/Finland

TELEPHONE:

+358 (0)18 - 29 029

MAIL:

info[at]naringsliv.ax forename.familyname[at]naringsliv.ax

LOCAL GOVERNMENT

Ålands landskapsstyrelse
Pb 60, 22101 Mariehamn, +358 18 25000
http://www.aland.fi

Jomala kommun
22150 Jomala, +358 18 32910
email: info@jomala.aland.fi
http://www.jomala.aland.fi

22320 Ödkarby, +358 18 48900
email: info@saltvik.aland.fi
22940 Åva, +358 18 56500
email: kom.dir@brando.inet.fi

http://www.brando.aland.fi Eckerö kommun

Överby, 22270 Eckerö, +358 18 32930
email: info@eckero.aland.fi
http://www.eckero.aland.fi Finströms kommun

Markusböle, 22310 Pålsböle, +358 18 42469
http://www.finstrom.aland.fi Föglö kommun

Degerby, 22710 Föglö, +358 18 50093
http://www.foglo.aland.fi Geta kommun

22340 Geta, +358 18 49300 Hammarlands kommun
22240 Hammarland, +358 18 36450 Kumlinge kommun

22820 Kumlinge, +358 18 55560
email: kumkom@aland.net
http://www.kumlinge.aland.fi Kökar kommun

22730 Kökar, +358 18 55829
http://www.kokar.aland.fi Lemlands kommun

22610 Lemland, +358 18 34100 Lumparlands kommun
22630 Lumparland, +358 18 35567, 35610 Mariehamns Stad
Pb 5, 22101 Mariehamn, +358 18 5310
email: info@mariehamn.aland.fi Sottunga Kommun

22720 Sottunga, +358 18 55125 Sunds kommun
22520 Kastelholm, +358 18 43270
email: rosmari.andersson@kommun.aland.fi
http://www.sund.aland.fi/ Vårdö kommun

22550 Vårdö, +358 18 47900
email: vardo@aland.net
http://www.vardo.aland.fi

Ålands Turistinformation
Storagatan 8, 22100 Mariehamn, +358 18 24000
email: info@turist.aland.fi

Open: Every day 9-16. 1.9-31.10 and 1.3-31.5 also saturday 10-15. 1.6-13.6 and 14.8-31.8 Mo-Fr 9-17 and Sa-Su 9-16. 14.6-13.8 Everyday 9-18. Godby Turistinformation
22410 Godby, +358 18 41890

Open: 4.6-19.8. Mo-fri 10-20, sa 10-16, su 12-16 Mariehamns Stads Turistinfo
Viking/Siljaterminalen i Västerhamn, 22100 Mariehamn, +358 18 531214
Open: Jun-Aug mon-sat, July daily Skärgårdens Turistinformation

Osnäs, 23360 Gustavs, +358 2 8413684
Open: 15.6-15.8 mon-sat 8.15-19.15 sun 9.15-19.15

Ålands Turistinformation

Storagatan 8, 22100 Mariehamn
Tel. +358 18 24000 **Fax** +358 18 24265
e-mail: info@turist.aland.fi

ADVENTURES

Alandia Escargot Ab
22520 Kastelholm, +358 18 43964

ART

Galleri Skarpans
Skarpansvägen 27, 22100 Mariehamn, +358 18 16030
email: skarpans.lind@aland.net
http://www.kulturfonden.fi/skarpans
Storagatan/Pb 60, 22101 Mariehamn, +358 18 25426
email: konst.info@aland-museum.aland.fi
http://www.aland-museum.aland.fi/konst
Open: Daily 10-16, tue 10-20. 1.9-30.4 Mon closed. Admission: Adults € 2,50, child. (0-12

BANQUETTES

Ulfsby Källarkrog
Ulfsby, 22150 Jomala, +358 18 31040, [0]40 738 0758
email: info@ulfsbykallarkrog.aland.fi
http://www.ulfsbykallarkrog.aland.fi/
Open year round by request.

BICYCLE FERRIES

Simskäla Fiskeresor
Västerövägen 176, 22550 Vårdö, +358 400 783 086
email: simskalafiskeresor@goaland.net

BICYCLE STORES

Sportcenter
Skarpansvägen 24, 22111 Mariehamn, +358 18 16489
email: sportcenter@aland.net
Inlines, slalom...

BOAT FUEL

Karlby Gästhamn Ab
Brudhäll, 22730 Kökar, +358 18 55926

No. of berths: 65. Nautical chart no.: 758.
Fiskeläget, 22270 Eckerö, +358 18 38530, [0]400 529 738
email: hamberg@aland.net
http://home.aland.net/hamberg/hamn.html
Open: 1.6-31.8. No. of berths: 50. Nautical chart no.: 761.

BOAT HIRE

Kasvikens camping
Haglundsväg 22, 22340 Geta, +358 18 41410, [0]457 313 5162
email: adventure@kasviken.com
http://www.aladventure.com

No. of overnight cottages: 3/19. 5/2 stars
Väster Hamnen, 22100 Mariehamn, +358 18 57500
email: info@midnightsunsailing.fi
http://www.midnightsunsailing.fi

Österhamn/Västerhamn, 22100 Mariehamn, +358 18 12820, 12821, [0]400 529 315
email: tony.anja@aland.net

BUSINESS SERVICES

Ålands Vattenskyddsförening

email: vattenskydd@GoAland.net Ålcom
Torggatan 10, 22100 Mariehamn, +358 18 23500
email: info@alcom.aland.fi
http://www.alcom.aland.fi

CASINOS

Hotel Arkipelag
Strandgatan 31, 22100 Åland, +358 18 24020
email: info@hotellarkipelag.aland.fi
http://www.hotellarkipelag.com
Open year round. No. of rooms: 86. No. of beds: 215.

CAR HIRE

Esso, Rundbergs Bil & Service Ab - Europcar
Strandgatan 1 B, 22100 Mariehamn, +358 18 525505, +358 18 15222
email: rbs@rundbergs.com
http://www.rundbergs.com

CLOTHING & ACCESSORIES

Martins
Torggatan 12, 22100 Mariehamn, +358 18 23600
email: martins@pp.inet.fi
Torggatan 5, 22100 Mariehamn, +358 18 13470
email: gskogberg@aland.net

COTTAGES

Alebo stugor
Käringsund, 22270 Eckerö, +358 18 38575
email: alebo@aland.net
http://home.aland.net/m04579
Open year round, camping 1.5.-30.9. No. of cottages/overnight cottages: 14/12.

Camping grounds 3 stars.
Bastöv. 531, 22310 Pålsböle, +358 18 42382
email: basto@aland.net
http://www.basto.aland.fi
Open: 1.5-30.8, year round for groups (min. 15 pers). No. of hotel rooms: 20. No. of beds: 50. No. of cottages/overnight cottages: 20/1

Norrbygatan 88, 22130 GOTTBY, +358 18 32511, [0]457 374 9819
Open: 14.3.-30.11. No. of cottages: 4
Frebbenby, 22240 Hammarland, +358 18 37800
email: bjorklidens@aland.net
http://www.bjorkliden.aland.fi
No. of cottages/overnight cottages: 14/14
Björksätersvägen 66, 22220 Emkarby, +358 18 38970; [0]457 0529 196
email: bjorksater@goaland.net
No. of cottages: 8

Björnhuvud, 22270 Eckerö, +358 18 38208, [0]457 526 7455
Stålsby, 22330 Tjudö, +358 18 48213, [0]457 522 1613
email: bomans.stugor@aland.net
No. of cottages: 12
22920 Brändö, +358 18 56221, [0]40 753 0514
email: lameta@alcom.aland.fi
http://come.to/brando.stugby
Open: 1.5.-30.9. No. of cottages: 10
22340 Geta, +358 18 48228, [0]40 83 39 236, [0]400 529 595
email: maria.haggblom@aland.net
No. of cottages: 8

Högbolstad, 22520 Kastelholm, +358 18 43959
email: ekers@aland.net
No. of cottages: 20
Norrbygatan 60, 22130 Gottby, +358 18 32509
email: ekstroms.stugor@aland.net
http://www.aland.net/ekstroms.stugor/
No. of cottages: 5

Korsö, 22920 Brändö, +358 18 56142, [0]457 3420734
No. of cottages: 10

Gäddviksvägen 17, 22240 Hammarland, +358 18 37650, [0]457 5958398
email: info@gaddviken.aland.fi
http://www.gaddviken.aland.fi
Open: 1.5-15.8 + the whole year for groups. No. of rooms: 37. No. of beds: 95. No. of overnight cottages: 6.
Varvsstigen 14, 22240 Hammarland, +358 18 37848, [0]457 52 44 248
email: info@holmgards.aland.fi
http://www.aland.net/holmgards
Open: 14.4.-31.10. No. of cottages/overnight cottages: 7/5

Käringsund, 22270 Eckerö, +358 18 31486, [0]457 0826 844
email: info@alandsresor.fi
http://home.aland.net/marianne.holmstrom
Open: 1.4-15.11 No. of cottages: 7
22270 Eckerö, +358 400 38403
email: agneta.andersson@pp.inet.fi
No. of cottages: 5
22270 Eckerö, +358 18 38510, 0400 47 4955; +46 70 600 1286
email: karlbergs.stugor@aland.net
No. of cottages: 11
Haglundsväg 22, 22340 Geta, +358 18 41410, [0]457 313 5162
email: adventure@kasviken.com
http://www.aladventure.com
No. of overnight cottages: 3/19. 5/2 stars
Hellsö, 22730 Kökar, +358 18 55709
http://www.klobbars.com
Open: 1.5-30.9, year round for groups. No. of beds (B&B): 58. No. of cottages: 7.

Hammarlandsvägen 1903 2 B, 22240 Hammarland, +358 18 38496, 0457 5417431
email: gudrun.kroken@aland.net
http://home.aland.net/m04444/
No. of cottages: 7
22270 Eckerö, +358 18 38000
email: info@karingsundsbyn.aland.fi
http://www.karingsundsbyn.aland.fi
No. of No. of cottages/overnight cottages: 46/15. (No. of rooms: 90. No. of beds: 260.)
Åvaby, 22940 Åva, +358 18 56519, [0]40 5640 619
22630 Lumparland, +358 400 529281
email: info@lumpostugby.com
http://www.lumpostugby.com
No. of cottages/overnight cottages: 10/6.

Bastö, 22310 Pålsböle, +358 18 48297, [0]40 72 63 972
email: isa.hallstrom@aland.net
Open: 15.4.-31.10. No. of cottages/overnight cottages: 4/1
Gottbyvägen 248, 22130 Gottby, +358 18 32540

email: mansas@aland.net
No. of cottages/overnight cottages: 6/6
Pl 6, 22270 Eckerö, +358 18 38594,[0]400 861 769, [0]40 733 9794
http://www.marbyfjarden.aland.fi
No. of cottages: 8
Öjvägen 15, 22610 Lemland, +358 18 34087, 34338
email: mellanvik@aland.net
http://home.aland.net/mellanvik/
No. of cottages: 10

Norröv.42, 22220 Emkarby, +358 40 548 6228
email: alexandra@norro.aland.fi
http://www.norro.aland.fi
No. of cottages: 5
Eckerövägen 252, 22270 Eckerö, +358 18 38611, [0]457522 1611
email: wikblom@aland.net
No. of cottages: 10
Stugbyvägen 24, 22630 Lumparland, +358 18 35781; [0]400 886558
email: svinostugby@aland.net
No. of overnight cottages: 11 No. of self-catering cottages: 10

Seglinge, 22820 Kumlinge, +358 18 55605, [0]40 052 4517
No. of cottages: 3
Torpvägen 465, 22270 Eckerö, +358 18 38268
email: osterangen@aland.net
http://www.osterangen.aland.fi
Open: 8.4 - 30.9. No. of hotel rooms: 21. No. of beds: 56. No. of cottages/overnight cottages: 23/7

HOTELS

Bastö Hotell & Stugby
Bastöv. 531, 22310 Pålsböle, +358 18 42382
email: basto@aland.net
http://www.basto.aland.fi
Open: 1.5-30.8, year round for groups (min. 15 pers). No. of hotel rooms: 20. No. of beds: 50. No. of cottages/overnight cottages: 20/1

Brudhäll Hotell och Restaurang
22730 Kökar, +358 18 55955/55953
email: brudhall@aland.net
Open: 15.4-30.9. (pets booked in advance). No. of rooms: 21. No. of beds: 62.

Eckerö Hotell & Restaurang
Käringsundsvägen 53, 22270 Eckerö, +358 18 38447
email: info@eckerohotell.aland.fi
http://www.eckerohotell.aland.fi
Open: Year round. No. of rooms: 40. No. of beds: 138.

Gäddviken Turisthotell & Sands Stugby
Gäddviksvägen 17, 22240 Hammarland, +358 18 37650, [0]457 5958398
email: info@gaddviken.aland.fi
http://www.gaddviken.aland.fi
Open: 1.5-15.8 + the whole year for groups. No. of rooms: 37. No. of beds: 95. No. of overnight cottages: 6.

Havsbandet Hotell & Restaurang
Sandmovägen 85, 22270 Eckerö, +358 18 38200
email: havsbandet@aland.net
Open: 1.5–30.9 (groups year round)

Hotel Arkipelag
Strandgatan 31, 22100 Åland, +358 18 24020
email: info@hotellarkipelag.aland.fi
http://www.hotellarkipelag.com
Open year round. No. of rooms: 86. No. of beds: 215.

Hotell Pommern
Norragatan 8-10, 22100 Mariehamn, +358 18 15555
email: info@hotellpommern.aland.fi
http://www.hotellpommern.aland.fi
Open year round. No. of rooms: 54. No. of beds: 104.

Park Alandia Hotell
Norra Esplanadgatan 3, 22100 Mariehamn, +358 18 14130
email: parkhotel@vikingline.fi
http://www.vikingline.se/parkalandiahotel
Open year round. No. of rooms: 79. No. of beds: 160.

Scandic Hotel Savoy
Nygatan 12, 22100 Mariehamn, +358 18 15400
email: info@alandhotels.fi
http://www.alandhotels.fi
Open year round. No. of rooms: 85. No. of beds: 170.

Åland Hotel Group Ab
Hamngatan 7, 22100 Mariehamn, +358 18 15300
email: info@alandhotels.fi
http://www.alandhotels.fi

Ålandhotels Hotell Adlon
Hamngatan 7, 22100 Mariehamn, +358 18 15300
email: info@alandhotels.fi
http://www.alandhotels.fi
Open: May - sept. & weekends

Ålandhotels Hotell Havsvidden
Geta, 22100 Mariehamn, +358 18 15300/15077

email: info@alandhotels.fi
http://www.alandhotels.fi
Open: May–Sept, year round for groups. No. of rooms: 30. No. of beds: 60.

Ålandhotels Kaptensgårdarna
Hamngatan 7, 22100 Mariehamn, +358 18 15300
email: info@alandhotels.fi
http://www.alandhotels.fi/
Open: May–Sept. & weekends.

Ålands Turist & Konferens Ab
c/o Hotell Arkipelag, Strandgatan 31, 22100 Mariehamn, +358 18 15349
email: info@turist-konferens.aland.fi
http://www.turist-konferens.aland.fi

Österängen Hotell och Restaurang
Torpvägen 465, 22270 Eckerö, +358 18 38268
email: osterangen@aland.net
http://www.osterangen.aland.fi
Open: 8.4 - 30.9. No. of hotel rooms: 21. No. of beds: 56. No. of cottages/overnight cottages: 23/7

HUNTING & FISHING EQPT

Jakt & Fiskebutiken Äventyret
Torggatan 12, 22100 Mariehamn, +358 18 23860
email: aventyret@goaland.net

LOCAL GOVERNMENT

Ålands landskapsstyrelse
Pb 60, 22101 Mariehamn, +358 18 25000
http://www.aland.fi

TOURIST INFORMATION OFFICES

Ålands Turistinformation
Storagatan 8, 22100 Mariehamn, +358 18 24000
email: info@turist.aland.fi
Open: Every day 9-16. 1.9-31.10 and 1.3-31.5 also saturday 10-15. 1.6-13.6 and 14.8-31.8 Mo-Fr 9-17 and Sa-Su 9-16. 14.6-13.8 Everyday 9-18.

VINEYARD

Tjudö Vingård
22330 Tjudö, +358 457 072 1192
email: bongo@aland.net

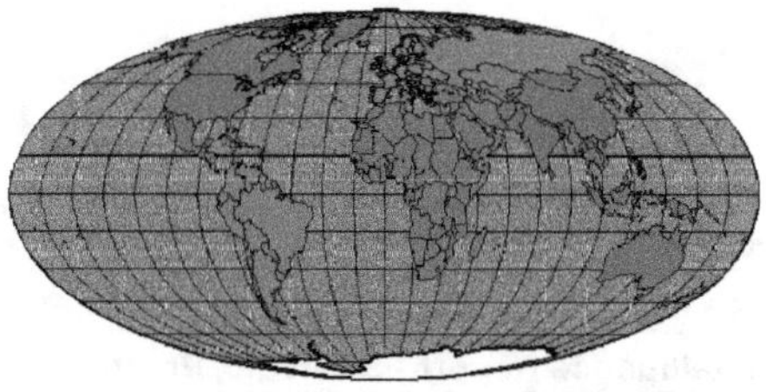

WORLD BUSINESS INTELLIGENCE REPORTS LIBRARY

World Business Information Catalog, USA: http://www.ibpus.com
Email: ibpusa3@gmail.com

Price: $99.95 Each

TITLE
Abkhazia (Republic of Abkhazia) Business Intelligence Report-- Strategic, Practical Information, Contacts
Afghanistan Business Intelligence Report-- Strategic, Practical Information, Contacts
Aland Business Intelligence Report-- Strategic, Practical Information, Contacts
Albania Business Intelligence Report-- Strategic, Practical Information, Contacts
Algeria Business Intelligence Report-- Strategic, Practical Information, Contacts
Andorra Business Intelligence Report-- Strategic, Practical Information, Contacts
Angola Business Intelligence Report-- Strategic, Practical Information, Contacts
Anguilla Business Intelligence Report-- Strategic, Practical Information, Contacts
Antigua and Barbuda Business Intelligence Report-- Strategic, Practical Information, Contacts
Antilles (Netherlands) Business Intelligence Report-- Strategic, Practical Information, Contacts
Argentina Business Intelligence Report-- Strategic, Practical Information, Contacts
Armenia Business Intelligence Report-- Strategic, Practical Information, Contacts
Aruba Business Intelligence Report-- Strategic, Practical Information, Contacts
Australia Business Intelligence Report-- Strategic, Practical Information, Contacts
Austria Business Intelligence Report-- Strategic, Practical Information, Contacts
Azerbaijan Business Intelligence Report-- Strategic, Practical Information, Contacts
Bahamas Business Intelligence Report-- Strategic, Practical Information, Contacts
Bahrain Business Intelligence Report-- Strategic, Practical Information, Contacts
Bangladesh Business Intelligence Report-- Strategic, Practical Information, Contacts
Barbados Business Intelligence Report-- Strategic, Practical Information, Contacts
Belarus Business Intelligence Report-- Strategic, Practical Information, Contacts
Belgium Business Intelligence Report-- Strategic, Practical Information, Contacts
Belize Business Intelligence Report-- Strategic, Practical Information, Contacts
Benin Business Intelligence Report-- Strategic, Practical Information, Contacts
Bermuda Business Intelligence Report-- Strategic, Practical Information, Contacts
Bhutan Business Intelligence Report-- Strategic, Practical Information, Contacts
Bolivia Business Intelligence Report-- Strategic, Practical Information, Contacts
Bosnia and Herzegovina Business Intelligence Report-- Strategic, Practical Information, Contacts
Botswana Business Intelligence Report-- Strategic, Practical Information, Contacts
Brazil Business Intelligence Report-- Strategic, Practical Information, Contacts
Brunei Business Intelligence Report-- Strategic, Practical Information, Contacts
Bulgaria Business Intelligence Report-- Strategic, Practical Information, Contacts
Burkina Faso Business Intelligence Report-- Strategic, Practical Information, Contacts
Burundi Business Intelligence Report-- Strategic, Practical Information, Contacts
Cambodia Business Intelligence Report-- Strategic, Practical Information, Contacts
Cameroon Business Intelligence Report-- Strategic, Practical Information, Contacts
Canada Business Intelligence Report-- Strategic, Practical Information, Contacts

For additional analytical, business and investment opportunities information,
Please contact Global Investment & Business Center, USA
at (202) 546-2103. Fax: (202) 546-3275. E-mail: ibpusa3@gmail.com

TITLE
Cape Verde Business Intelligence Report-- Strategic, Practical Information, Contacts
Cayman Islands Business Intelligence Report-- Strategic, Practical Information, Contacts
Central African Republic Business Intelligence Report-- Strategic, Practical Information, Contacts
Chad Business Intelligence Report-- Strategic, Practical Information, Contacts
Chile Business Intelligence Report-- Strategic, Practical Information, Contacts
China Business Intelligence Report-- Strategic, Practical Information, Contacts
Colombia Business Intelligence Report-- Strategic, Practical Information, Contacts
Comoros Business Intelligence Report-- Strategic, Practical Information, Contacts
Congo Business Intelligence Report-- Strategic, Practical Information, Contacts
Congo, Democratic Republic Business Intelligence Report-- Strategic, Practical Information, Contacts
Cook Islands Business Intelligence Report-- Strategic, Practical Information, Contacts
Costa Rica Business Intelligence Report-- Strategic, Practical Information, Contacts
Cote d'Ivoire Business Intelligence Report-- Strategic, Practical Information, Contacts
Croatia Business Intelligence Report-- Strategic, Practical Information, Contacts
Cuba Business Intelligence Report-- Strategic, Practical Information, Contacts
Cyprus Business Intelligence Report-- Strategic, Practical Information, Contacts
Czech Republic Business Intelligence Report-- Strategic, Practical Information, Contacts
Denmark Business Intelligence Report-- Strategic, Practical Information, Contacts
Djibouti Business Intelligence Report-- Strategic, Practical Information, Contacts
Dominica Business Intelligence Report-- Strategic, Practical Information, Contacts
Dominican Republic Business Intelligence Report-- Strategic, Practical Information, Contacts
Ecuador Business Intelligence Report-- Strategic, Practical Information, Contacts
Egypt Business Intelligence Report-- Strategic, Practical Information, Contacts
El Salvador Business Intelligence Report-- Strategic, Practical Information, Contacts
Equatorial Guinea Business Intelligence Report-- Strategic, Practical Information, Contacts
Eritrea Business Intelligence Report-- Strategic, Practical Information, Contacts
Estonia Business Intelligence Report-- Strategic, Practical Information, Contacts
Ethiopia Business Intelligence Report-- Strategic, Practical Information, Contacts
Falkland Islands Business Intelligence Report-- Strategic, Practical Information, Contacts
Faroes Islands Business Intelligence Report-- Strategic, Practical Information, Contacts
Fiji Business Intelligence Report-- Strategic, Practical Information, Contacts
Finland Business Intelligence Report-- Strategic, Practical Information, Contacts
France Business Intelligence Report-- Strategic, Practical Information, Contacts
Gabon Business Intelligence Report-- Strategic, Practical Information, Contacts
Gambia Business Intelligence Report-- Strategic, Practical Information, Contacts
Georgia Business Intelligence Report-- Strategic, Practical Information, Contacts
Germany Business Intelligence Report-- Strategic, Practical Information, Contacts
Ghana Business Intelligence Report-- Strategic, Practical Information, Contacts
Gibraltar Business Intelligence Report-- Strategic, Practical Information, Contacts
Greece Business Intelligence Report-- Strategic, Practical Information, Contacts
Greenland Business Intelligence Report-- Strategic, Practical Information, Contacts
Grenada Business Intelligence Report-- Strategic, Practical Information, Contacts
Guam Business Intelligence Report-- Strategic, Practical Information, Contacts
Guatemala Business Intelligence Report-- Strategic, Practical Information, Contacts
Guernsey Business Intelligence Report-- Strategic, Practical Information, Contacts
Guinea Business Intelligence Report-- Strategic, Practical Information, Contacts

TITLE
Guinea-Bissau Business Intelligence Report-- Strategic, Practical Information, Contacts
Guyana Business Intelligence Report-- Strategic, Practical Information, Contacts
Haiti Business Intelligence Report-- Strategic, Practical Information, Contacts
Honduras Business Intelligence Report-- Strategic, Practical Information, Contacts
Hungary Business Intelligence Report-- Strategic, Practical Information, Contacts
Iceland Business Intelligence Report-- Strategic, Practical Information, Contacts
India Business Intelligence Report-- Strategic, Practical Information, Contacts
Indonesia Business Intelligence Report-- Strategic, Practical Information, Contacts
Iran Business Intelligence Report-- Strategic, Practical Information, Contacts
Iraq Business Intelligence Report-- Strategic, Practical Information, Contacts
Ireland Business Intelligence Report-- Strategic, Practical Information, Contacts
Israel Business Intelligence Report-- Strategic, Practical Information, Contacts
Italy Business Intelligence Report-- Strategic, Practical Information, Contacts
Jamaica Business Intelligence Report-- Strategic, Practical Information, Contacts
Japan Business Intelligence Report-- Strategic, Practical Information, Contacts
Jersey Business Intelligence Report-- Strategic, Practical Information, Contacts
Jordan Business Intelligence Report-- Strategic, Practical Information, Contacts
Kazakhstan Business Intelligence Report-- Strategic, Practical Information, Contacts
Kenya Business Intelligence Report-- Strategic, Practical Information, Contacts
Kiribati Business Intelligence Report-- Strategic, Practical Information, Contacts
Korea, North Business Intelligence Report-- Strategic, Practical Information, Contacts
Korea, South Business Intelligence Report-- Strategic, Practical Information, Contacts
Kosovo Business Intelligence Report-- Strategic, Practical Information, Contacts
Kurdistan Business Intelligence Report-- Strategic, Practical Information, Contacts
Kuwait Business Intelligence Report-- Strategic, Practical Information, Contacts
Kyrgyzstan Business Intelligence Report-- Strategic, Practical Information, Contacts
Laos Business Intelligence Report-- Strategic, Practical Information, Contacts
Latvia Business Intelligence Report-- Strategic, Practical Information, Contacts
Lebanon Business Intelligence Report-- Strategic, Practical Information, Contacts
Lesotho Business Intelligence Report-- Strategic, Practical Information, Contacts
Liberia Business Intelligence Report-- Strategic, Practical Information, Contacts
Libya Business Intelligence Report-- Strategic, Practical Information, Contacts
Liechtenstein Business Intelligence Report-- Strategic, Practical Information, Contacts
Lithuania Business Intelligence Report-- Strategic, Practical Information, Contacts
Luxembourg Business Intelligence Report-- Strategic, Practical Information, Contacts
Macao Business Intelligence Report-- Strategic, Practical Information, Contacts
Macedonia Business Intelligence Report-- Strategic, Practical Information, Contacts
Madagascar Business Intelligence Report-- Strategic, Practical Information, Contacts
Madeira Business Intelligence Report-- Strategic, Practical Information, Contacts
Malawi Business Intelligence Report-- Strategic, Practical Information, Contacts
Malaysia Business Intelligence Report-- Strategic, Practical Information, Contacts
Maldives Business Intelligence Report-- Strategic, Practical Information, Contacts
Mali Business Intelligence Report-- Strategic, Practical Information, Contacts
Malta Business Intelligence Report-- Strategic, Practical Information, Contacts
Man Business Intelligence Report-- Strategic, Practical Information, Contacts
Marshall Islands Business Intelligence Report-- Strategic, Practical Information, Contacts

TITLE
Mauritania Business Intelligence Report-- Strategic, Practical Information, Contacts
Mauritius Business Intelligence Report-- Strategic, Practical Information, Contacts
Mayotte Business Intelligence Report-- Strategic, Practical Information, Contacts
Mexico Business Intelligence Report-- Strategic, Practical Information, Contacts
Micronesia Business Intelligence Report-- Strategic, Practical Information, Contacts
Moldova Business Intelligence Report-- Strategic, Practical Information, Contacts
Monaco Business Intelligence Report-- Strategic, Practical Information, Contacts
Mongolia Business Intelligence Report-- Strategic, Practical Information, Contacts
Montserrat Business Intelligence Report-- Strategic, Practical Information, Contacts
Montenegro Business Intelligence Report-- Strategic, Practical Information, Contacts
Morocco Business Intelligence Report-- Strategic, Practical Information, Contacts
Mozambique Business Intelligence Report-- Strategic, Practical Information, Contacts
Myanmar Business Intelligence Report-- Strategic, Practical Information, Contacts
Nagorno-Karabakh Republic Business Intelligence Report-- Strategic, Practical Information, Contacts
Namibia Business Intelligence Report-- Strategic, Practical Information, Contacts
Nauru Business Intelligence Report-- Strategic, Practical Information, Contacts
Nepal Business Intelligence Report-- Strategic, Practical Information, Contacts
Netherlands Business Intelligence Report-- Strategic, Practical Information, Contacts
New Caledonia Business Intelligence Report-- Strategic, Practical Information, Contacts
New Zealand Business Intelligence Report-- Strategic, Practical Information, Contacts
Nicaragua Business Intelligence Report-- Strategic, Practical Information, Contacts
Niger Business Intelligence Report-- Strategic, Practical Information, Contacts
Nigeria Business Intelligence Report-- Strategic, Practical Information, Contacts
Niue Business Intelligence Report-- Strategic, Practical Information, Contacts
Northern Cyprus (Turkish Republic of Northern Cyprus) Business Intelligence Report-- Strategic, Practical Information, Contacts
Northern Mariana Islands Business Intelligence Report-- Strategic, Practical Information, Contacts
Norway Business Intelligence Report-- Strategic, Practical Information, Contacts
Oman Business Intelligence Report-- Strategic, Practical Information, Contacts
Pakistan Business Intelligence Report-- Strategic, Practical Information, Contacts
Palau Business Intelligence Report-- Strategic, Practical Information, Contacts
Palestine (West Bank & Gaza) Business Intelligence Report-- Strategic, Practical Information, Contacts
Panama Business Intelligence Report-- Strategic, Practical Information, Contacts
Papua New Guinea Business Intelligence Report-- Strategic, Practical Information, Contacts
Paraguay Business Intelligence Report-- Strategic, Practical Information, Contacts
Peru Business Intelligence Report-- Strategic, Practical Information, Contacts
Philippines Business Intelligence Report-- Strategic, Practical Information, Contacts
Pitcairn Islands Business Intelligence Report-- Strategic, Practical Information, Contacts
Poland Business Intelligence Report-- Strategic, Practical Information, Contacts
Polynesia French Business Intelligence Report-- Strategic, Practical Information, Contacts
Portugal Business Intelligence Report-- Strategic, Practical Information, Contacts
Qatar Business Intelligence Report-- Strategic, Practical Information, Contacts
Romania Business Intelligence Report-- Strategic, Practical Information, Contacts
Russia Business Intelligence Report-- Strategic, Practical Information, Contacts
Rwanda Business Intelligence Report-- Strategic, Practical Information, Contacts
Sahrawi Arab Democratic Republic Volume 1 Strategic Information and Developments

TITLE
Saint Kitts and Nevis Business Intelligence Report-- Strategic, Practical Information, Contacts
Saint Lucia Business Intelligence Report-- Strategic, Practical Information, Contacts
Saint Vincent and The Grenadines Business Intelligence Report-- Strategic, Practical Information, Contacts
Samoa (American) A Business Intelligence Report-- Strategic, Practical Information, Contacts
Samoa (Western) Business Intelligence Report-- Strategic, Practical Information, Contacts
San Marino Business Intelligence Report-- Strategic, Practical Information, Contacts
Sao Tome and Principe Business Intelligence Report-- Strategic, Practical Information, Contacts
Saudi Arabia Business Intelligence Report-- Strategic, Practical Information, Contacts
Scotland Business Intelligence Report-- Strategic, Practical Information, Contacts
Senegal Business Intelligence Report-- Strategic, Practical Information, Contacts
Serbia Business Intelligence Report-- Strategic, Practical Information, Contacts
Seychelles Business Intelligence Report-- Strategic, Practical Information, Contacts
Sierra Leone Business Intelligence Report-- Strategic, Practical Information, Contacts
Singapore Business Intelligence Report-- Strategic, Practical Information, Contacts
Slovakia Business Intelligence Report-- Strategic, Practical Information, Contacts
Slovenia Business Intelligence Report-- Strategic, Practical Information, Contacts
Solomon Islands Business Intelligence Report-- Strategic, Practical Information, Contacts
Somalia Business Intelligence Report-- Strategic, Practical Information, Contacts
South Africa Business Intelligence Report-- Strategic, Practical Information, Contacts
Spain Business Intelligence Report-- Strategic, Practical Information, Contacts
Sri Lanka Business Intelligence Report-- Strategic, Practical Information, Contacts
St. Helena Business Intelligence Report-- Strategic, Practical Information, Contacts
St. Pierre & Miquelon Business Intelligence Report-- Strategic, Practical Information, Contacts
Sudan (Republic of the Sudan) Business Intelligence Report-- Strategic, Practical Information, Contacts
Sudan South Business Intelligence Report-- Strategic, Practical Information, Contacts
Suriname Business Intelligence Report-- Strategic, Practical Information, Contacts
Swaziland Business Intelligence Report-- Strategic, Practical Information, Contacts
Sweden Business Intelligence Report-- Strategic, Practical Information, Contacts
Switzerland Business Intelligence Report-- Strategic, Practical Information, Contacts
Syria Business Intelligence Report-- Strategic, Practical Information, Contacts
Taiwan Business Intelligence Report-- Strategic, Practical Information, Contacts
Tajikistan Business Intelligence Report-- Strategic, Practical Information, Contacts
Tanzania Business Intelligence Report-- Strategic, Practical Information, Contacts
Thailand Business Intelligence Report-- Strategic, Practical Information, Contacts
Timor Leste (Democratic Republic of Timor-Leste) Business Intelligence Report-- Strategic, Practical Information, Contacts
Togo Business Intelligence Report-- Strategic, Practical Information, Contacts
Tonga Business Intelligence Report-- Strategic, Practical Information, Contacts
Trinidad and Tobago Business Intelligence Report-- Strategic, Practical Information, Contacts
Tunisia Business Intelligence Report-- Strategic, Practical Information, Contacts
Turkey Business Intelligence Report-- Strategic, Practical Information, Contacts
Turkmenistan Business Intelligence Report-- Strategic, Practical Information, Contacts
Turks & Caicos Business Intelligence Report-- Strategic, Practical Information, Contacts
Tuvalu Business Intelligence Report-- Strategic, Practical Information, Contacts
Uganda Business Intelligence Report-- Strategic, Practical Information, Contacts
Ukraine Business Intelligence Report-- Strategic, Practical Information, Contacts

TITLE
United Arab Emirates Business Intelligence Report-- Strategic, Practical Information, Contacts
United Kingdom Business Intelligence Report-- Strategic, Practical Information, Contacts
United States Business Intelligence Report-- Strategic, Practical Information, Contacts
Uruguay Business Intelligence Report-- Strategic, Practical Information, Contacts
Uzbekistan Business Intelligence Report-- Strategic, Practical Information, Contacts
Vanuatu Business Intelligence Report-- Strategic, Practical Information, Contacts
Vatican City (Holy See) Business Intelligence Report-- Strategic, Practical Information, Contacts
Venezuela Business Intelligence Report-- Strategic, Practical Information, Contacts
Vietnam Business Intelligence Report-- Strategic, Practical Information, Contacts
Virgin Islands, British Business Intelligence Report-- Strategic, Practical Information, Contacts
Wake Atoll Business Intelligence Report-- Strategic, Practical Information, Contacts
Wallis & Futuna Business Intelligence Report-- Strategic, Practical Information, Contacts
Western Sahara Business Intelligence Report-- Strategic, Practical Information, Contacts
Yemen Business Intelligence Report-- Strategic, Practical Information, Contacts
Zambia Business Intelligence Report-- Strategic, Practical Information, Contacts
Zimbabwe Business Intelligence Report-- Strategic, Practical Information, Contacts

www.ingramcontent.com/pod-product-compliance
Lightning Source LLC
LaVergne TN
LVHW080043210926
848481LV00011B/3264